BEI MIR BIST DU SCHÖN

THE LIFE OF
SHOLOM SECUNDA

BY VICTORIA SECUNDA

Foreword by Walter Matthau

MagiCircle PRESS

Published by Magic Circle Press
Weston, Connecticut

Distributed by   Walker & Company
                  720 Fifth Avenue
                  New York, New York 10019

LC#: 81-82532
ISBN: 0-913660-15-9

Grateful acknowledgment is made to the following for permission to reprint published materials: *The Silent Millions: A History of the Jews in the Soviet Union* by Joel Cang (Taplinger Publishing Co., Inc., 1970) © 1969 by Joel Cang, reprinted by permission; *The Book of Jewish Knowledge* by Nathan Ausubel (Crown Publishers, Inc., 1964) © 1964 by Nathan Ausubel; *A History of the Jewish Experience* by Leo Trepp (Behrman House, Inc., 1962, revised 1973) © 1962, Revisions 1973 by Leo Trepp; *World of Our Fathers* by Irving Howe (Harcourt Brace Jovanovich 1976) copyright © 1976 by Irving Howe; *Nicholas and Alexandra* by Robert K. Massie (New York: Atheneum, 1967) copyright © 1967 by Robert K. Massie, used with permission of Atheneum Publishers; *Zanuck: Hollywood's Last Tycoon* by Leo Guild (Los Angeles: Holloway House Publishing Company, 1970), copyright © 1970 by Leo Guild; *The Only Way to Cross* by John Maxtone-Graham (Macmillan Publishing Co., Inc. 1972) copyright © 1972 by John Maxtone-Graham; *The Yiddish Theater in America* by David S. Lifson, by permission of the publisher, A.S. Barnes & Company, Inc., copyright © 1965 by David S. Lifson, all rights reserved; *How We Lived: A Documentary History of Immigrant Jews in America 1880-1930* by Irving Howe and Kenneth Libo (Richard Marek Publishers, Inc., 1979) copyright © 1979 by Irving Howe and Kenneth Libo; *Finding Our Fathers: A Guidebook to Jewish Genealogy* by Dan Rottenberg (Random House, 1977) copyright © 1977 by Dan Rottenberg; *A History of Russia* by Jesse D. Clarkson (Random House, 1961) copyright © 1961 by Jesse D. Clarkson; *The Fervent Years: The Story of the Group Theatre and the Thirties* by Harold Clurman (Alfred A. Knopf, 1945) copyright © 1945 by Harold Clurman; *A History of Russia*, Definitive Edition, by Bernard Pares (Alfred A. Knopf 1968, new edition of 1926 original), copyright © 1926, 1928 by Alfred A. Knopf Inc.; *Concise Encyclopedia of Jewish Music* by Macy Nulman, copyright © 1975 by McGraw-Hill, Inc., used with the permission of McGraw-Hill Book Company; *A Journey to Greatness: The Life and Music of George Gershwin* by David Ewen (Henry Holt & Co., 1956) copyright © 1956 by David Ewen, used with the permission of the author; *The Celluloid Empire: A History of the American Movie Industry* by Robert H. Stanley (Communication Art Books 1978), copyright © 1978 by Robert H. Stanley, reprinted by permission of Hastings House, Publishers, Inc.; *The Birth of the Talkies: From Edison to Jolson* by Harry M. Geduld (Indiana University Press, 1975) copyright © 1975 by Indiana University Press; *I Should Care: The Sammy Cahn Story* by Sammy Cahn, copyright © 1974 by Sammy Cahn, reprinted by permission of Arbor House Publishing Company; *The Borscht Belt* by Joey Adams with Henry Tobias (Bobbs-Merrill 1966) copyright © 1966 by Joey Adams and Henry Tobias, used with permission of the author; *Bright Star of Exile: Jacob Adler and the Yiddish Theatre* by Lulla Rosenfeld (Thomas Y. Crowell Company, 1977) copyright © 1977 by Lulla Rosenfeld, used by permission of the author; *The Downtown Jews* by Ronald Sanders (Signet 1977) copyright © 1969 by Ronald Sanders; *The Bluebird of Happiness: The Memoirs of Jan Peerce* by Alan Levy (Harper & Row, Publishers, 1976), copyright © 1976 by Alan Levy and Jan Peerce; *Vagabond Stars: A World History of Yiddish Theater* by Nahma Sandrow (Harper & Row Publishers, 1977) copyright © 1977 by Nahma Sandrow; *A Survey of Early Jewish-American Sheet Music (1898-1921)*, Working Papers in Yiddish and East European Jewish Studies Number 17, by Mark Slobin, issued by the Max Weinreich Center for Advanced Jewish Studies of the YIVO Institute for Jewish Research, copyright © 1976 by Mark Slobin; English lyrics from "Bei Mir Bist Du Schön" by Sholom Secunda, Sammy Cahn and Saul Chaplin, copyright © 1937 (renewed), Warner Bros. Inc., All Rights Reserved, Used by Permission; Lyrics from "Yiskor" by Sholom Secunda and Samuel Rosenbaum, copyright © 1967 by Ethnic Music Publishing Co.

FOR BETTY

ACKNOWLEDGMENTS

I heartily confess to a certain bias in writing this biography. Although I have been a journalist for many years, I am nevertheless Sholom Secunda's daughter-in-law, and having spent three years researching and writing this book, it is hard to deny that the result is a combination of those facts.

When Betty Secunda, Sholom's widow, asked me to take on the project, I agreed to do it, but with some doubts. I had never met my subject (he died in 1974, three years before I married his son, Sheldon), and I fretted about being given the freedom by his family to write about him without tears.

I needn't have worried. Betty gave me her collection of 1,000 letters to and from Sholom, theater programs and memorabilia that filled her closets over nearly 50 years of marriage. She also provided me with a translation of his memoirs, written in Yiddish from memory (but without documentation) for a series in the *Jewish Daily Forward*. Betty and her sons, Sheldon and Eugene, were extraordinarily candid and cooperative in hours of interviews, many of them painful, that recalled Sholom in a light that was not always favorable, but which made him human.

In addition, I interviewed the following colleagues, friends and relatives of Sholom's to whom I owe a great debt: Celia Adler, Julius Adler, Maxene Andrews, Charles Azenberg, Emanuel Azenberg, Ceil Beckman, Alex Blau, Sammy Cahn, Saul Chaplin, Alan Chester, Doris Cohen, Fyvush Finkel, Florence Franzman, Norman Furman, Dinah Goldberg, Betty Goodfriend, Isaac Goodfriend, Henrietta Jacobson, Miriam Kressyn, Ginetta La Bianca, Jack Lefkowitz, Leon Liebgold, Lily Liliana, Herman Malamood, Vic Marinello, Danny Marsik, Saul Meisels, Chaim Miller, Jan Peerce, Frank Petrocelli, Molly Picon, Larry Ravdin, Seymour Rexsite, Sam Rosenbaum, Sonny Rossi, Zvee Scooler, Anna Skulnik, Sylvia Snyder, Sara Tucker, Norman Warembud, Ruth Warembud, Simon Weber, Lottie Weintrop, Lou Weintrop, Sondra Weintrop, Frances Winarick, Gloria Winarick, Gordon Winarick, Bella Yablokoff and Herman Yablokoff.

For research assistance, I am indebted also to Dina Abramowicz, Librarian for the YIVO Institute for Jewish Research; Diane Cypkin, Yiddish Theatre Consultant for the Museum of the City of New York; Walter Evans, Warner Bros. Music, Inc.; Professor Herbert Marshall of the Center for Soviet and East European Research at Southern Illinois University; the staff of the Lincoln Center Library for the Performing Arts in New York; Joshua K. Klapper of ASCAP; and Burt Koral of BMI.

For reading the manuscript and editorial suggestions, I am grateful to Meredith Bernstein, Barbara Coats, Leslie Rubin Darhansoff, Neil Hickey, Enid Moore, Charles Powell, Jane Burman Powell, Michael Remer, Ann McGovern Scheiner, Arthur Secunda, Shirley Secunda and Max Weintraub.

Valerie Harms, publisher of Magic Circle Press, edited the manuscript with professionalism, cheerfulness and enthusiasm.

Finally, I wish to thank my daughter, Jennifer Heller, who between the ages of 8 and 12 learned what it means to have a mother who works in the house but who may not necessarily be at home. Her patience, interest and ability to amuse herself for hours deserve special praise, many hugs, and possibly an increase in her allowance.

Victoria Secunda
December 1981

FOREWORD

Sholom Secunda was the composer-conductor at the Second Avenue Theater which was located on Second Avenue and 2nd Street in New York City. I was working for "Lena" (I never knew her last name) as a Cherry Soda Vendor. I would walk up and down the aisles during the intermissions carrying paper cups of cherry soda, which were ensconced in a deep tray. I was able to stretch my commissions by spilling enough soda into the tray to fill some empty cups, which allowed me to pocket ten cents for each cup filled. Lena was on to the scam but she went along with it. She'd say things like, "Oh what a steady hand you have; didn't even spill a drop onto the tray." She said it so we wouldn't think she didn't know what was going on. When we became too efficient with the sodas we would be promoted to ice-cream bricks.

After a while I picked up another 50 cents a night as a "super." A "super" played different roles on the stage to make it appear as though they were employing a "cast of thousands". In the play "The Dishwasher," I was an immigration officer in the first act and a cellist in a symphony orchestra in the third act. In "The Organ Grinder" I was an old woman in a wedding scene. I hollered "MAZEL TOV!" in a loud, high voice. It was easy for me when I was twelve.

I envied Sholom Secunda. I envied him getting applause just by appearing on the podium in the pit. It's still my biggest satisfaction to appear on a stage and get a big hand before I open my mouth.

Sholom Secunda enriched sixty years of a history that made an indelible impression on me and millions more.

Walter Matthau

CONTENTS

INTRODUCTION

How do you measure the life of a man? One yardstick is the size of his obituary in *The New York Times:* when he died in 1974 at the age of 79, Sholom Secunda's took up a quarter of a page. Another is the size of his estate: Secunda's was large enough to provide security for his widow, Betty, but little more. A third is the recognizability of his name: the greatest recognition factor of Secunda's 1,000 songs and 65 Yiddish operettas, his oratorios and liturgical music, is the title of a single song, "Bei Mir Bist Du Schön," and people are more inclined to remember it than the name of its composer.

The measure of Sholom Secunda's life can be found in the memories of a generation of immigrant Americans whose hair is white and whose speech is flavored with an accent that is unmistakably Yiddish, who still sing his songs. It can be found, too, among the now-middle-aged children of those immigrants who can recall the first time their parents *shlepped* them to a Yiddish musical production on lower Second Avenue in Manhattan, Yiddish theater's "Broadway."

But Secunda's life was significant not only because he achieved fame in a now dwindling corner of early 20th Century culture—the Yiddish theater—but because of the odds against his having done so. His life and accomplishments must be assessed in terms of his roots.

Secunda died just two years short of the centennial of the Yiddish theater. In his childhood in the Russian Ukraine, he had learned the songs of Abraham Goldfaden, the "father" of the Yiddish theater, music that punctuated a youth that was touched by typhus, pogroms and grinding poverty. To escape persecution because of their Jewishness, Sholom and his family fled to the United States in 1907, enduring a filthy steerage voyage in the bowels of a steamship across the Atlantic Ocean and the painful probes of doctors on Ellis Island. They settled in New York, living in a cramped, rat-infested tenement on the Lower East Side among millions of other immigrant, downtown Jews.

As a teenager, Sholom experienced the humiliation of being one of the oldest children in a public school class in New York that spoke a language he did not understand. He worked his way through the Institute of Musical Art (now called Juilliard) giving piano lessons by day and working as a Yiddish theater extra by night, sandwiching in his studies and snatches of sleep.

He paid his figurative dues to the Musicians Union by its banishment of him to Philadelphia, where he served a three-year apprenticeship before being allowed to conduct and compose in a New York theater. Yiddish theater flowered in America, and Secunda flourished with it, learning American words and ways and shedding his *greener* Russian mannerisms and dress.

On Second Avenue today one finds few reminders of the time when Yiddish theater hummed with life and of the era in American history that it so uniquely symbolized. Its 27 New York theaters—ornate palaces seating up to 3,000 ardent *patriots,* as Yiddish theater fans were called—are gone, reincarnated as parking lots, movie theaters and office buildings. The Hebrew Actors Union, which once boasted a membership of 1,500, today has 200 members, of whom only about 50 are active.

Still, there are keepers of the Yiddish flame who regard these facts as so much circumstantial evidence. Secunda's was a generation that traveled light, bringing with it from Eastern Europe not spinning wheels and pewter but skits and song. In place of antiques, their legacy is a culture that is surely as deserving of preservation. "As long as there is one Jew," says veteran actor Seymour Rexsite, "there will be a Yiddish theater."

But Sholom's position as the last leading composer of a theater that has lost its immigrant audience is not what lingers when thinking of him. Rather, it is that he got the most out of an era that is gone for good, a time of high hopes, a time when America was a Golden Land of unlimited dreams.

Sholom Secunda had his share of disappointments. But he also had his share of realized promises, more than the vast majority of his fellow immigrants. And he gave it back, through his music, his intellect, his humor and above all, his zest. He was a hero to a generation whose children would say, "Talk English!" If he could make good in America, sharing with his *patriots* the tempering of Russian persecution and the terror of a new language and land, then so could they.

And they did. The legacy of immigrants like Sholom who made good in the film, publishing, music, Broadway theater and business worlds is immeasurable.

But in Secunda's case, there is this caveat: in a world that forced many Jews to change their names, Sholom kept his. Like the theater for which he wrote, he became Americanized, but never totally assimilated. He planted his Russian-Jewish roots in the United States, talking English, but at the same time—figuratively and literally— talking Yiddish. While some immigrants achieved power and prestige downplaying their heritage, Sholom chorused his. He was a transitional American—a man who was never totally Old World or New, but both. He was an immigrant who made good in the Golden Land on his own, Jewish terms.

To understand what that meant and how he did it, in the words of a comedian, you had to be there. From the beginning.

🎵 ALEXANDRIA AND NICHOLAYEV

Until he entered *chedar* (Hebrew elementary school) at the age of six in Alexandria, Russia, Sholom Secunda was called *lemeshke,* the Yiddish word for "loser," by everyone in his family. His mother justified the sobriquet by telling him that as a child he had been listless. He sat alone, she said, until somebody pulled him out of his reverie. Often his mother said that God had punished her by sending her a child who turned out so poorly.

Sholom Secunda's mother was not an easy woman to please. She was born Anna Rebecca Nedabeika in Yelisavetgrad (now called Kirovgrad) in the Russian Ukraine in 1860. When she was a child, she and her family moved to Alexandria, fifty miles away. There, she met and married Abraham Secunda* and bore him seven of their nine children.

Abraham, who was exactly her age, was not the husband of her choosing. The marriage was arranged by her parents, although she was in love, she later said, with someone else—a man who "wore a top hat." Abraham was many things, but "elegant" was not one of them.

Anna was a proud woman and carried herself with an imperiousness that belied her height—she was four feet, ten inches—and her poverty. She endured the stress of nine pregnancies and ghetto squalor by assuming the role of critic. Although her children would remember her singing lullabies to them, she seldom smiled and frequently found fault, a marked contrast to Abraham's earthy sense of humor. Over the years, her children would find it difficult to measure

---

*The Secundas believe that they are descendants of Italian Jews who were expelled from Italy in the 16th Century and who settled in Russia.

up to her demands for filial devotion and financial success.

The circumstances of Sholom's birth did little to endear him to his parents. Anna went into labor early in the morning of the Sabbath, August 23, 1894. Among Jews, the most sacred day of the week was the Sabbath, a day that culminated a week of hard labor and prayer, a day when members of the family wore their best clothes to synagogue. Even in the summer, men wore neat (although threadbare), coarse black wool suits and stiff white collars. The Sabbath was the one day in the week when tradition, heritage and ceremony briefly blotted out the daily dreariness of ghetto life.

It was unusually hot that Sabbath. A midwife had come to the Secundas' two-room apartment to help Anna through her time. Abraham took his five sons to the tiny, dank synagogue where they sat, sweating, crowded among the other Jewish men.

Berel, who was eight years old, was the second oldest and most mischievous of the children. While his father was praying, he sneaked out of the synagogue and joined two of his Gentile friends who were on their way to the Ingulets River for a soothing swim. Berel estimated that, if he hurried, he could take a quick dip, dress, and be back in time for the Blessing of the New Month, before his father would notice his absence.

While Berel was swimming, Anna gave birth to Sholom, who was named after a former *shammes* (sexton) at the synagogue who had died childless. What Anna did not know was that within minutes of Sholom's birth, Berel was dead. A strong current had carried him out to the deepest channel in the river. His friends had been unable to save him, and they ran to the Secunda house to tell the family about the tragedy.

The midwife sent the boys to the synagogue to inform Abraham. He went to the river with his sons and pulled Berel's lifeless body, which had floated toward shore, out of the river. The next day, in keeping with Orthodox Jewish tradition, the child was buried.

Anna's sorrow was compounded by her keen disappointment that her sixth child was not female. "I wanted a girl," Sholom once heard her say bitterly to Abraham, "and a boy arrived. Berel was a joy—he used to sing and dance, and he was a good student. God took Berel away and gave me a *lemeshke* instead."

Berel's death was but one tragic element in what was a harsh life not only for the Secundas, but for all Russian Jews. Five million Jews —fully half the world's Jewish population—lived in Tsarist Russia, most of them in the Jewish Pale of Settlement.[1] The Pale, which had been established by Catherine the Great in the late 1700s, consisted of regions of Poland annexed to Russia, and the Ukraine in Southern Russia.[2] Jews were forced from the countryside, many of them in chains, into cities in the Ukraine, where they could be carefully policed.[3] These cities became overcrowded, and the paucity of jobs impoverished their residents.

Alexandria, a town of about 14,000 in the province of Kherson, was fairly typical of cities in the Pale.[4] The Jews who lived there were tailors, cobblers, small-time merchants, miners and metalworkers (Abraham Secunda was a tinsmith who covered roofs with tin and repaired them after heavy rain and snow storms).[5] A few Jews were professionals—doctors, dentists, lawyers—and a handful were wealthy, able to send their children to universities in other cities.

But even for affluent Jews, imperial anti-Semitism was a horror that gnawed at their daily lives. Tsarist hatred of Jews stemmed from Russian Orthodox tenets which blamed Jews for the murder of Christ.[6] Restrictions on Jewish travel and residence were severe.[7] In an effort to assimilate Jews, in the middle of the 1800s young Jewish boys were forced to serve in the army for up to 25 years in the hope of weaning them from their heritage.[8] At the same time, seeds for the Russian Revolution of 1917 were being sown all over Russia, and unrest among workers was increasing.

Russia's most anti-Semitic tsar was Alexander III, whose reign began in 1881. During his regime, Yiddish theater was banned, Jewish newspapers were censored (a policy begun before him), and Jews were not allowed to own property outside their towns.[9] His over-all policy toward Jews was to convert one-third, starve one-third, and allow the rest to emigrate.[10] Between 1881 and 1918, nearly 1.3 million Jews would accommodate him by leaving Russia, most of them for the United States.[11] The Secundas would be among them.

On November 1, 1894—three months after Sholom Secunda's birth—Alexander III suddenly died. His successor, Nicholas II, became the last tsar of Russia. The man who claimed he did not want to be emperor would nevertheless energetically pursue the anti-Semitic cruelties of his predecessors.[12] During his reign, unrest and terrorism in Russia would put a violent end to imperial rule, culminating with the Russian Revolution and Nicholas' execution.

Jews, who were not only considered "Christ killers" but scapegoats for peasant uprisings as well, were caught between tsarist and peasant hatred. In 1902, a series of pogroms against Jews that shocked the world was unleashed in Russia. The militia was not permitted to stop these violent attacks, at least not until the damage was done.[13].

The weight of repression and starvation resulted in desperate efforts by Jews to get out of Russia and start life anew in the United States. But leaving Russia meant abandoning homes, however humble, and families. It also cost money, which Russian Jews seldom had.

In overcrowded towns like Alexandria, jobs were scarce. Jewish workers and tradesmen had to work up to 20 hours daily to feed their families, on a diet consisting primarily of bread, potatoes and herring —"the poor man's chicken."[14] Only the rich ate well, and they were generous: at the turn of the century, nearly half of Russia's Jews were kept alive by benevolent, fellow Jews.

Abraham Secunda was able to put food on the table by crawling on tin roofs and repairing them, six days a week, from dawn to sundown. "You don't live in comfort in my house," he would say at the Sabbath table, "but no one starves, either." But the threat of starvation grew critical in 1896. That year Anna gave birth to her seventh son, Yankele. Abraham and Anna decided that only by moving to a larger city would business prospects be brighter. They chose Nicholayev, a thriving port city of 175,000, located at the mouth of the Bug River on the Black Sea.

Nicholayev, whose Jewish population numbered 20,000, had large factories and businesses, great synagogues with celebrated cantors and choirs, and 15 Jewish schools.[15] Abraham's and Anna's four eldest sons were reaching an age when the quality of their schooling was of increasing concern. At 12, Velvel, their first-born, showed great promise. He had done well in *chedar*. From the time he was 10, he had occasionally read the Sabbath portion of the Torah and had sung prayers in the synagogue in Alexandria where Abraham was a trustee. Velvel had a lovely voice, which particularly pleased his parents.

Music, like the Sabbath candles, helped to brighten the Secunda home. In Nicholayev, it was hoped, Velvel might be able to sing in a synagogue with a first-rate choir and to learn something about music. The other sons—Aaron (8), Yosele (6), Meyer (4)—Sholom and Yankele were still infants—were in varied stages of their education, and would also profit from a better choice of *chedars*.

In addition to business and educational opportunities, Nicholayev beckoned also because Abraham had friends who lived there. Seeking a better life by moving was something of a family tradition. At least, that's what Abraham always said. His parents, who were originally from Lithuania, had moved to Alexandria from Dinenburg, near the Latvian border, probably because they were forced into the Pale. They had often used the expression, "change of place, change of luck." In Nicholayev, perhaps Abraham's luck, and that of his sons, would improve.

Abraham wrote to his friends of his decision to move there. Since it would have been too expensive to take their meager furniture, it was sold. The only belongings taken, aside from clothing, were pillows, blankets, and the large brass samovar. "Until God knows when," Anna said, "we will at least have something to sleep on and be able to make tea."

The journey from Alexandria to Nicholayev by train, a trip of 200 miles, took all night. Anna would later recall the tearful farewell at the railroad station. All the relatives on both sides of the family came to say goodby, believing, accurately, that they would never see each other again. With lumbering trains and no telephones, Nicholayev seemed a lifetime away. For Abraham Secunda, whose future was so uncertain, it was an awesome moment. But for Sholom, it would indeed be a change of luck. If not for Nicholayev, like his brothers he would almost certainly have begun to learn his father's trade at the age of eight.

The train pulled into Nicholayev at dawn, and the exhausted family walked to the new home that Abraham, through a friend, had secured for them. It was a small, two-story building that surrounded a courtyard. The rooms on the first floor were used for cottage industry, and included one small apartment into which the Secundas moved. The second floor was used as a hotel.

The Secundas' apartment consisted of three small rooms. One room was used by day as a kitchen-dining room and by night as a bedroom for all six sons, with bedding spread out on the floor. The second room was Abraham's and Anna's bedroom. The third room became Abraham's workroom.

Abraham had decided to change his trade in Nicholayev, but pride precluded his working for someone else. In the courtyard outside their apartment, he found a variety of discarded pieces of iron. The day he arrived, while Anna unpacked their few belongings, he spent several hours in the courtyard, studying the iron shapes. At last he came into the house.

"I'm going to manufacture beds," he announced. "Velvel and Aaron will help me make them. Then we'll take them to the furniture stores in town and sell them."

"Yes," Anna said, "but won't you need tools to work and bend the iron?"

"Leave it to me."

Abraham was nóthing if not inventive. Within a few days, he had made his tools out of the iron scraps he found. He and his sons used other found metal and made a dozen beds. Early one morning, they left the house, carrying all twelve beds. They did not return until after dark.

"What happened?" Anna asked.

"We sold them all! What's more, the shopowners gave us orders for more!"

That evening, the family celebrated. For the first time since they had moved to Nicholayev, Anna was able to cook a hot supper for her family, a meal that included fish, not just bread and tea. In the evening they sang, and laughed, and thanked God that the old family homily seemed to be coming true. Perhaps their luck had changed.

Until he was five, Sholom's recollections of his earliest years were filtered through the reminiscences of his parents. Like most children, his memories began when he started school. Education seems to underscore events that are often, until the beginning of literacy, a blur. This was certainly true of Sholom. His personal remembrances began the day when his father first brought him to the *chedar* where his brothers had been students for three years.

Most people can remember their first, terrifying day of school. But in Tsarist Russia, *chedar* took on a special urgency. Leo Trepp, in his book, *A History of the Jewish Experience,* writes:

Sinking deeply into despondency, (Russian Jews) had only Torah to sustain them spiritually and intellectually, but as they were cut off from life, they lost themselves in overly refined talmudic disputations. . .The rabbis formed the elite. Children, from the tenderest age, were pressed into the routine of eternal study. They knew none of the joys of normal childhood.[16]

Sholom's first day at *chedar* began painfully. At seven o'clock in the morning Abraham led Sholom into the *chedar,* which was across the street from their house. The *chedar* had one small room with a long table. Around the table were narrow benches on which the pupils sat. The rabbi sat in the middle of one bench. Abraham introduced Sholom to the rabbi by saying, "This is Sholom. He's no good for anything. I hope he's better at learning than at other things."

The boys at the *chedar* ranged in age from five to thirteen. Sholom's father left, and the rabbi told Sholom to join the other boys his age on one side of the table. Once the sting of his father's remarks began to fade, Sholom became fascinated by the activities of the older boys. The bar mitzvah students put on their phylacteries. He marveled at how they wound the leather straps attached to the small, black leather boxes around their left arms, and how they tied more little boxes to their foreheads. The phylacteries, he learned, contained tiny slips of paper inscribed with scriptural passages. The rabbi went through the same ritual, praying incessantly, and completed the process by draping a long prayer shawl over his head.

One of the bar mitzvah candidates stood by himself at the head of the table. He began chanting prayers, and the children chanted or hummed along. Except for the five- and six-year-olds, who were not yet able to read Hebrew, everyone took part. The act of praying was not strange to Sholom, since he had seen his father doing the same every morning. But seeing the *chedar* boys praying was different. He wanted to be like them.

In *chedar,* little Sholom, the *lemeshke,* found his niche, away from the taunting of his brothers and the sighs of his mother. He ran home after school bursting with descriptions of his first day, and imitated for Anna the garbled sounds of the boys' prayers. He mimicked the rabbi's rocking back and forth in physical devotion. That night, Abraham bent over Sholom as he lay on the floor before going to sleep.

"Papa," Sholom asked, "do you think I will be able to chant in *chedar?*"

"If you are a good boy and learn well and are not lazy, you too will pray before the cantor's desk," Abraham said gently, "just like the other boys."

It was not simply the ceremony of the phylacteries that made Sholom eager for school each morning. Certainly it was not the *Minchah* and *Maariv,* the afternoon and evening prayers, that were sung at the end of the school day. What excited Sholom was the music of the prayers. He proved to be an astonishingly quick study. Soon he was singing the prayers from memory, and he particularly loved the prayers with the most lyrical melodies.

"I sang myself to sleep and I woke up singing," Sholom wrote. "At breakfast, my older brothers would tease, 'He just got up, and he's singing already!'"

But Abraham would look at his son and beam. Other fathers would proudly boast of their sons' prowess in *chedar* or with their fists. The way to Abraham's heart was through music. He was not a trained musician, but he loved music. Song and Purim plays were an integral part of the lives of Sholom's parents. Anna had a strong, clear soprano voice. She knew all the early songs by Abraham Goldfaden, father of the Yiddish theater.

Abraham, a brilliant raconteur, was the family comedian. Years later in the United States he was still known as a wit, even with his fractured English. "Muzzer's Day, Muzzer's Day," he would say with a wink, "every day is Muzzer's Day. Even Fazzer's Day." His reputation in the Twenties as a dandy on Manhattan's Lower East Side sprang from his affection for spats and sharply tailored suits.

In Russia he lacked funds for the latest fashions, but he loved to dress up, and was able to put together a wardrobe of costumes to accompany his jokes and songs. Abraham, too, had learned the early lyrics of Goldfaden that had been published in Russia during the lenient years before Alexander III. In time Abraham and Anna became an amateur theatrical team and were invited frequently to perform at celebrations in Alexandria and Nicholayev.

Abraham was an early *patriot* of the Yiddish theater. After the family moved to Nicholayev, he discovered the delights of Odessa, a prosperous port city some 75 miles away. There, from time to time, he would spend the weekend and immerse himself in Jewish culture. Odessa had a full spectrum of Jewish arts, and Abraham enjoyed every hue, from the great synagogues with famous cantors and choirs to illegal productions of Yiddish plays and the winecellars where Jewish actors and entertainers would perform Yiddish theatrical scenes and songs.

On Friday morning Abraham would board a ship in the Nicholayev harbor and sail to Odessa. Saturday morning he would go from synagogue to synagogue to hear each cantor. At night he would prowl the winecellars. Each scrap of music he committed to memory, and in the winecellars he would pay the singers a few coins to write down the lyrics for him.

On his return to Nicholayev Sunday night, Abraham would teach his sons all the music he had learned over the weekend. The children grew up knowing a mix of folk, theater and liturgical music that would have an enduring influence on Sholom's work. At home the entire family would perform the songs and plays that Abraham had picked up as souvenirs of his Odessa wanderings. Eventually he and Anna stopped performing, even in these home-grown productions, because they did not wish to look foolish in front of their impressionable children. But the children loved putting on little plays for their parents. "My father took great pleasure in that," Sholom later recalled.

And so, Abraham was especially touched by Sholom's earnest desire to learn the music of the prayers in *chedar*. His small son, who for so long had shown no enthusiasm for other things, came alive with music. Having that gift brought Sholom closer to the heart of his father and of the family. Particularly on the Sabbath.

The Sabbath dinner was, for the Secunda family, not only a liturgical benchmark of the week. It was the one meal during the week when the entire family ate at the same time. On other days meals had no routine. During the day, while Abraham and his sons worked on the beds, they would slip into the kitchen when the stomach commanded attention and grab a hunk of bread. At *chedar* the other boys carried some bread and chicken fat for munching between prayers. But on Friday the family had a consistent and unifying routine. With the workday ended, Abraham would lock up his tools. He would then take the boys to a bath house, as there was no bathtub at home (a bucket of cold water stood in the kitchen for washing of faces and hands). One by one, he would stand each son on a bench and lather him with soap and a brush, scrubbing until the boy's skin was scarlet. After they dried off and got dressed, they would slowly walk home.

Anna dressed her sons in Sabbath clothes and Abraham led them to the synagogue for the Welcoming of the Sabbath. This particular synagogue was for the poor families of Nicholayev. It did not have a well-known cantor, and certainly not a choir. Abraham did not have enough money to belong to the Hatters' and Furriers' Synagogue, which had no choir but did have a good cantor. Totally beyond his reach was the Choir Synagogue, where the rich Jews prayed, although occasionally he would take his sons there to give them some exposure to the music. The Secundas belonged to the Cobblers' Synagogue.

When the men returned from services, Anna would bless the Sabbath candles, and the warmth of her table would dispel the gloom of their cramped, chilly apartment. The supper table would be covered with a white cloth. A bottle of wine would be placed in the middle of the table, surrounded by small glasses for the children and a large one for Abraham. An enormous loaf of braided challah sat next to it.

Abraham had a good singing voice, and he would stand holding aloft his glass and sing the blessing of the wine. The children and Anna would sing responsively. "We sounded almost like a professional choir," Sholom recalled. The children would then each bless the wine. Abraham would summon Sholom and Yankele and give them a taste of the wine from his glass. Then they all ate a full dinner. To the children it seemed like a feast for royalty: gefilte fish, soup with noodles, chicken, noodle pudding and cookies. Between courses, Abraham led his family in Sabbath songs.

But the Sabbath was not merely for festivities alone. After the meal Abraham would examine his sons as to their Hebrew scholarship acquired in *chedar* that week. Each son would be questioned and each was required to read a specific prayer. One son would be asked to read part of the portion of the week from the prayerbook and translate it into Yiddish; another would chant the portion from the Prophetic writings.

The ritual terrified Sholom—when he was called upon to be examined his brothers would hoot, "Let's see what the *lemeshke* knows!"—until one Friday, several months after his *chedar* training had begun. He reluctantly walked over to his father and opened the first page of his prayerbook. Everyone was laughing, as usual. He began singing "How goodly are thy tents, Oh Jacob," from memory, just as the boys in *chedar* had chanted it by the cantor's desk every day. Suddenly the room was still, save for his singing, and the family listened in astonishment. When he finished, there was a hush in the room.

Abraham pulled Sholom to him in an embrace and, turning to the family, said, "Well, what do you say to that? He's not such a *lemeshke* after all!" Anna kissed his head and said, "What a sweet voice he has. He may surprise us yet." Sholom was embarrassed, but ecstatic.

He was never called "lemeshke" again.

Abraham was a robust man who could crush or overjoy his sons with a word. He was not a man to abuse his authority as head of the family, but he was always held in awe by his children. Not only was he clever and industrious and a strict observer of Orthodoxy, he was also as strong as a horse. Despite his height—he was five feet, two inches—and slender body, his physical strength was a family legend. In Alexandria, all the peasants, it was said, had feared him. In short order he made his neighbors in Nicholayev aware of his reputation as well.

Abraham was a hero, Anna would later tell her grandchildren. She particularly loved telling the story of the time that a beefy Gentile peasant had asked Abraham to repair a samovar on the Sabbath, and Abraham had refused. The peasant, she said, had threatened Abraham and had taken a swing at him. Abraham responded, she said, by beating him up.

All of Abraham's sons inherited their father's strength. All, that is, except Sholom. "I remember as a little child watching my brothers fight with the little Gentile boys," he later said, "but I cannot ever remember having been in a fight myself."

Nor was he interested in playing with the other children in the street after school. For them the hours in *chedar* ground slowly by, but for Sholom they flew. After school he would go straight home and sit with his prayerbook. His older brothers would continue to work on the beds; the younger boys would play and fight in the street. Sholom would practice for hours, chanting the prayers again and again.

Anna, who was then pregnant with her first daughter, would stand by the stove and listen to Sholom sing. She said nothing to him. She just listened.

🎵 LITTLE CANTOR

For most artists, pursuing a natural, creative gift can be a lonesome business, particularly for a boy with no talent for physical daring. Among Russian Jews, however, music when combined with Orthodoxy attracted special approbation. Status for a family was guaranteed if one of its members was a rabbi. Having a cantor in the family was almost as honorable.

In the Secunda family there was prestige in the fact that Velvel, the oldest son, had secured a place in the choir of one of Nicholayev's large synagogues. Although the position was non-paying, it was a source of family pride. Velvel, they believed, was the musician in the family.

Until Sholom turned seven.

One evening, the *chedar* rabbi paid a visit to the Secunda home. "Your child has a special gift for singing," he said to Abraham. Then, turning to Sholom, he said, "Come, sing something for your parents."

Anna, Abraham and all the children sat in a circle. Sholom, standing in the middle of the room, began to chant a prayer, from memory, in the cantorial style. When he finished, everyone smiled and applauded. Like any child caught in the momentum of hard-won family approval, he continued singing, this time several of the theater songs that his father had taught him. The family and their visitor applauded again, laughing in delight at the little boy's wondrous voice and obvious pleasure.

The moment of shared enthusiasm extended to Velvel, who said to Abraham, "Why don't you take Sholom to Cantor Lev at the Great Synagogue for an audition?" Abraham agreed to the suggestion. The following Saturday Sholom, accompanied by his father and Velvel,

sang for Cantor Lev. On Lev's recommendations, Sholom was engaged—for no pay—by Monsieur Kurich, the choir director.

At the age of seven, Sholom began what was to be a lifetime habit
of working long hours. Every day, except Friday and Saturday, he
went to the synagogue to rehearse. Sholom couldn't wait for those
rehearsals. He would rush home after *chedar,* wolf down some bread
and tea, and run two miles to the synagogue. He and the other young
choristers would arrive an hour before the rest of the choir for their
music studies.

When Sholom first joined the choir, he was tenth alto. Before the
year was half over, he was soloist of the alto section. He had begun
the year learning the music by rote, and ended it by sight reading
with few mistakes.

Because of his size, Sholom at eight looked three years younger.
The worshipers at the synagogue became curious about and amused
by the alto whom they could hear but not see—because he was so
small—during his lovely solos. After services, the men would ask the
cantor to point out "the child who sings." Before long, news of
Sholom, the singing prodigy, began to spread beyond the temple
walls.

In Nicholayev, the largest and wealthiest synagogue was the Choir
Synagogue. Its choir director was Bezalel Brown, a musician of considerable repute. Brown, who was also an opera singer, was a recognized composer whose liturgical music was later sung in many
American synagogues.

One evening before the end of Sholom's first year as a choir singer,
Brown called unexpectedly on the Secundas. He had, he said, heard
Sholom sing at the Great Synagogue. He offered Sholom a position as
soloist in his choir, for an annual fee of 30 rubles.

Anna and Abraham were dumbfounded.

"There is a vast difference," Brown continued, "between singing
with Monsieur Kurich and singing with Monsieur Brown. Kurich
teaches him notes. I will teach him music."

Abraham and Brown shook hands on it. Sholom would, at the end
of his commitment to Kurich, begin rehearsals at the Choir Synagogue. After Brown departed, Abraham and Anna stared at each
other in disbelief. Their son would be singing with the greatest choir
director in Nicholayev, and for this he would even be paid money!

Sholom's eighth year marked the beginning of his professional career in music, a career that would span 72 years. Because of his extraordinary talent, and his ability to earn wages, his father did not force him to learn the bed-manufacturing trade. The older brothers, however, had to continue their work in the shop, which they did with varying degrees of enthusiasm.

Velvel, the firstborn, was industrious in school and in his father's workshop. Of all the boys he most resembled Abraham. He had a quick sense of humor. He loved to dress up in costumes. He loved to act (years later he would be a singer and actor in New York's Yiddish theater), and organized a dramatics club whose members were choirboys from the synagogues in Nicholayev. He was, Sholom later said, his parents' favorite.

Aaron was the antithesis of Velvel. A somber child, he was earnest in his *chedar* studies, but happiest when working on the beds. Long after his brothers had finished their tasks, he would remain in the shop, hammering until his mother summoned him to dinner.

Yosele. *Oy,* Yosele. He was the family headache. He hated *chedar.* He had no ear for music. He was lazy, and frequently fought with his parents.

"You don't understand me!" he would shriek. "The chickens understand me better than you do!"

Yosele wasn't kidding. Anna always had a hen, to provide eggs for the table, and a rooster to announce daybreak and awaken everyone for work and school. Yosele preferred poultry to people. Chickens were not *nudges.*

Yosele's best friend was Petkeh ("little Peter"), the rooster. Every day after *chedar,* Yosele would trot into the courtyard and teach Petkeh the lesson he had learned that day. His daily chats with the chicken made his father furious. One day when Yosele was chanting a prayer at Petkeh, Abraham came out into the courtyard and angrily reprimanded him.

"You spend all day talking to a bird," he shouted, "when you should be inside, working in the shop, like your brothers!" Yosele was mortified. His father had embarrassed him in front of his feathered friend. He ran out of the courtyard and disappeared, and did not return for a week. When he had bolted, Yosele had but two kopecks in his pocket. On the seventh morning of his absence, he strolled into Anna's kitchen.

"Where have you been!" Anna cried.

"In Sevastopol," Yosele casually replied.

"But that's 200 miles away," she gasped. "How did you eat? How did you live?"

He did not answer. Instead, he reached into his pocket and put his two kopecks on the table. Then he grinned at his mother.

Yosele was the most exasperating child.

Meyer was the athlete in the family. Often he would skip school, and later would be found doing acrobatic stunts on a bicycle. He was the smallest of his peers, but had the distinction of being able to beat up any kid on the block.

Yankele, the youngest brother, was still too young to have a distinct personality, but he beguiled his parents with his energetic, stomping dances.

Taybele at two was the only daughter in the family. For the moment.

In his second year as a professional singer, Sholom doubled his income. Monsieur Kurich came to see Abraham and persuaded him to allow Sholom to return to the Great Synagogue. To sweeten his proposal, he promised to train Sholom to be a cantor, and to pay him 60 rubles a year. It was an offer Abraham couldn't refuse.

Sholom was not only becoming a famous singer, he was also the star pupil in *chedar*. Buoyed by increasing self-esteem, he finally found his tongue.

"I want to be a cantor," he announced to his father.

"My son, you are not even bar mitzvah," Abraham replied. "You are too young."

"I want to be a cantor," Sholom repeated.

To appease his son's new-found stubbornness, Abraham approached the trustees of the Cobblers' Synagogue. "Let the boy chant the prayers at just one Sabbath," he pleaded, "not, God forbid, for money. I promise he won't disappoint you."

On a Friday soon after, the family, including Anna, went to the evening service at the Cobblers' Synagogue, accompanied by a claque of friends. Sholom sat by the eastern wall at the front of the synagogue. He was nearly engulfed by a mushroom-shaped yarmulke that was suspended on his ears.

The service began. Sholom covered his slender shoulders with a prayer shawl that trailed on the ground, and walked to the cantor's lectern. Tapping his tuning fork, he found the correct pitch and began singing, ''Come, let us sing. . . .'' The congregants were astounded by the young boy's authority, his poise, silver voice.

Sholom was asked to repeat his performance at the Sabbath service the following morning. This time, the tiny temple was overflowing with visitors. News of the little cantor's debut had spread among Jews throughout the city, and worshipers from the Choir Synagogue, the Tailors' Synagogue, the Hatters' and Furriers' Synagogue all came to hear the boy. People who couldn't fit into the room spilled out onto the steps and street. After the service Abraham shook hands with members of the Jewish community of Nicholayev.

''You son will be another Rumzumni, Russia's greatest cantor!'' one man said. ''He's going to be a famous man someday,'' said another. Abraham smiled and nodded.

Until he was eleven, Sholom's life had been a struggle, but not unhappy. At eleven he had known more praise than he could imagine. If the attention paid him caused his siblings to envy him, he was not, until years later, aware of it. But his uncluttered euphoria was not to last.

Between 1903 and 1905, a series of pogroms against the Jews erupted all over Russia, particularly in the Ukraine. Many pogroms occurred in cities simultaneously, carefully choreographed by the Minister of the Interior. Although they seemed so, there was nothing spontaneous about these pogroms. Jews had traditionally been scapegoats for Imperial wrath, and the years immediately following the turn of the century were especially threatening to the crown.

Between 1904 and 1905, Russia had engaged in war against Japan and had suffered a humiliating military defeat at Port Arthur. The disgrace stoked simmering unrest among Russia's peasants and workers to the boiling point. On Sunday, January 22, 1905, an estimated 120,000 workers marched peacefully toward the Winter Palace in St. Petersburg to deliver their grievances to Tsar Nicholas II.[1] Imperial soldiers opened fire on the crowd that included women and children, killing several hundred people and wounding thousands. ''Bloody Sunday'' touched off a series of strikes that paralyzed Russia's industry and culminated in the October Manifesto which promised freedoms of conscience, speech, assembly and representation in an electoral parliament, the Duma.[2]

On paper the Russian Revolution of 1905 seemed to be a success. In fact, it inflamed reactionary forces eager to punish the revolutionaries, however peaceful their original intent. The day after the October Manifesto was issued, several organizations known as the "Black Hundreds," funded by the secret police, incited mob brutality against the revolutionaries.[3] Jews were singled out for the harshest attacks, because it was believed that they were the backbone of the revolutionary movement, having the most to gain by Imperial reform. Russian soldiers ignored the anti-Semitic bloodletting. During one pogrom in Odessa, soldiers were not called in until the fourth day of rioting.[4]

Members of the Secunda family still living in Alexandria had written to Abraham about a pogrom in their town. An account of the Alexandria pogrom survives in a St. Petersburg periodical that was published in 1904:

On September 6, . . . a mob of local hooligans, joined by a few recently drafted soldiers, began to loot Jewish stores and businesses. Within an hour more than a score of stores were looted, and one could observe interesting metamorphoses. The women suddenly paraded in new scarves on their heads and new shoes. The men clad themselves in new boots and caftans. Some looters, those who are fond of somebody else's property, carried away from the stores whole bundles, which they immediately loaded onto their wagons, and left in a hurry.

In broad daylight, a robbery took place before the eyes of everybody. Whistling and shouting of the looters filled the air. The rest of the mob went about appropriating the merchandise from the Jewish stores very quietly, businesslike, without shouting and yelling. The victims of the robbery did not display any anger. They were simply deprived of their possessions.

On their way, the looters encountered a synagogue, and here something terrible happened. It has been reported that some shooting provoked the mob, and it forced its way into the synagogue. The mob began beating the worshipers. More than two scores of Jews were wounded, and one of them died. In this terrible moment Father Aleksei Aleksandrowitch arrived to help the Jews. He appeared in the square with banners and started to officiate a (Russian Orthodox) service under the open sky. By this action, he stopped, for a time, the pogrom.

But at the end of the service, the pogrom resumed and was aimed primarily at the better stores. Again about 50 men started to loot and destroy, and the mob, several thousand strong, took away the robbed goods by foot and by horse. At nightfall the looters stopped their "work," and the following day a hundred cossacks arrived to put an end to the pogrom.[5]

Another report tallied the casualties: three dead, hundreds wounded.[6]

Sholom almost certainly knew about the Alexandria pogrom but, like most young people, was protected from premature panic by feelings of immortality. Unless tragedy is experienced, it does not truly exist, especially when you are eleven.

The tragic implication of being a Russian Jew exploded before his eyes in 1905, just thirteen months after the Alexandria pogrom. Nicholayev had a pogrom of its own.

The owner of the building in which the Secundas lived was a Christian man of compassion. When the pogrom began on the outskirts of Nicholayev, he tried to protect his Jewish tenants. He hung crosses in all the windows facing the street, and he allowed Jews in the building to go up to the hotel on the second floor and hide themselves there. He was sure that the pogromists—soldiers, cossacks, rioters— wouldn't venture into the hotel.

Abraham heard the rioters running through the streets toward their building and yelled at his family to go upstairs. The four older sons led the way into the courtyard and up the steps leading to the second-floor entrance to the hotel. Abraham carried Yankele and Anna held Taybele in her arms. Sholom, holding onto his mother's dress, brought up the rear.

Just as they got to the hotel entrance, the rioters, many of them carrying clubs, ran into the courtyard, like a crack spreading through glass. They began looting the lower apartments as Abraham pushed his family through the hotel door and slammed it shut. In his haste he did not notice that Sholom was still standing outside on the steps.

Sholom, paralyzed, peered through the banister and watched the bullies below. They smashed the shutters and windows. They shouted and sang and demolished everything in sight. Sholom watched as though he were standing in another time—it never occurred to him that he was in danger.

Inside, Abraham made a head count of the children and realized that Sholom was missing. He threw open the hotel door, ignoring the risk to himself and the others, and ran outside. He saw Sholom staring at the savagery in the courtyard, ran down the few steps to where his son stood, scooped him up in his arms and carried him up to the hotel. Once the door was locked, he slapped Sholom hard across the face. Anna, with tears streaming down her cheeks, grabbed her son and covered his face with kisses.

The Nicholayev pogrom lasted for three days. The Secundas huddled with the other Jewish tenants in hushed clusters on the corridor floors, hungry and terrified. The landlord brought up a little food each day, and with it stories of atrocities to Jews in other parts of the city. One pregnant Jewish woman, he was told, had foolishly gone out into the street and had been trapped by a band of rioters. They threw her to the ground, slit open her abdomen with a knife and stuffed it with feathers. Other stories filtered up to the frightened group, stories that would haunt them for the rest of their lives, stories that Anna would bring to America.

On the fourth day, the city was quiet. The Secundas and their neighbors made a blessing for having escaped with their lives. The men cautiously led their wives and children down the stairs and back to their apartments. Because of the icons and crosses, there was little damage to the Secundas' rooms, save for broken windows.

Life resumed its former rhythm, but not the thoughts or the nights of the survivors. The constant fear of another pogrom made the Sabbath prayers more profound, the pleasure of music more poignant, the adherence to Judaism more urgent.

That moment, watching the rioters from the steps, was the moment when Sholom lost his childhood. From that time on, he would consider his religion before nationalism or professional gain. From that time on, the horror of the Nicholayev pogrom would define him in all his decisions: he was a Jew.

Russia's difficulties, domestic and foreign, began to tear apart Jewish families. The Russo-Japanese debacle had depleted Russia's male population. Hardest hit by the draft were the Jews. In Nicholayev, over 200 Jewish men were drafted, depriving 600 children of support. Charitable Jewish societies were formed to help the fatherless families. A report of these philanthropic efforts appeared in the *Voskhod,* a St. Petersburg weekly, in 1904:

> We welcome most warmly the response of the whole Jewish population to the appeal of the society to help poor Jews of the city of Nicholayev to establish a new, special fund for the needs of families of the soldiers called up for military service. Hundreds of people of various sexes and ages have placed themselves at the disposal of the society. They spend all their free time covering the districts allotted to them, collecting small and large donations, registering the unfortunate families. The information gathered by the registrars reveals for us a terrible picture of poverty and misery. From among the 200 families deprived of their husbands, (many) go hungry the day after the departure of their husbands.[7]

Abraham Secunda had been able to avoid the draft—probably because of his age—but he feared for his sons, especially Velvel, 19, who had received his draft notice. Abraham had learned from Jewish friends that it was possible to smuggle his son out of Russia and to obtain the immigration papers needed for Velvel to enter the United States.

In 1903, Velvel managed to escape to America. The details of his journey do not survive, but he probably crossed the Austro-Hungarian border illegally, the route frequently used by politically vulnerable Russian Jews who were in a hurry. Velvel settled in New York.

With the escape of Velvel, Abraham realized that his position and that of his family were untenable. Once again, the brightest hopes for them lay elsewhere—this time, across the Atlantic Ocean. Lacking the money to take his entire family out of Russia simultaneously, he began their piecemeal evacuation.

Sholom was the next to leave home, but not for the United States. Following the Nicholayev pogrom, and the resumption of daily family routines, Sholom's cantorial career progressed. Although still too young to be an official cantor, his reputation for virtuoso cantorial singing grew.

Sholom continued to sing at the Great Synagogue, largely because of its cantor, Monsieur Lakhman, whose tenor voice was brilliant. Within the year, Lakhman was hired as the cantor of the Choir Synagogue of Yekaterinaslav (present name: Dnieprapetravsk), a large city 175 miles away. With Lakhman, Sholom had learned the subtle intricacies of cantorial improvisation, and he had grown fond of his musical mentor.

Shortly after his departure for Yekaterinaslav, Lakhman returned to Nicholayev for a brief visit. His mission: to hire Sholom as the soloist in Lakhman's new choir. Sholom was then only eleven, and had never been separated from his parents. But Cantor Lakhman could be very persuasive.

"I have spoken to my choir director, Monsieur Shargaradski, about your son," Lakhman said. "We both believe Sholom and our choir would benefit from his being our soloist. In Yekaterinaslav, his opportunities are greater than they are here. He will live at my house. We will pay him 18 rubles a month, and he will have no expenses. This is an extraordinary opportunity for him."

The offer was tempting, but Abraham was dubious. "Sholom is now in government school and is still going to *chedar*," he hedged. "We don't want his education to stop."

"Think about it," Lakhman said. "I'll come back tomorrow."

As soon as Lakhman left, Sholom, who had overheard the conversation, burst into tears. "Please let me go," he begged. "I promise I'll write every day, and I can send home my earnings." His parents refused.

"One son is already in America," Anna said, "and this would mean another son away from home."

Sholom wailed.

The following morning, he applied more pressure. That evening, Cantor Lakhman returned and resumed his compelling arguments.

At last, Abraham and Anna relented. A week later, Abraham and Sholom boarded the overnight train to Yekaterinaslav. "It was the solemnest day of my life," Sholom later wrote. He looked out the window and saw his mother, brothers and sister standing on the platform, crying, as the train pulled out of the station.

The next morning, Cantor Lakhman met Abraham and Sholom at

the railroad station and took them in a droshky to an inn, having reserved a room for them. Then he took them to his house.

Mrs. Lakhman greeted Sholom with a hug and a kiss. She introduced him to her four children, and showed Abraham where Sholom would be sleeping. In a corner of the dining room there was a large, wooden chest where she kept clothing and linen.

"I'll make the chest up with good bedding," she said reassuringly to Abraham, "and it will be comfortable for your son." Her own children slept on iron beds—not on the floor, as Sholom did at home—in a second room. The house was airy and roomy, and reflected its owners' prosperity.

Abraham had decided to stay in Yekaterinaslav for two days to help Sholom orient himself to his new surroundings. In the afternoon they strolled back to the inn.

"Are you sure you want to stay, Sholom?" Abraham asked. "You can still change your mind."

"I want to stay," Sholom replied, with only slightly faltering conviction.

The following morning Sholom went to his first rehearsal at the synagogue. Although the repertoire was entirely new to him, he sight-read the material easily. At the end of the rehearsal Monsieur Shargaradski, the choir director, walked up to Sholom and patted him on the head. "Ah," he said with a grin, "you gobble down notes like potatoes."

At the inn that night Sholom and his father went to bed early so that Abraham could rest up for the long journey back to Nicholayev the next morning. Sholom waited until his father's breathing was slow and rhythmic, a certainty that he was asleep. The little boy wept quietly through most of the night, and was awake when his father got up. They dressed and had a breakfast of bread and tea.

Abraham carried his packed bag to the street and hailed a droshky. Father and son were silent all the way to the station. The train was due to depart, and Abraham hurriedly bought a ticket. Sholom clung to his father as onlookers watched the poignant farewell. At last, Abraham disengaged himself from his son's arms and ran for the train. Sholom stood on the platform for a long time, watching the train until it was out of sight.

Abraham had given Sholom enough money to take a droshky back to the Lakhmans', but he decided to walk instead (all his life Sholom would walk rather than ride, to save carfare). He wanted to explore Yekaterinaslav.

That day Sholom saw his first trolley. "In Nicholayev," he wrote, "everybody rode with horses. Here, there were trolleys without horses, and faster than horses. I couldn't tear my eyes away from such a wonder. The boulevard where I walked was wider than any I had ever seen. The trolleys seemed to fly past me on both sides. The stores lining the street seemed like pyramids. The bigness of everything made such an impression on me that I forgot about my misery at being left alone."

Sholom followed the trolley tracks to Ayordunskaya Street, where the Lakhmans lived, and found their house. He arrived just as the family was sitting down to their midday meal. He took his seat next to the oldest son, Isaac, and looked around the room admiringly at the polished floors and crisp curtains at the windows. But what impressed him most was the food.

It was the first time he had ever eaten such a meal in the middle of the week. The Lakhmans' routine lunch consisted of soup, meat and white bread. In the Secunda family such a meal was served only on the Sabbath, and not always then.

After lunch the Lakhmans and their younger children lay down for a nap. Cantor Lakhman gave the two older boys permission to go for a walk.

Out on the street, Isaac said, "You want to go for a trolley ride for free?"

"Yes," Sholom said, "but how?"

"When the conductor is in the front of the car collecting the passengers' fares, you and I will climb on the back of the car. He'll be too busy to notice. When he sees me, I'll give a shout and jump off, and you follow me. I do it every day with the other boys."

Sholom didn't dare admit he was scared. "All right," he said bravely, "I'll try it."

A trolley stopped and picked up the queue of passengers. It started up slowly, giving the boys time to grab onto the railings at the rear of the car. In a couple of minutes the conductor spotted the hangers-on and headed for the rear. Isaac shouted at Sholom and jumped off. Sholom looked down between his feet at the tracks that were streaking below him in silver blurs, and clung in terror to the railing, afraid of killing himself in a fall.

The conductor reached the terrified boy and yanked him roughly onto the trolley. He stood, holding Sholom by the ear, who blushed with embarrassment as the other passengers giggled, until the trolley came to a stop, and shoved him into the middle of the street. Sholom sat in the dirt, his ego and knees bruised, until Isaac trotted up to him. He helped Sholom to his feet, and led his limping companion home.

Sholom's beginnings with the choir were as awkward as his first trolley ride. In the evening there was a general rehearsal at the Great Synagogue, and Sholom was greeted with a chill from the other boys in the choir. He overheard one of them ask the choir director, "What's he doing here? Aren't my solos good enough any more?"

It wasn't the newness of Sholom's position alone that threatened them; it was also his uncanny talent for sight-reading. The boys conspired to find a way to sabotage Sholom's musicianship, and they very nearly succeeded. When Sholom rose to sing a solo over the choir's harmony, the boys sang so softly they nearly whispered, and Sholom was unable to hear them. The idea was to force him to lose his place. Sholom, however, quickly caught on, and the trick worked only once.

When they returned to the Lakhmans' house, Cantor Lakhman told his wife of Sholom's triumph and she beamed in approval. "That makes you worth a glass of milk and a piece of bread and butter," she said. Sholom got into his nightclothes. Mrs. Lakhman tucked him in, put out the light, and retired with her husband for the night.

The jousts of the day behind him, Sholom lay awake in the dark dining room. He was seized by an attack of homesickness. He couldn't bear sleeping alone, having shared one room with all his brothers for eleven years. Sholom was terrified by solitude, a terror that would linger a lifetime. He cried himself to sleep.

In the middle of the night he woke up with an urgent need to go to the bathroom. There were no bathrooms in the house, and although the Lakhman children had chamber pots under their beds, Mrs. Lakhman had failed to give one to Sholom. The only alternative was to go out into the courtyard where there was an outhouse. Unfortunately Mrs. Lakhman had also failed to tell Sholom its exact location. Sholom's need was so great that he was in pain, but he dared not wake up the household with so private a matter. He felt his way along the walls until he found the front door. Once outside he peered through the darkness, but could not see the outhouse. In desperation, he relieved himself in a corner of the courtyard.

In the darkness, Sholom had become disoriented, and he could not find the door to the Lakhmans' apartment. Chilled, miserable and exhausted, he dropped onto the cobbled street by a wall and fell asleep.

At dawn, Sholom was shaken awake by the yardkeeper, who directed him back to the Lakhmans' apartment. Everyone was still asleep when he slipped back onto the linen chest. He drew the covers around his trembling shoulders and fell asleep. So soundly did he sleep that he didn't hear the Cantor and his family gathering around the dining table for breakfast. Mrs. Lakhman gently stroked his face until he was awake and said softly, "Here we don't sleep so late. You'll have to learn to get up a little earlier. Now get dressed. It's time to eat."

Sholom did as he was told, saying nothing about the previous night's misadventure. The yardkeeper, however, was not bound to keep Sholom's wanderings a secret, and informed the Cantor of them shortly after breakfast.

Mrs. Lakhman led Sholom outside to show him the outhouse and said she would give him a chamberpot each night. Then she ordered him back to bed. "You must rest," she said. "Tonight you'll be singing for the congregation for the first time, and you have to take care of your voice."

Sholom slept for most of the day, and in the evening he and the Lakhman family went to the synagogue. He joined the other boys in the choir room and, like them, dressed in a tall, velvet yarmulke and a prayer shawl.

His singing debut in Yekaterinaslav resembled his previous debuts. News of the small boy with the big voice attracted a capacity crowd to the synagogue. Sholom was, as before, inspired by an audience. After the service, the boys slapped him on the back and several elders in the congregation squeezed his hand and said, "Well done."

The Lakhmans returned to the house, where the Sabbath meal was waiting. They buzzed about Sholom's singing, everyone sang Sabbath songs, and Sholom melted into the warmth of his new, temporary family.

At bedtime, Mrs. Lakhman took Sholom aside and said in mock

anger, "Now, young man, if you will be so kind as to follow me, I will accompany you to the courtyard. I want to be sure there is no repetition of last night's incident."

Sholom blended into his new life and routine with the ease with which most children adapt to change, always to their own astonishment in adult hindsight. He wrote to his parents every day, as promised, and sent them his monthly salary and a few extra rubles he picked up at outside singing engagements—25 kopecks for an average wedding, as much as 35 kopecks for the funeral of a very rich man.

Since he was not attending school or *chedar,* Sholom had to find ways to amuse himself. In the morning he usually went with the Cantor to the synagogue for morning prayers. In the afternoon Sholom would practice jumping off trolley cars. In the evening he went to rehearsals.

Mornings were his favorite part of the day. "I became a drinker at the age of 11," he later said with a laugh. Nearly every morning at the synagogue there was someone observing the anniversary of a relative's death, which called for a ceremonial drink. It was customary for the mourner to bring a couple of bottles of vodka and some herring and bread. Sholom would be asked to join in for a *l'chaim,* a glass of vodka and a bite to eat. His early acquaintance with vodka resulted in spontaneous naps on a synagogue bench and a good deal of laughter from the older men. In time the little drinker could hold his liquor nearly as well as his elders.

With his extra earnings—minus a bit spent daily on ice cream and chocolates—he also sent home theater programs. Most of the boys in the synagogue choir belonged to a children's drama club, and Sholom sang leading roles in productions such as Goldfaden's "Shulamis" (for which, many years later, he would write his own score). He also appeared with the synagogue's adult drama club, which mounted plays in a public theater.

Sholom passed the winter months growing in size and confidence. Although he missed his family, for the first time he was aware of an identity apart from them.

Life was smooth, until spring. One unseasonably warm afternoon, Sholom and his fellow choir-members were walking back from the outskirts of the city, where they had sung at the funeral of a wealthy congregant. For his solo Sholom had been paid 50 kopecks, and he and his friends crowded into a candy store and exchanged a bit of their fees for chocolates. The dusty road back to town followed the banks of the Dnieper River.

"Let's go for a swim," one of the boys suggested, his mouth full of candy. The boys ran to the shore and took off their clothes, swam out a short distance into the murky, frigid water, and turned back.

One by one the shivering boys clambered out of the water, and suddenly they turned to watch Sholom struggling for shore. "My hands refused to move," Sholom wrote, "and I could barely move my legs. I had a terrific pain in my head and I felt very drowsy." Thoughts of his brother's death by drowning must have contributed to his panic. When he pulled himself onto the bank, he was trembling. His friends helped him to dress and walked him home. The Cantor and his family had just sat down to dinner when the small band deposited Sholom on the front steps and fled, afraid that the Cantor would think they had played some kind of cruel prank. When Sholom walked in the door, Mrs. Lakhman asked him to wash up for dinner.

"If you don't mind," Sholom said softly, "I'm not very hungry. I don't feel too well."

Mrs. Lakhman walked over to Sholom and felt his forehead. "You're burning with fever," she said. "Get right to bed." After he put on his night things, she tucked him in and gave him two teaspoons of castor oil—the universal home remedy for any illness—hopeful that the awful-tasting liquid would by morning produce a cure.

It did not. By the following afternoon, he still had a raging fever. Fearful that he had a contagious disease, Mrs. Lakhman fetched an older member of the choir, a young man who lived next door, and asked him to take Sholom to the hospital. There he was examined by a doctor who agreed that Sholom's illness was severe. However, there wasn't a free bed in the hospital, the doctor said, and he advised the young man to take Sholom back home. In the hospital corridor, however, Sholom collapsed and his companion ran back for the doctor. Sholom lost consciousness and was placed in an isolation room. He did not wake up for a week.

He had typhus.

When Sholom finally regained consciousness, he woke to a bright, crystal morning. Next to his bed was a large window that looked out onto a courtyard of the hospital. At first, he thought he was dreaming—he imagined that he saw his mother standing on a ladder outside the window. Sholom screamed, "That's my mother! That's my mother!"

A nurse came into the room, quieted the hysterical boy, and said gently, "She's been standing on that ladder every day for nearly a week."

It had been a harrowing six days for Anna. She had received a telegram from Cantor Lakhman informing her of Sholom's illness, and had taken the first available train from Nicholayev.

The morning of her arrival she was met by the Cantor, who took her directly to the hospital.

"I want to see my son," she announced to the doctor.

"No one is permitted in his room because of contagion," the doctor replied.

"I am not leaving until I see my son," Anna said, setting her jaw. "If you won't let me see him, then I must assume that he is dead."

Anna was not a woman to be put off, particularly when it came to her cubs. At last the hospital personnel allowed her to climb the ladder, held securely by two orderlies, to see for herself. In his sleep, Sholom had inadvertently covered his face with the covers, and no one had taken the precaution of checking him before letting Anna witness his condition. When she climbed to the top of the ladder, what she saw through the window was a small mound covered by a sheet. Believing that her son had died, she fainted into the arms of the two men below. A doctor revived her and assured her that Sholom was alive. Finally she climbed back onto the ladder. A nurse folded back the covers to reveal the semiconscious boy.

Sholom remained in the hospital for three weeks. The doctors told Anna that she should take her son to Nicholayev, where he could begin what would be a slow recovery. Sholom's career in Yekaterinaslav was finished.

On the last morning of his stay in the hospital, a nurse walked into his room carrying a little box and handed it to Sholom. "What's this?" he asked, shaking the box. He heard a clanking noise.

"Open it up and see," the nurse said, smiling. Sholom lifted the cover and saw an assortment of silver coins. "While you were sick," the nurse explained, "the boys in the choir came to look at you through the window. Every time they came, they brought a few coins.

They told me that the money is your share of the funerals and weddings they sang at during your stay in the hospital.''

Sholom was touched by the act of friendship from the same boys who, a few months before, had tried to elbow him out of the choir. The day Sholom was released from the hospital, Cantor Lakhman picked him and his mother up and took them to the railroad station. The man and boy embraced, both of them weeping, and said goodby.

Sholom's recovery was agonizing, particularly for an 11-year-old boy on the brink of puberty. He lost his hair and his voice. Both occurrences had been predicted by the doctors, and both were temporary. Within a few weeks, his blond curls returned and eventually his voice was as strong as ever.

But the family Sholom returned to was very different from the family he had left. Anna had given birth to her second daughter, Saratshke. Abraham had launched the second phase of the evacuation of his family from Russia. He had taken Yosele and Meyer to America, probably by the same illegal route Velvel had taken, since his sons had reached draft age. Aaron remained as the senior male breadwinner. Although he was the second oldest, he was also the smallest of the brothers, and his parents believed that his diminutive size would keep him out of the army.

Life in the Secunda home took on a tenuousness. Aaron continued to make beds in the shop. Anna took Abraham's place and carried the beds to stores to be sold. Every week letters arrived from America. Abraham wrote,

We are living in one room and all working and making a living. The time will come soon, please God, when I can send you boat tickets so that our family can be together again. This place is a golden land with wonderful synagogues and Yiddish theaters. Here you don't have to be afraid of Fonye (the Tsar), or pogroms.

Anna kept her husband abreast of the news, chatting to him in her letters about the children. Sholom wrote letters as well, but not of the usual sort. He wrote his news in rhymes and set them to music. Velvel, being a musician, would sing the letters to his father and brothers, and write back to Sholom, begging for more.

Across the ocean, both halves of the family tried to keep up their spirits in the limbo of their indefinite plans. Abraham sent a letter that was designed to encourage his family:

> I have recently met and become acquainted with the famous Jewish composer and choir-director Herman Wohl. I have told him about our talented little boy. Mr. Wohl assures me that if Sholom is really such a gem, he will take him under his wing and develop him. Choirboys like that aren't born in America, he says. I told him I do not yet have enough money for boat tickets to bring you all here. Wohl says he will help me find a way to secure boat tickets for the whole family.

The letter frustrated Sholom, partly because, as a professional singer, he believed he was able to earn extra money to help the family leave Russia more quickly, and partly because he was tantalized by what Wohl had said about him. Sholom suggested to his mother that he officiate, for a fee, at prayer services on Sabbaths in the small synagogues in Nicholayev.

Anna must have admired her son's resourcefulness, and most certainly was exhausted by work, caring for an infant, and worry about her truncated family. In any case she agreed to Sholom's plan. After all he had just passed his twelfth birthday—he was nearly a man.

Sholom persuaded the trustees of the Hatters' and Furriers' Synagogue to allow him to chant the prayer services the following Sabbath. After the service the *shammes* stood before the congregation with a plate into which the men threw coins. A trustee wrapped the small pile of coins into a handkerchief and gave it to Sholom. At home Anna sat down at the table and opened the bundle. She counted out 25 rubles.

Sholom began to sing in a different synagogue each week. It wasn't enough. The family was barely able to subsist on their small, combined income. So he began singing in towns within a 20-mile radius of Nicholayev.

His first on-the-road job was in Dabrinka. Sholom had never traveled alone before. He had heard, however, that it was possible to go on a train without paying for the ticket. All you do, he was told, is hide under a seat so the conductor won't notice you. As the train is pulling into your destination, you simply crawl out and hop off the train. Sholom's trolley capers had provided useful seasoning for the ploy.

Anna gave her son sufficient money to pay for his trip, innocent of his plan to enjoy the largesse of the tsar's railroads. But the trick was not to be as easy as he had been told.

Sholom went to the Nicholayev station, where the conductor was standing on the platform. When his back was turned, Sholom scrambled onto the train and crept under the first seat he saw, before the other passengers were even on board. Although he was twelve, he still looked like a child, and his smallness made it easier to curl up under the seat.

The passengers began boarding the train. Many of them carried baskets containing their belongings which they slid under their seats. One of the baskets struck Sholom in the face, but he bit his lip and kept silent. At last the conductor shouted, "Pervi zvanak" (first bell), then "Vtaroy zvanak" (second bell), and finally, "Treti zvanak" (third bell), which meant that the train was about to start.

As the train eased out of the station, the conductor asked the passengers for their tickets. Knowledgeable about stowaways, he kicked under each seat to ferret out clandestine travelers. Being hit by the basket was, for Sholom, fortuitous—the conductor kicked it, rather than him. Sholom silently held his cramped position until the conductor called, "Dabrinka Station!" As the passengers rose to file out of the car, Sholom crawled out from under the seat and mingled among them until he was safely out onto the platform.

Carrying his own basket, which Anna had packed with bread and his tall, white yarmulke, he looked about the station and spotted a man with a beard and sidelocks, who directed Sholom to the synagogue.

Morning prayers were in progress, shared by only the *shammes* and a few ancient worshipers. After the service, Sholom spoke to the *shammes,* listing his cantorial credentials, however ex-officio, to the puzzled man, adding that in a year he would be bar mitzvah.

"This boy says he is a cantor," the *shammes* said, turning to the group of old men who were hunched over the sacred books. "Oh, really?" one of them replied sardonically. "Let's hear him sing something."

Sholom rapped his tuning fork and sang, as he had done so many times before. The *shammes* took him to the trustee's office in town, where Sholom sang again. He was hired for the Sabbath. The trustee instructed the *shammes* to give the boy something to eat and a place to sleep.

On Friday evening and Saturday morning Sholom sang the Sabbath services. Sunday morning he was given a pile of loose coins and a small bundle of food. Again he went to the station, and crawled under a seat on the train, thereby saving his return fee as well. At home he gave the money to Anna: 30 rubles.

For weeks the Dabrinka scenario was repeated in town after town, and each week Sholom returned with more and more coins. In preparation for Abraham's letter about boat tickets, Anna collected enough money to buy railroad tickets for herself and the children from Nicholayev to the Latvian city of Libau (now called Liepaja), an ice-free port on the Baltic Sea.

The long-awaited letter from Abraham arrived in November of 1907:

> Mr. Wohl has introduced me to a Mr. Wolf, a manager of cantors and concert artists. Mr. Wolf told me that if Sholom is as good as I say he is, he will make us rich. He will buy your boat tickets and take the money out of Sholom's earnings when he begins singing here in New York. In the meantime, Mr. Wolf is preparing advertisements about Sholom's arrival, and will engage him to sing at Sabbath services and concerts.

> And so, my dearest, the time has finally come. I want you to sell all the household goods and shop equipment. In one week I will send you the boat tickets for you and the children. You must arrange for a passport yourself. That I cannot do from so great a distance.

Anna's hands trembled as she read the letter. It had been a year since she had seen her husband, two years since she had seen her first-born son.

The countdown for their emigration to the United States began immediately. The first order of business was the passport. Anna knew that the safest journey for herself and the children would be a legal one, through Libau. It would also be the trickiest. Aaron was draft age, and the government was not issuing passports to young men who were slated for service in the army. Wisely, Anna had squirreled away bribe money as well.

The next morning she visited the commissioner of police in Nicholayev. "I would like to obtain a passport as quickly as possible for myself and my children," she said, smiling sweetly. "I am sure you will be able to arrange this for me, and I hope, when the papers are ready, you will be kind enough to accept a generous gift." The police commissioner, long accustomed to the generosity of Jews desperate to leave Russia, nodded, returning her smile in conspiratorial warmth.

A week later the commissioner delivered the passport to Anna. He promised her that her journey across the border into Latvia would be smooth, and that she could take all her children—regardless of their ages—with her. Anna clasped his hand and into it placed a bag full of rubles.

Next, she began selling their belongings except, once again, for the bedding and the samovar. With the tools sold, Anna and Aaron were no longer able to make and sell the beds. Sholom continued to sing for the family's food.

At the end of November a package from Abraham arrived with the boat tickets and instructions for their departure. Anna sat at the kitchen table—which was still unsold—and opened the package.

"You will take the train to Libau," Abraham wrote, "then a ship to Liverpool, England. From there you will take the ocean-liner *Carmania* to New York." When she finished reading the letter, she put her head on the table and wept.

On the first Sabbath in December, Sholom sang his final service at the Hatters' and Furriers' Synagogue. The other synagogues in Nicholayev had arranged to shorten their services so that the choirs could attend Sholom's farewell performance. After the service the trustees of the synagogue came to Anna's house to personally say their goodbys. They gave her 25 rubles, and then turned to Sholom. "This is for you," one of them said, putting into his hands a silver watch on a long, silver chain. On the back of the watch was engraved, "We will never forget your sweet singing."

Sholom nodded his thanks—the emotion that clogged his throat had rendered him speechless. Of all the leave-takings in his twelve years, this was the most painful. Nicholayev—its bitter cold, its warm music, its poverty, its friendships, its bloodshed—was his home. With an uncertain future Sholom said goodby to the familiarity of his sometimes rocky past.

♫ AMERICA

It was customary for husbands or relatives in the United States to send steamship tickets to Russian immigrants. The flight from Russia required knowledge of bureaucratic red tape. To help Jews escape, a number of East European Jewish agencies were established to guide refugees through the maze of hotel, railroad and ship connections, as well as customs and language barriers.

As Irving Howe points out in *World of Our Fathers,* the Jew passed through many hands, some oiled by greed: "Con men, cheap-Jacks, sharpers, white slavers, thieves, money changers, thugs: a rich assortment of villains drawn from all races worked the ports of the north Atlantic."[1] The Jewish agencies managed to either eliminate, or work around, the unscrupulous.

Other institutional shepherds from Russia were the steamship companies. It was not political or humane compassion that motivated them; it was profit. John Maxtone-Graham, in *The Only Way to Cross,* writes:

In the last decade before the First World War, emigration involved a huge volume of business for the steamship companies. It was no accident that the peak year of all time, 1907, when one million two hundred thousand were admitted to the United States, also saw the maiden voyage of the Lusitania and Mauretania. Other superliners that followed on their heels were designed with this huge demand in mind, and the economic foundation that made such fleets of enormous vessels feasible was the seemingly endless flow of humble passengers. Half of the Imperator's thirty-five hundred passengers were immigrants. Companies might publicize the splendor of their swimming pools and restaurants, but their most profitable clients never used them. . .Like all gigantic human enterprises, the emigrant boom was not merely subject to natural fluctuations. There was also judicious manipulation on the part of the companies who, having ordered the ships, now promoted a hard-sell campaign to keep them filled.[2]

Many of the steamship companies also provided railroad tickets and arranged lodging along the route to the United States, a sort of steerage package deal.[3]

Abraham worked through American representatives of one such company and Anna followed its directives, outlined in a final letter from her husband.

On the Tuesday evening following Sholom's farewell Sabbath service, Anna, Aaron, Sholom, Yankele, Saratshke and Taybele boarded the train for the two-day trip to Libau. They were met at the Libau railroad station by a steamship representative, taken to a large inn which was crowded with other refugees, and told they would remain there for a few days until it was time to board a ship for Liverpool. The agent told them not to leave the inn, a precaution, he said, against the wiles of crooks.

Conditions at the inn were, at best, cramped and uncomfortable. Two things eased the Secundas' stopover. One was the momentum of finally leaving the land of the Tsars and the prospect of freedom and family reunion. The other was that at the inn, Anna ran into an old friend from her home town whom she had not seen in 25 years. Her friend was the mother of Abba Ostrovski, who earned a respected reputation later as an artist in the United States. Abba was by then in America, and his father, mother and sisters were traveling to join him. The two families spent most of their time at the inn together (in years to come, they would be neighbors in Manhattan and Brooklyn).

Three days later, several droshkys gathered up the England-bound refugees and took them to a small ship. The crossing was uneventful, thanks to calm seas, and in three more days they were in Liverpool. There they were taken to another inn where they stayed for another three days. "The facilities were of poor quality," Sholom wrote, "but they were good enough for us, because in Nicholayev we didn't have better. Still, all the passengers felt like prisoners."

At last the travelers were taken to the *Carmania,* a Cunard ocean-liner built around the turn of the century that was driven by the latest in navigational power—turbine engines (because of its speed, during World War I the ship was converted into an armed merchant cruiser).[4] January was not the most propitious time of the year to cross the North Atlantic. John Maxtone-Graham writes:

> The natural hazards to be met on this ocean defy invention and read like a seasonal catalogue from hell. Hulls of all ocean-going vessels carry a painted symbol called a load-line, indicating permissible displacements for various seasons and types of water. The lowest level bears the terse abbreviation "WNA"—Winter North Atlantic. No other ocean has this specific billing.[5]

Steerage in ocean-going vessels at the turn of the century was hell within a hell. Passengers were crammed together in the lowest reaches of a ship; slop that passed for stew was dealt from a common kettle; toilets and berths were filthy. Because of the profitability of steerage with the immigration boom, some steamship companies improved conditions, provided stewards and clean dining rooms, in order to insure that passengers would recommend the facilities to relatives in Eastern Europe.[6]

Still there was always the crush of too many bodies in too little space, and at best, this is what a Russian immigrant could expect for the approximately $35 he paid to cross the Atlantic.[7]

> . . .compartments were little more than hold space, filled with sixteen bunk units. The bunks, or rather shelves, were about six by three feet, four to a tier separated by an eight-inch board, and served not only as bed but bureau and closet as well. In the center of the compartment was a table, on which three meals were served daily. . .Despite this vast improvement over the communal potato pot of the Britannia, it was still customary for passengers to bring supplementary rations of their own. . .[8]

Each bunk was cushioned by straw, thrown overboard at the end of the crossing, and a blanket.[9] In many cases eating utensils were not provided, although the more ambitious companies did by 1905 furnish them. One of the lower open-air decks was earmarked for steerage passengers' use, but deck chairs were an accoutrement only for first and second class. In any case they would have taken up too much space. There were too many people to make room for such comforts. This is Sholom's recollection of his family's voyage:

The *Carmania,* in comparison with modern ships, was not big. We were traveling twelve days. The ocean raged, and the waves rolled the ship back and forth. Most of the passengers, including my mother, were sick during the entire voyage.

Since we were a family of six, we were given a cabin with double-deck bunk beds. My poor mother lay in the cabin day and night. The children who were not sick ran around the deck of the ship all day. Some of the passengers found out that I was a cantor, and I was put to work on Friday and Saturday night, singing cantorial recitatives. People on deck also asked me to sing Yiddish songs to distract them from their seasickness.

Passengers who were not seasick gathered on deck and each one unburdened his heart. Most of them were going to children or husbands already in America. Each one was leaving some cruelty and going with great hopes to the Golden Land. Some of the women told how their husbands had gone away to America and, after a short time, had stopped writing. They didn't even know where their husbands were. So they were going to New York to find them —where else would a Jew go? Others complained that their sons who had run away to America from the Russian draft had never written a letter. I listened to these sad accounts and was moved to tears. I remember thinking, thank God my father and brothers are different. To pass the time on board, I wrote songs about everything I learned from the passengers. I wrote a play about the events I had heard about and called it, "Ungrateful Children." I set the play to music, mostly American songs I had learned while in Nicholayev. With the famous song, "Come, Yisroelik, Come Home," I changed the words and, instead of implying that Jews should go home to Palestine, I wrote that everyone should go home to America. I taught the songs to some of the other children, and we performed the play. The passengers were delighted.

Snow was falling on December 31, 1907, as the *Carmania* approached the shores of New York. Most of the passengers ran out onto the steerage deck to look at the building. "A great joy spread among us when we saw the Statue of Liberty," Sholom wrote. "Everyone marveled at the Singer Building, then the tallest building in New York. To us it was a miracle."

In writing about his arrival in the United States, Sholom recalled that his fellow passengers referred to Ellis Island as "Kessel Garden." From 1855 to 1892, the point of entry for immigrants had been Castle Garden, a former fort in Manhattan's Battery Park.[10] By 1890 Castle Garden simply could not process the growing influx of immigrants. Ellis Island, which opened in 1892, had been built to handle a maximum of 5,000 immigrants daily. By 1907 as many as 15,000 immigrants arrived in New York in one day.[11]

The *Carmania* was guided into its berth by harbor tugboats and secured to the mooring. Cabin passengers disembarked first, and immigrants in steerage were herded into lighters (flat-bottomed boats) for the short trip to Ellis Island. There they were led into a large auditorium filled with long benches.

When the voyagers were seated, officials started calling out names. Those whose names were called stood up, and an official led them into another room. When Anna heard the name "Secunda," she and her children followed the official to an examining room where rows of doctors, dressed in white coats and wearing rubber gloves, poked at their eyes and bodies. Next they were led to an interrogation room where immigration inspectors asked Anna where they were going, who would meet them and take care of them, lest they become a public burden.

While they were being questioned (through an interpreter), they saw Abraham, who was sitting off to one side of the room, looking anxiously at them. A clerk yelled "Abraham Secunda!" and Abraham quickly walked over to the table where the inspectors were sitting. One of the inspectors said something to him in English that neither he nor his family understood. A translator told him in Russian that they would not let his family leave Ellis Island that day because one of the children would have to be re-examined by a doctor. If, in the doctor's judgment, everything was all right, he could then take his wife and children home.

Abraham looked with anguish at Anna, and reluctantly left. The family was taken to the examining room once more. It was Yankele who needed re-examining—the doctors suspected that something was wrong with his eyes and had marked his coat with chalk, color-coded to indicate the possible disease. (They undoubtedly thought that the ten-year-old boy might have trachoma, a highly contagious infection of the mucous membrane of the eyelids. The disease, which is as common as the common cold, was widespread in Asia and Africa due to poor hygiene, and was the cause of half of the medical detentions at Ellis Island, as well as deportations if diagnosed.[12]

In the evening Anna and her children, along with hundreds of other immigrants who had been detained, were led to a large eating hall. Sitting at a long table, they learned that some of the immigrants had been there for days and hadn't been told why they were being detained. Their stories depressed Sholom and his family utterly. "That night," he recalled later, "we all slept on long benches. At least the children slept. My mother sat up all night crying in terror and anger, not knowing when my father would return or how long we would have to stay there, or worse, if we would have to be sent back to Russia."

The next morning they were fed again in the eating hall and returned to the vast waiting room. Every minute crawled by. It was almost noon before their name was announced. Anna and the children grabbed their bags and bundles and were taken to the interrogation room. Abraham, looking haggard, was there. An inspector spoke to him out of earshot of his exhausted, impatient family. Finally a smile spread across his face. He turned toward Anna and vigorously waved for her to follow him.

The family ran through the door that led outdoors. Abraham and Anna clung to each other, kissing and weeping as the gentle snowfall melted on their faces. The children wept and hooted. Abraham looked at them and said, "Where's Sholom?" Anna laughed and pushed Sholom toward him. "Don't you recognize your own son?" she said. Abraham stared at Sholom, who had been so gravely ill six months before, to see for himself that he was well.

"The last time I saw you," he said somberly, "you were a baby." Then he grinned and crushed Sholom in his arms.

The processed immigrants, which included the Secundas, were herded to a dock where they were to wait for a ferry to take them to Manhattan. Abraham spotted the boat as it churned through the gray, icy water toward them. "That's the boat that will take us to our new life," he said.

On the ferry Abraham and Anna talked excitedly. The children ran from window to window craning their necks to watch the buildings grow as the boat pushed toward Manhattan. One can only imagine the shock of seeing that gigantic, stone skyline up close after a lifetime of muddy shtetls and towns. The ferry landed at the Battery and Abraham led his family out to the street and up a flight of stairs.

"Where are you taking us?" Anna inquired nervously.

"This is the elevated," Abraham said authoritatively. "It is a train that runs above the street all over the city. We'll ride on it until we get to Fourteenth Street Station. They we'll get off and go to our apartment on Twelfth Street (he pronounced it 'strit')."

Sholom was literate in Russian, Hebrew and Yiddish, but he also knew a smattering of Roman characters because the prayers in his synagogue songbook were written under the staff in Roman letters (the music was written from left to right and so, too, were the prayers, phonetically). At each station Sholom tried to read the names of the streets. At 14th Street the Secundas piled through the train door, walked downstairs to First Avenue, and followed Abraham to 12th Street between Avenues B and C.

Abraham had rented a three-room apartment on the top floor of a five-story building in the heart of the Lower East Side, where most Jewish immigrants lived. The Lower East Side was then the most densely populated area in the city with over 700 people per square acre.[13] A quarter of the city's population—one million people—was Jewish, and most of them lived there.[14]

Jewish ghetto life was a clutter of overcrowded, rat-infested tenements, and a clatter of pushcarts, loaded with every imaginable ware, filling the streets from early morning until past dark. Sewing machines could be heard whirring in apartments as three generations of Jews, including small children, worked up to eighteen hours a day sewing piecework for garment industries.

If eight people sleeping in one room was not an unfamiliar ratio to the Secunda family, surely the press of so much city flesh in the street was. The routine city noise must have been deafening and frightening. But to a child of twelve, there were miracles of the new world that, for a time at least, made America seem like a carnival. The bigness of it all, the rush of people, the gadgets!

Sholom wrote,

We entered the house and climbed up the stairs to the fifth floor.
Going up all those stairs didn't bother us, because we couldn't get
over the height of the building. The neighborhood and our building were dirty—it was dark in the stairwells because there were no
lights—but who cared? This was America!

The Secundas' apartment was one of five on the top floor. "You
don't have to go out into the courtyard to go to the bathroom in winter here," Abraham boasted. He took his family down the narrow
hall and opened a door. "See? This is called a 'toilet.' Every floor in
the building has one." Sholom reached for the knob at the end of a
long chain that hung from the tank near the ceiling. He jumped as
water rushed into the toilet bowl. "All day long we children ran to
the bathroom and pulled the chain," Sholom later recalled. "To us it
was another miracle."

Then Abraham demonstrated how to use the sink, one faucet for
cold water, the other for hot water. The children stared. "No more
washing in a bucket," Abraham said.

In the apartment the best was yet to come. As dusk crept over the
city, Anna asked Abraham to light some candles. Abraham laughed.

"Wait!" he shouted. "You see that little box up there near the
ceiling? It's called a 'kvoder mitter.' Into it I will put a kvoder, which
is twenty-five cents. Then I will turn up the hanging lamp. Watch
this."

Abraham crawled onto a table and stood up so as to reach the box,
into which he put a quarter. He jumped down, went to the gas lamp,
turned on the gas (25¢ would buy a week's worth), and struck a
match. He stood back and to his gaping family announced, "And
then there was light."

Velvel, Yosele and Meyer had not yet returned from work, although by now it was dark. Abraham and his sons worked in a small
metal shop, for which they were paid $6 each for a week of eleven-
hour days. The shop was on Christie Street between Rivington and
Stanton, and they usually walked some 16 blocks home to avoid having to pay carfare. At 9:00 p.m. their footsteps were heard outside
the apartment door. "There they are!" Abraham shouted, running
to open it.

Anna threw her arms around each of her sons, the older sons hugged their younger brothers and sisters, everyone laughed and kissed. Then Anna turned to her husband and said, "Is there any food in the house?"

"Tonight you will not cook," he replied. He sent Velvel to the corner delicatessen. Velvel returned with corned beef and pastrami sandwiches and sour pickles. In the meantime Abraham had boiled water in the samovar. Sandwiches were a revelation to Sholom. So were the speech mannerisms and unusual clothing his father had adopted in America. Gone was Abraham's beard, worn by most Jewish men in Russia. In its place was a well-manicured goatee. For his family's homecoming, Abraham wore his best American suit, complete with tight-fitting vest, and a Panama hat, although it was winter.

In America Abraham also changed everyone's name. Velvel became "Willie," Yankele became "Jack," Yosele became "Joe," Taybele became "Thelma," Saratshke became "Shirley," and Sholom became "Sam" (his early compositions would have the name "Samuel Secunda" written on them, which in later life he would change back to "Sholom Secunda"). Only Aaron and Meyer were spared.

The Americanization of the Secundas had begun. Abraham told the newcomers that they were "green ones" or "greenhorns." But he and Willie, Joe and Meyer were, he said, "yellow ones" because they were oldtimers in the new world.

"It's getting late," Abraham said after dinner, "and the 'yellow ones' have to get up early for work." Sleeping arrangements adopted a familiar pattern. The eight children bedded down on the floor in the kitchen. Before he and Anna retired to their bedroom, Abraham came into the children's room.

"Don't forget," he whispered to the greenhorns, "you don't use a courtyard in America. You walk across the hall. And don't forget to pull the chain."

The five newcomers quietly recited the *krishme,* or evening prayer. The three oldtimers did not. Sholom wondered about that for a moment, but he was too exhausted to raise the subject. He slipped into a deep sleep.

At 7:00 a.m. the next morning Abraham woke his older sons, who hastily wolfed down scraps of the previous evening's sandwiches, and rushed off to work. Abraham did not go to the shop that day, because he wanted to show Anna how and where to shop. By the time the other children had av .kened, Abraham and Anna had returned with armloads of packages. Breakfast included eggs and tea, which Anna dispensed from the samovar, and she smiled at her reflection in their only surviving possession from Russia.

With six extra mouths to feed, and with Sholom rapidly approaching the end of his days as a soprano, Abraham decided to take Sholom that Saturday to neighboring synagogues to arrange a possible engagement. On the Sabbath morning Willie, Abraham and Sholom went to the Belchatover Synagogue on Sixth Street, between Avenues B and C. The Sabbath services were in progress. Abraham asked the *shammes* if Sholom could finish out the service as cantor. With the permission of the president of the temple, Sholom sang the remaining prayers, visibly pleasing the congregants. One of them, Reuben Sadovski, the owner of a large cloak and suit factory, pledged a donation for Sholom's services that exceeded the combined wages of Abraham and his working sons. Mr. Sadovski told Abraham that Sholom would be asked to sing again on special holidays, possibly all year around.

That afternoon Willie, Abraham and Sholom met with Mr. Wolf, the theatrical manager who had assisted with boat tickets. Again, Sholom sang.

"He's everything you said he is," Wolf said heartily.

In the next few months Wolf placed advertisements in the Jewish press with a photograph of Sholom holding his tuning fork in one hand and his prayer book in the other. He wore his yarmulke, prayer shawl, and an appropriately solemn expression. The copy for the ad was worthy of Barnum & Bailey:

> Come, friends, and you will see a wonder that no one has yet seen or heard! This 13 year old child, only a few months in this country, whose name is Sholom Secunda, will stand forth as Cantor and his sweet and delicious tenor voice and talent will overwhelm you. All the greatest Cantors say that such a talent is born once in a thousand years! Therefore, friends, if you wish this pleasure, supply yourself with your tickets early. Without tickets, positively no one will be allowed to attend.

The diminutive cantor was certainly a novelty, and for 25¢ he could be heard in Manhattan and Brooklyn synagogues nearly every weekend.

Sholom and his brothers were enrolled at P.S. 22 on the corner of Sheriff and Stanton Streets. They were placed in special classes that had been established by the Board of Education to help immigrant students grapple with English in order to qualify for regular grade level.[15] In some cases it took several years to catch up. Sholom spent a month in the special class before being transferred to the fourth grade. The transition period was relatively short, owing to his experience in government school in Nicholayev and his acquaintance with the Roman alphabet. He was four years older than his American classmates, but as his English improved, he was transferred to more advanced grade levels.

Jack and Thelma struggled a bit longer in the interim classes (the girls attended girls' schools). Shirley, who was placed in kindergarten, probably had the easiest time of it, given her youth.

During his first year in the United States, Sholom became a minor celebrity on the Lower East Side, and in time Wolf was able to command, and get, a fee of $100 for Sabbath services. Occasionally the weekend deal would include a Sunday evening concert, for an additional $50. Those were staggering sums in 1908, particularly for ghetto Jews. But Sholom's fees were for performances in the city's biggest synagogues. The gate included a lot of 25¢ tickets, as well as donations by wealthy temple members.

It seemed too good to be true and, of course, it didn't last. The backlash that chronically haunted Sholom's successes took the form, again, of illness. Jack came home from school one afternoon with a perilously high fever, and he was shipped off to a hospital. Soon Shirley and Thelma were infected as well. They had scarlet fever.

Sholom contracted diphtheria.

The Secunda apartment was put under quarantine, and Anna was given instructions by a doctor on how to run her domestic hospital. Willie, Aaron and Joe slept in the kitchen. Sholom slept by himself in one bedroom, and the remainder of the children slept with Abraham and Anna. It was six weeks before the quarantine sign was removed and the children were able to go back to school.

Mr. Wolf was not at all happy about Sholom's indisposition. He had laid out funds for advertisements and had booked concerts, all of which had to be canceled. Sholom recovered, however, in time for the High Holy Days, and for this Wolf had a master plan.

The elders of the synagogues for which Sholom had sung were pleased to have him grace their regular services, but they did not want a schoolboy to officiate on the solemnest days of the Jewish calendar —Rosh Hashonah and Yom Kippur. Wolf decided to book Sholom in a theater instead. He pitched the idea to Max R. Wilner, manager of the Thalia on the Bowery, the largest Yiddish theater in New York. Although Wilner was not a particularly religious man, he recognized the box office potential of the young cantor.

"Why don't you discuss it with Kessler?" Wilner said to Abraham and Wolf.

David Kessler. The name was magic in the Yiddish theater. If one were to ask any devotee of Second Avenue who its greatest actor was, one would hear two names—Kessler and Jacob Adler. Indeed, the two men jockeyed for position in the hearts of audiences and the tills of theaters throughout their tandem careers.

Sholom had heard of Kessler while still in Russia. Willie had written enthusiastic letters extolling Kessler's electrifying performances. Among Yiddish actors, though, the name Kessler struck terror in the heart. Lulla Rosenfeld, author of *Bright Star of Exile,* quotes Sara Adler's description of Kessler's behavior:

> It got so that the rehearsal without trouble was like heaven. . . Kessler was not just a strong-tempered man, he had a fiery charcter. His soul kindled even at rehearsal. At times he became so enraged with the actors that I wondered how a human heart would take it. I was afraid he would kill someone, or drop dead himself of heart failure.[16]

Kessler was not only an incandescent actor, he also possessed a superb tenor voice. In 1908 he was at the peak of his career, and was the star-manager of the Thalia.

Yiddish theater itself was at its zenith, a cultural product of New York whose influence exceeded its geographic and language barriers. The week Sholom had arrived in the United States, Abraham Goldfaden, the father of the Yiddish theater, had died in New York. Over 75,000 New Yorkers turned up at his funeral. The following day *The New York Times* carried this editorial:

Many in the vast crowd that thronged the streets may have been impelled by curiosity, but there was more evidence of genuine sympathy and admiration for the man and his work than is likely to be manifested at the funeral of any poet now writing in the English language.[17]

Sholom was aware, when he was presented to David Kessler on the empty stage of the Thalia, that he was meeting a cultural giant, as well as an ego capable of dressing down inattentive audiences.

"This is a cantor?" Kessler said impishly, eyeing Sholom. "Let's hear what he can do."

Kessler, Abraham and Wilner took seats in the front row of the theater. Sholom sang a prayer for his small but powerful audience. When he finished, Kessler bounded onto the stage.

"You have a wonderful voice," Kessler said, "but it's not enough. The face also has to be expressive. I'm going to sing something, and I want you to watch my face."

Kessler repeated the prayer that Sholom had sung.

"You see?" he continued. "My face expresses what I sing. It expresses the words *and* music. You have to do the same. Try it again."

Sholom repeated the prayer, trying to implement the great man's directions.

Kessler agreed with Wilner and Abraham that Sholom would be a box office hit conducting the High Holy Days services at the Thalia. Abraham asked for $100, to which Kessler agreed. The sum pleased everyone but Sholom, who later wrote, "My father was not a good businessman. Although the theater was packed, I earned no more for that appearance than for a Sabbath service and Sunday concert. However, in the process I formed an intimate acquaintance with David Kessler, and I went to the Thalia Theater every night and saw all the shows without paying."

Sholom's Yiddish theater debut was not without rumblings. Handbills had been posted outside the theater and all over New York announcing Sholom's upcoming performance. Lower East Side Jews believed it to be disrespectful and exploitive to have a boy conduct the services, and said so at a meeting with the Thalia's management. To placate the protestors, a rabbi was engaged to stand by the lectern and chant some prayers at the beginning of the service. To augment his clout, Sholom became a bar mitzvah just before the High Holy

Days at the Second Rumanian Synagogue on Rivington Street. He officiated at his own bar mitzvah, which included a choir, and the event was widely publicized to enhance the young man's authority.

Sholom's Thalia performance created a sensation, and from that moment on, until his death, his name would be recognized by New York Jews. (Because he became famous at such an early age, when he was in his 50s and was introduced to Yiddish theater *patriots,* they would invariably respond, "Sholom Secunda! You're still alive?")

With Sholom's increased earnings, the family was able to improve its living conditions. They moved to a four-room apartment on the corner of Houston and Columbia Streets. The apartment even had its own bathroom. It was in this apartment that Sholom began writing all the cantorial music he sang, and studying secular music. Abraham bought an upright piano, paying for it in installments, and hired a piano teacher. "He called himself 'professor,'" Sholom wrote of his teacher. "On the Lower East Side, every hack wedding musician proclaimed himself 'professor.'" In a short time, however, the "professor" ran out of lessons, and told Abraham and Anna that they would have to find another teacher. He had taught Sholom all he knew.

Sholom's eagerness to be thoroughly educated in music was not entirely a product of aesthetic ambition. He knew that his days as a soprano were numbered, and that in order to earn a living in music, he would have to be trained in other areas.

Abraham, however, did not share his son's objectivity. He and Willie had quit their jobs to spend all their time promoting Sholom. Sholom's fees made it possible for the family to move yet again, this time to 24 Attorney Street on the corner of Grand Street, in the Yiddish theater district. This apartment had five rooms, electric lights instead of gas, and was heated by steam. The rent was $31 a month. Because the Secundas did not have boarders, for whom there was ample room, they were considered by their neighbors to be rich.

At 14, while still attending school, Sholom had become the chief breadwinner in the family. Although he would spend the rest of his life either partially or totally supporting his family, he was not unique among immigrant Jews. Hutchins Hapgood, a young non-Jewish journalist, wrote a series of articles at the turn of the century about the Jewish quarter in New York that appeared in the "Atlantic Monthly" and the *Commercial Advertiser,* a daily New York newspaper. The pieces were assembled into a book, *The Spirit of the*

Ghetto, and included this analysis of the subtle changes within the immigrant family that occur when one of its sons supports the rest:

> An important circumstance in helping to determine the boy's attitude toward his father is the tendency to reverse the ordinary and normal educational and economical relations existing between father and son. In Russia, the father gives the son an education and supports him until his marriage, and often afterward, until the young man is able to take care of his wife and children. The father is, therefore, the head of the house in reality. But in the New World the boy contributes very early to the family's support. The father is in this country less able to make an economic place for himself than is the son. The little fellow sells papers, blacks boots, and becomes a street merchant on a small scale. As he speaks English, and his parents do not, he is commonly the interpreter in business transactions, and tends generally to take things into his own hands. There is a tendency, therefore, for the father to respect the son.[18]

The analysis is apt. In years to come, Sholom would be the family's success story, which would cause his siblings to feel the competitive bends, some of them justified. (His sister, Thelma, went to her grave harboring resentment toward her talented brother. An accomplished pianist and piano teacher, she never forgave Sholom for referring to himself—to the exclusion of his brothers and sisters—during a television interview as being the only musician in the family. Sholom was often hoist by his own hyperbole.) But his sensitivity to Abraham's paternal authority and to Russian Jewish tradition would later cause tension within his own marriage. Sholom tried to please too many people and often got into trouble because of it.

Like thousands of other immigrant children, Sholom outdistanced his father not only financially, but educationally as well. According to Irving Howe, this, too, was not uncommon.

> In 1905, the peak year of immigration, the Jewish pupils on the East Side were concentrated in thirty-eight elementary schools. These contained 65,000 students, of whom some 61,000 or almost 95 per cent, were Jewish. . .That condition which a half-century later would be called de facto segregation did not deeply trouble

the Jewish immigrants—on the contrary, they found a certain comfort in sending their children to public schools overwhelmingly Jewish. Children who knew a little English served as translators for those who a week or two earlier had stepped off the boats.[19]

At P.S. 22, students anxious not to remain "greenhorns" blended quickly into the Yankee scene. At Sholom's school, this cheer, while essentially American in spirit, still sounded vaguely Russian:

Hee haw! See-saw!
Hallo Baloo! Gazinka pop!
Hee-haw! See-saw!
Twenty-two is on the top!

Still, students could see the humor of their own awkwardness. Gentle fun was poked at their own malapropisms, the result of cram-course English lessons. The following essay appeared in the January 1911 issue of the *Advocate,* P.S. 22's school newspaper:

Definitions That Don't Define

Because a boy can give a definition of a word, it does not follow that he can use that word or that he really knows its meaning. Pupils often make ludicrous blunders in trying to use words after having studied their definitions. Here are a few samples culled from actual class work:

Frantic, wild, frenzied; as "She gathered frantic flowers."
Athletic, vigorous, strong; as "The butter is athletic."
Clandestine, secret; as "We shall keep our own clandestines."
Converge, to tend together; as "John and his sister converged the baby."
Cordial, hearty; as "I have a cordial appetite."

By 1910 Sholom was in the seventh grade, although, at 16, he was three years older than his American classmates. While earning a living, he found enough time to earn a place on the school's honor roll and a position on the staff of the *Advocate.* He duplicated his achievements the following year, the year he graduated from elementary school.

In the graduation issue of the *Advocate,* Sholom appears in a photograph of the Class of 1911—162 somber-looking young men who range, it appears, from 14 to 18 years of age. Sholom played a piano solo at the commencement exercises in June. Abraham and Anna took pride in the fact that within three years, Sholom's literacy in English had become total. (Not so his parents'. Abraham could awkwardly read and write English. Anna knew a very few words and could not write in English at all.)

Although students were not legally required to attend high school —it wasn't until 1914 that they were required to even finish the sixth grade—Sholom nevertheless enrolled in DeWitt Clinton High School.[20]

By the time Sholom graduated from grammar school, his singing career had ground to a halt. For months he had had to strain to reach notes in his upper register, and physiology forced him to sing a tone lower from week to week. By the High Holy Days he was totally unable to sing as a soprano. His loss of income sent his family back into financial struggle.

Anna had to take in three boarders to help make ends meet. The dining-room table could barely accommodate the thirteen people who now lived in five rooms.

Abraham leased a cellar on Grand Street and opened a shop to repair baby carriages, assisted by Willie and Aaron. It occurred to Abraham that he could put his ability to work metal to maximum urban use. Every apartment in the ghetto was crowded, and the item that took most space was the bed. Abraham fashioned a metal bed frame that would fold up. When he and his sons had made several of the folding beds, he rented a pushcart and sold them to furniture stores around the city. Eventually he was able to hire a horse and wagon to carry the beds from store to store. His sole concern was feeding his family. Of less concern was expanding the business, although he could not make enough beds to fill the demand. (Abraham was, indeed, a lousy businessman. One of his clients was Max Englander, a Hungarian refugee who had a mattress and parlor furniture factory on West 17th Street. Englander asked Abraham to join him in the business. Abraham declined, saying that he wanted to stick with the folding beds, an invention he never troubled to have patented.

Englander's company, the Englander Couch and Bedding Company, became a multimillion-dollar business that exists to this day.)

Sholom was less easily satisfied than his father, and he grew impatient with the pace of his musical education. He enrolled in the Third Street Music Settlement where, for 25¢ a lesson, he received piano instruction and studied solfeggio and theory after school. He practiced several hours a day and within a few months was sufficiently qualified to teach piano himself.

"I didn't have the heart to take 25¢ a week from my mother to pay for my lessons," he wrote, "not to mention the 10¢ a day carfare to travel to high school."

Jewish parents, no matter how poor, were eager to enhance the cultural lives of their children. Many of them had pianos, so there was no dearth of students. Sholom took on eight students, earning $2.00 a week, $1.00 of which he gave to his mother to help pay for his room and board.

Sholom's DeWitt Clinton career lasted one year. He noticed an ad in a newspaper for the Eron Preparatory School on East Broadway that prepared its students for college and Regents examinations. Mr. Eron told Sholom that he could study at his own pace for Regents examinations in all high-school subjects which, once passed, would enable him to enter college. To pay for Eron Prep, Sholom took on several more piano students.

He also worked as choir-director in several synagogues for the High Holy Days and occasional Sabbaths. Sholom's love for vocal music grew more ardent, and he read everything he could about the opera in newspapers. He particularly wanted to hear Caruso, and began putting aside a little money in order to buy a ticket to the Metropolitan Opera.

One day he read an article about an afternoon performance of Caruso in "Pagliacci." He had, by this time, saved $1.50. Sholom walked from Grand Street to 34th, and asked the ticket office employee for a seat. The ticket seller told him that for $1.50, he could stand during the performance, but not sit. Stung by disappointment, he wandered into Macy's on his way home, a store he had heard of but not seen. On the second floor he saw little tables with paper and envelopes for writing letters. He sat down and wrote to Mr. Gatti-Cassasa, the manager of the Metropolitan Opera House:

I am 17 years old, and I have never seen an opera. I used to be a singer, until my voice changed. I would give anything to hear Caruso, and all I have is $1.50 which, I'm told, is not enough to pay for a seat. Is there anything you can do to help me?

Two days later Sholom received a reply from Gatti-Cassasa stating that he should come to the Met on the day of the performance, show the letter at the door, and he would be let in.

Sholom did as he was told, looking ashen, having been unable to sleep the night before. The doors had not yet opened, but a double line of opera-lovers wound around the block. He went to the outer lobby, which was crammed with people who were bidding for tickets to the sold-out performance.

When the doors opened, Sholom ran in and exhibited his letter. The ticket-taker asked Sholom to stand to one side. In a few minutes a man with a top hat and cutaway greeted him, looked at the letter, and asked Sholom to accompany him. He led Sholom up the stairs and, with a key, opened a door to a box. Sholom, clutching his cap, sat on the edge of a fragile, red-velvet chair, and gaped at the splendor of the opera house. Of the experience he wrote:

No one was in the box besides me. In the surrounding boxes I noticed bedecked ladies and gentlemen taking their seats. Musicians were warming up in the pit. At last, the conductor raised his baton and the orchestra began to play. The heavy, gold curtain opened and a clown appeared and began to sing. At first, I thought it was Caruso, but the man had a baritone voice, and I knew Caruso was a tenor. He sang very well, and soon the curtain was drawn. In the next scene, a wagon, drawn by a donkey, was pulled on stage. On the wagon stood *another* clown, and he started to sing. I didn't know who he was either, but his voice was incredible.

I hadn't noticed that the box had filled up, until a man with a gray beard put his hand on my shoulder and whispered, "Deez iz Caruso." Later I discovered that the man with the strange accent was Mr. Gatti-Cassasa. I also discovered that this was a benefit performance, with a variety of singers performing in selected scenes from "Pagliacci."

Sholom studied diligently at Eron Prep School and within a year and a half, he was qualified to take the Regents Examinations, a task that would have taken three years at DeWitt Clinton. During that time his family saw little of him. He did his Eron Prep homework on the elevated, on trolleys and on horse-drawn street cars, while traveling to and from his piano students in Brooklyn, the Lower East Side and Harlem.

Sholom excelled in mathematics, and he began considering career alternatives. Medicine was his first choice, in part because a classmate of his wanted to become a doctor, and in part because a career in medicine was a noble and lucrative ambition for the children of Jewish immigrants. To be a doctor or a lawyer was a visa uptown, and indeed, the proportion of Jewish students in medicine and law to non-Jewish students in those fields at that time was nearly double.[21] But medical school took years of expensive study, and Sholom was not sufficiently motivated to make the sacrifices necessary to pursue a career that was not, after all, an affair of his heart.

The Eron faculty encouraged Sholom to become an engineer, and they recommended that he apply to Cooper Union.

He took the entrance examination and was accepted. But the lure of physics and chemistry was pale compared to that of Wanamaker's Department Store on Fourth Avenue and Eighth Street, just around the corner from Cooper Union. Every day at noon, concerts were given at the Store's auditorium featuring New York's finest pianists, violinists and singers.

At the end of Sholom's first year at Cooper Union, Professor Henderson of the chemistry department wrote Sholom a note requesting a meeting.

"Mr. Secunda," the professor said, "in spite of your excellent grades, you have not qualified for matriculation because of your absenteeism. You have missed so many classes that, I'm afraid, you will have to take your first year over again."

Sholom told Henderson that he had skipped classes in order to attend the Wanamaker's concerts. Henderson smiled at Sholom's ingenuousness and said, "Which would you rather be? An engineer or a musician?"

"I want to be a composer," Sholom blurted.

"If that's the case, then you should forget engineering. Even if you complete the program, you'll be a terrible engineer."

Henderson suggested that Sholom apply to Columbia College, where he could take courses in the music department. Sholom was accepted by Columbia and began his second start in college. His attention span, this time, lasted six months. Irritated by having to take courses unrelated to music, he expressed his frustration to Professor Farnsworth of the music department. Farnsworth, sympathetic to Sholom's need for total musical immersion, suggested that he talk with Dr. Frank Damrosch (brother of the conductor-composer Walter Damrosch) who, with James Loeb, had co-founded the Institute of Musical Art in 1905 (it became the Juilliard School in 1926). Sholom took his advice, met with Dr. Damrosch, and told him about his career as a cantor, his abortive stint at Cooper Union, his piano teaching, his study of music. Damrosch quizzed Sholom on his general knowledge of harmony and solfeggio and told him he would be accepted by the Institute for the following fall. The esteemed Percy Goetscius would be among his instructors.

Sholom's parents were unaware that he was finishing his first year at Columbia, or that he had studied at Cooper Union. They knew only that he disappeared every morning, returned late at night, and that he was contributing a modicum of money to the family income. His brothers continued working with Abraham in the bed shop on Canal Street, and Willie, pursuing his interest in theater, joined a dramatics club.

Sholom desperately needed money to pay for his tuition, and Willie found a solution to his financial pinch. Willie had befriended a professional Yiddish theater actor who was in the company of producer Max Gabel's Yiddish Comedy Theater on Suffolk Street. Gabel, a former vaudevillian, was a performer and writer. He was mounting a play called "Grigori Gershuni" for which he needed extras to play as revolutionaries. Willie and Sholom were hired, and they were paid a dollar a performance. It was the beginning of Sholom's career on Second Avenue.

🎵 YIDDISH THEATER BEGINNINGS

Sholom Secunda's years in the Yiddish theater began at its zenith in New York. That Sholom should be a composer on Second Avenue has a logic that borders on preordination, and so a brief history of Yiddish theater is in order

That there ever existed a Yiddish theater at all is, on one level, surprising. Among Orthodox Jews, theater was forbidden because it was considered frivolous, a violation of the daily discipline of prayer, religious ceremony and Talmudic study. But on the Jewish calendar there was one day during which rigidity and sobriety were enthusiastically forgotten: Purim. On that day, Jews could drink alcoholic beverages and have parties. Purim, which occurs just before spring, has its roots in the Book of Esther. During the Purim festival, plays dramatizing the salvation of Persian Jews from a massacre were performed, and men took the parts of women (who were not allowed on a stage), even wearing women's clothing.[1]

By the middle of the 19th Century constraints on Jewish behavior were relaxed in some East European communities, and Jews attended performances of traveling Yiddish entertainers—acrobats, singers and minstrels.[2] The first of these troupes was the "Brody Singers," from the Galician town of Brody, founded by a Jew named Yakovka.[3] These performances were musical, with bits of dialogue inserted at first, and then whole scenarios, usually depicting Chasidic life.

Abraham Goldfaden, a Yiddish songwriter from Odessa, persuaded the Brody Singers to perform an operetta he had composed, in a winecellar in Jassy, Romania, in 1876.[4] That performance is considered the official birth of the Yiddish theater as an ongoing institution.

The first Yiddish play produced in the United States occurred six years later. The play, in five acts, was Goldfaden's "The Sorceress," performed by six men and two women (although women were still discouraged from becoming actresses), and aided by a choir from a local synagogue. The play, starring Boris Thomashevsky, was performed at Turn Hall on Fourth Street between Second Avenue and Third Avenue.[5]

The acceptability of Yiddish theater among Jews can be traced to synagogue life itself. As Sholom's childhood illustrated, Russian and East European synagogues would vie for the services of cantors. The ardor with which these men performed was nothing if not theatrical, and congregants, hungry for some kind of entertainment to enliven the days of unrelieved hard work and worry, would speak as much about these performances as they would about the prayers. The synagogue choirs were the source of many Yiddish actors and singers who later performed in America. It is small wonder, then, that much of the music written for the New York Yiddish stage was based on cantorial harmonies and configurations learned in the old country.[6]

The quality of Yiddish theater in America was inexorably intertwined with immigrant Jewish life on the Lower East Side. By the turn of the century, there were three Yiddish theaters in New York—the People's, the Windsor and the Thalia. (By 1921, when the United States Bureau of Immigration put a lid on the influx of millions of European Jews, there were over twenty Yiddish theaters. By contrast, by 1929 there were seventy legitimate, English-language theaters in New York.)

The nature of immigrant concerns dictated how the theater was structured. The Lower East Side was dotted with organizations, guilds and clubs, whose function was to aid fellow countrymen in New York and back home. These societies, called *landsmanshaftn*, were based on nationality or occupation. They were havens for the newest arrivals of refugees at Ellis Island, putting them in touch with former neighbors already in New York, often aiding sick members or paying for their burials. These societies kept alive memories of villages and families left behind: thus societies existed for exiles of Alexandria, Tarnopol, Minsk, Odessa, Kiev, and bore their names (Sholom is buried in a family cemetery plot purchased by the Alexandria Society in the early 1900s).[7] They even had their own cafes. The muddy shtetl was transported to the streets of New York.

In order to finance their philanthropic work, the societies would

hire a block of seats, or an entire theater, for a Yiddish theater performance at as much as a 75% discount, and sell the tickets at full
price—sometimes more—to its members.[8] The proceeds would go into the society's treasury.

Because there were no "angels" as such in the Yiddish theater,
these "benefits" were the backbone of the Yiddish theater economy,
and so on the first four days of the week, theater performances were
for benefits only. Friday, Saturday and Sunday performances were
open to the public at large. Plays mounted for benefit nights were
different from those on the weekends. During the week, because the
gate was fairly predictable, a certain degree of experimentation in
scheduling of plays was possible. On weekends plays tended to be
from a familiar repertoire, crowd-pleasers that would be a draw.

Because of this schedule, the actors, who would sign with a theater
for an entire season, became in essence a repertory company. Often
the same cast would appear in a different play each night. During a
single week in November, 1914, David Kessler's theater advertised
seven plays in five days (including matinees).[9] Most theaters had nine
performances a week (matinees as well as evening performances on
Saturdays and Sundays), with no days off for the actor.

The hectic and ambitious pace of plays necessitated a prompter's
box—there was little time for rehearsals—and resulted in departures
from the script and frequent sloppiness in performance. But it provided experience in the theater accorded few Broadway actors, experience that was the extra edge for Yiddish actors who moved on to
Broadway and Hollywood: Molly Picon, Jacob Ben-Ami, Menashe
Skulnik, Paul Muni, Celia, Stella and Luther Adler, Joseph Buloff,
John Garfield and Edward G. Robinson.

In the early 1900s the Yiddish community on New York's Lower
East Side was the largest in the world. Between 1881 and 1914, nearly
two million Jews emigrated to the United States, most of them from
Eastern Europe.[10] It is estimated that there were in New York in 1918
a quarter of a million Yiddish theater-goers.[11] The Yiddish press had
a readership of half a million.[12] Its periodicals included the *Tageblatt,*
Yidisher Kemfer, Feder, Groyser Kundes, Morgen Zhurnal, Tag,
and, of course, the *Forward.*

Until the immigration quotas of the 1920s, the Yiddish theater
had a constant supply of new audiences for recycled plays. No other
factor so significantly explains the variety of Yiddish theater, which

ranged from profitable musical soap operas and *shund* (trash) to the brilliantly acted but poorly attended Yiddish Art Theater. The audience of immigrants, once it learned English and moved uptown or out to the suburbs, took its business to Broadway and movie houses. The Yiddish theater in America depended on greenhorns.

And so, if one were a producer on Second Avenue, it would not be unusual to mount Yiddish translations of the plays of Shakespeare, Ibsen or Chekhov, plays that many immigrants brought with them, or at least a taste for them, from Europe. But such a producer would go broke if that were the only fare. As David Kessler said to a reporter from the *Forward* in 1909, "*Shund* is more profitable; I must offer plays that attract the public, if I want to pay my rent. But as an actor, I prefer good plays. When I play trash, it's like drinking castor oil. My actors will tell you I would prefer to drink poison. But what can I do if a good play brings in only half the revenue?"[14]

On Second Avenue in the first two decades of the 20th Century, immigrants who were not, on the whole, sophisticated, wanted to be amused in a vernacular they understood (Yiddish was a bond that connected Jews from varied cultures and countries around the world). They also knew what they liked, and were not reticent to register their feelings. Russian Jews brought with them from the homeland a habit of responding vocally to the action of the play before them. Hutchins Hapgood wrote his observations of Yiddish theater audiences in the early 1900s:

Poor workingmen and women with their babies of all ages fill the theatres. Great enthusiasm is manifested, sincere laughter and tears accompany the sincere acting on the stage. Pedlars [sic] of soda-water, candy, of fantastic geegaws of many kinds, mix freely with the audience between the acts.

Conversation during the play is received with strenuous hisses, but the falling of the curtain is the signal for groups of friends to get together and gossip about the play or the affairs of the week. Introductions are not necessary, and the Yiddish community can then be seen and approached with great freedom. . .

The Yiddish actors. . .take themselves with peculiar seriousness, justified by the enthusiasm, almost worship, with which they are regarded by the people. Many a poor Jew, man or girl, who makes no more than $10 a week in the sweatshop, will spend $5 of it on the theatre, which is practically the only amusement of the Ghetto Jew. He has not the loafing and sporting instincts of the poor Christian, and spends his money for the theatre rather than for drink. It is not only to see the play that the poor Jew goes to the theatre. It is to see his friends and the actors.[15]

The hero worship of Yiddish theater stars is understandable when one considers the content of the plays in which they performed. Second Avenue dramatists wrote for and about immigrants. The first act of the play was often set in Russia or Poland, and the second act depicted ghetto life on the Lower East Side. Lyrics of songs from operettas chronicled troubles left in the Old World and found in the New:

Brothers of the free states, you're lucky, you're free/
Russia seeks false accusations against us/
The accusation of ritual murder is renewed. . .
Just as one Jew is always a guarantor for another/
One pays for another's guilt/
So help your friend, protect your relative/
Save us from the evil Tsarist land.

—"A brivele fun Russland"
(A letter from Russia)[16]

. . .Misfortunes happen here at every step/
And yet this hell is called the land of the free/
They put a family out on the street/
Because they can't pay the rent on time.

—"Di nyu-yorken trern"
(The New York tears)[17]

"Whether they specialized in art or *shund,*" writes Lulla Rosenfeld, "the theaters downtown were the cultural center of immigrant life. Every public event found its echo on the stage. When news of the Kishinev pogrom horrified the world, the three-year-old Stella Adler stood center stage, arms thrown wide, and in a voice that carried to the farthest gallery cried: 'Jews, for the love of mercy/Give of your charity!/For the dead, burial/For the living, bread!' "[18]

As immigrants became assimilated, English crept into Yiddish scripts. "We worked with the material that was relevant to the audience," Molly Picon says, "that the audience understood. Otherwise we would have had no theater." The high drama of most plays was catnip to audiences. Dramatists wrote about infidelity, incest, loss of religion, the dreaded Tsar, the dreaded *goyim,* (Gentiles), violent death, patriotism, mama. As long as some aspect of the play related to the immigrant's life, audiences were hooked.

The importance of identification with plots often had bizarre consequences. "Classics sufficiently 'adapted' to Jewish life," writes Irving Howe, "won over the audiences. *Romeo and Juliet,* starring (Boris) Thomashefsky, was given an old-country setting, with the Capulets and Montagues turning into feuding religious parties, the rationalist Mithnagdim and the pietist Chasidim. Romeo, now Raphael, and Juliet, now Shaindele, played the balcony scene in a synagogue, with Raphael telling his beloved, 'Look yonder! See the Eternal Light! It is a sign that the Jewish love of God is everlasting.' A witty touch was the transformation of Friar Lawrence into a Reform rabbi."[19]

Efforts to improve Yiddish theater were the concerns of such actors as David Kessler, Jacob Adler and, later, Maurice Schwartz—efforts that were, in the early 1900s, far more daring than the plays being offered on Broadway. Harold Clurman writes, ". . .the Yiddish theater, as Lincoln Steffens. . .and other observers of the period point out, 'was about the best in New York at that time in stuff and in acting.' . . .The actors were among the best I have ever seen in many years of playgoing all over the world."[20]

Sholom Secunda, a music student in 1914, was thrilled to be a part of the Yiddish theater—the pulse of the Lower East Side—even as a spear carrier. Following his stint as an extra (he played a revolutionary) in "Grigori Gershuni," he was hired for Gabel's next production, "Joseph and His Brothers," to sing in the chorus.

To assist featured players and chorus members in learning the music of new productions, Gabel had hired a trained singer to teach them the songs (most of them could not read music). But a member of the company had told Gabel that Sholom was studying music and that he could probably teach the songs for nothing. The idea appealed to Gabel's sense of budget, and Sholom, who was eager to ingratiate himself to the producer, agreed to take on the assignment.

Sholom continued his studies at the Institute of Musical Art during the day and his work in the theater at night, saving up for his second year's tuition. By the spring of 1915 he was a fixture at Gabel's Comedy Theater, in particular the actors' dressing room. At 19 he still looked like an adolescent, and the actors teased him about his budding beard. They vied for the privilege of being the first to shave the fuzz from his chin, but Sholom demurred, certain that by shaving at all he would encourage whiskers and the chore of daily shearing.

One evening Sholom got wind of another Gabel production, "Our Children," that was being planned for the 1915-1916 season, and he approached Gabel about writing a song for the prima donna, Jennie Goldstein. Gabel replied that Joseph Rumshinsky would probably do the music. Rumshinsky, however, was then the leading composer of the Yiddish theater, and could command high fees. A song by Secunda could cost nothing.

"Give it a try," Gabel said to Sholom. "If Jennie likes your song, she'll probably do it in the show."

The song was called "America," for which the lyrics had already been written. Sholom took the lyrics home after his performance that night. He ran up the four flights of stairs to his parents' apartment, grabbed some blank sheet music, and sat down at the upright piano to compose music. He worked on the tune through most of the night.

The following afternoon after his classes, Sholom took the song to the Comedy Theater. During a break in the rehearsal, he handed the song to Gabel.

"Don't give it to me," Gabel said, "take it to Jennie. She's at home now."

Jennie Goldstein lived on Forsythe Street, near Houston, with her parents—she may have been an actress, but she was still a respectable Jewish girl. Sholom climbed to the fifth-floor flat, knocked on the door, and was panting from his exertion as Jennie opened the door.

He told her about the song, and that Gabel had suggested he bring it to her house. Impatiently she led the out-of-breath composer to her piano.

Sholom sang the topical song—a rousing patriotic tune was a guaranteed crowd-pleaser—staring bashfully at the keys as he played. When he finished, the young, pretty woman asked him to play it again. As he sang through the song, Jennie rose from the sofa and walked behind him to read over his shoulder. She began to sing with him. At the end of the song, Jennie smiled for the first time.

"It's a good song," she said. "I like it."

Then she stared closely at his face. "Don't I know you?" she asked.

She invited Sholom to have a glass of tea with her, and they sat in the parlor, chatting about their respective histories. Jennie had had a small part in David Kessler's production of "Dos Yiddishe Harts" at the same time that Sholom had made his cantorial debut at the Thalia Theater some years before. She remembered him from the Rosh Hashonah services at the theater. In the course of their amiable conversation, Jennie promised to sing Sholom's "America" in Gabel's new show.

Sholom went to the Comedy theater every night, whether or not he was needed. In a few days posters announcing Gabel's next production were plastered all over the Lower East Side, in windows of grocery stores and butcher shops and bakeries. Sholom paused in front of each shop to proudly read his credit below Rumshinsky's: "Additional Music By Sholom Secunda."

Sholom's euphoria was short-lived. Gabel was forced to close the theater because it was being torn down by the City to be replaced by a post office. His debut as a Second Avenue composer was inauspicious.

By the end of June, 1916, Sholom had finished his second year at the Institute, and he was looking for work for the summer. He had heard that the Odeon Theater on Clinton Street was to become a Yiddish theater the following season, and that Egon Brecher, an actor-manager, had engaged a troupe, many of whom had appeared at Gabel's. Sholom was hired to sing in the chorus, again for a dollar a performance, and he earned $6 a week.

The star of the Brecher troupe was Sam Morris. One of Morris' closest friends was actor-dancer Hymie Jacobson, who was temporarily without work. Morris persuaded Brecher to fire Sholom and to hire

Jacobson to be a chorus boy and an occasional comic buffoon, Jacobson's specialty. A man of extraordinary talent, Jacobson soon landed a speaking part in another theater, and Sholom was re-hired. What started as a rivalry became a lifelong friendship and professional collaboration.

At the same time, however, a lifetime of mutual enmity began between Sholom and Joseph Rumshinsky.

The backgrounds of the two composers were strikingly similar. Rumshinsky was born in Vilna, Russia, and had come to the United States in 1904 at the age of 23. As a child he, too, had sung in Russian synagogues, he had taught piano, and he had conducted synagogue choirs. In his long career he wrote over 100 Yiddish operettas, and by 1917 he was in great demand by the stars of Second Avenue.[21] His melodies, according to *Forward,* were more popular than the stars. "But he murdered a lyric," Molly Picon says. He came close to murdering many of the actors he worked with as well.

"He was a very hated person," recalls a former chorus girl who appeared in many of his operettas. "He would insult people and make them feel like two cents. Once, Madame (Regina) Prager, a distinguished prima donna in the European style, was saying a prayer before going onstage. She was very religious and very dignified. Rumshinsky went over to her and growled, 'Get moving, you old hag,' because he wanted her to hurry. She didn't say a word.

"Another time Hymie Jacobson was rehearsing a number and suggested a change. Rumshinsky leaped from the orchestra onto the stage with fire in his eyes. Jacobson ran through the dressing room and jumped through the window to escape him."

Dinah Goldberg, a lively and popular soubrette in the Yiddish theater beginning in the 1920s, worked with all the prominent Second Avenue composers—Alexander Olshanetsky, Abraham Ellstein, Sholom Secunda—but her most vivid memories are of Rumshinsky:

Once during a show called "Song of Israel" at the Rolland Theater, there was a scene involving a hora song and dance. The ensemble was supposed to dance off the stage and then there was a pause in the music and the wailing note of an Arab girl was supposed to be heard from off stage. Betty Siminoff played the role of the Arab girl. Rumshinsky was conducting and came to the pause, but there was no singing from off stage. He tapped his baton,

tion again, and still no Betty singing—she was busy talking to someone and didn't hear her cue. Once again, Rumshinsky came to her cue, and this time the audience was stunned to hear the portly conductor wailing like Tarzan calling the apes.

At intermission, Betty said, "He'll kill me!" and we told her to go into the dressing room and take off all her clothes—he'd never go in there if she were nude. She ran in and undressed. Suddenly the door burst open—it was Rumshinsky. He screamed at her, "Du pishiker! Du cocker! (You pisser! You shitter!)." Then he turned around and stormed out. He never even noticed that she was naked.

For all his unpleasantness, Rumshinsky nevertheless had an enormous influence on the quality of Yiddish musical theater. Under his aegis, Second Avenue orchestras grew from a half-dozen instruments to two dozen. He hired choreographers from Broadway and directors from Hollywood. The chorus girl who remembers his disagreeable personality recalls also his extraordinary directorial inventiveness: "Rumshinsky wrote 'The Gypsy Girl,' which starred Molly Picon. It was put up on a huge scale. For a song about bells, they had bells wired to all the boxes around the theater, and during the song the bells rang. All the people in the audience looked around, trying to figure out how they did it. It was a sensation."

Rumshinsky's attention to detail, however exasperatingly executed, was profitable. He was always engaged for, and filled, the biggest houses on Second Avenue, some of which had 2,000 seats stretching up two tiers of balconies, and bigger than any house on Broadway. "The money just rolled in," a former actress recalls. "When we went on the road, we had very good advance agents, and the money kept pouring in. Maxie Siegel used to come backstage on Tuesday and say, 'Girls, please take your salary now. I don't want to carry it until Sunday.' His pockets would be bulging, because people would hang from the rafters to come and see Molly Picon in a Rumshinsky production."

It was with mixed emotions that Sholom, who knew of Rumshinsky's reputation, first met the great Yiddish theater composer. Brecher had agreed in 1916 to let Sholom write the score for "Justice," by Solomon Shmulevitsh (who had also written the lyrics for "A Letter to My Mother," which Sholom had sung as a boy).

Sholom was not, however, permitted to do the orchestrations because he was not a member of the powerful Musicians' Union. "Justice" was a flop.

Brecher decided that his next venture, "Home Sweet Home," needed a star to avert another box office disaster. Regina Prager, a reigning (and aging) prima donna, was engaged. As a star, she had clout in the choice of music she would sing. Rumshinsky's music she knew; Sholom's, she did not.

To Sholom, Madame Prager was a legend. He had seen her perform in her three crowning productions: "Bar Kochbah," "Shulamis," and "Akeydes Yitskhok." Although well into middle age, she nevertheless retained a pure, dramatic soprano voice, a voice that in her younger years would have been worthy of the Metropolitan Opera.

Sholom asked Brecher if a composer had been hired. Brecher replied that no decision had been made, but that Madame Prager favored Rumshinsky. He advised Sholom to seek out Madame Prager the following day and to propose that he write something for her.

The next afternoon at rehearsal Sholom told Prager about his musical background, and she agreed to let him work on the lyrics of some of the songs she had given to Rumshinsky. That evening he picked up the lyrics at her apartment on Second Avenue. One song was the title song, "Home Sweet Home," the other, a patriotic song. By 2 a.m. Sholom had completed the music for both songs. The next day he went to class, gave three piano lessons, and urged the sun to go down—he had an appointment with Madame Prager that evening.

At 8:00 p.m., he arrived promptly at her apartment. Madame Prager ushered Sholom into her parlor, a lavish room with framed pictures of the actress on the walls, heavy green velvet draperies at the windows, an enormous oriental rug on the floor.

They were not alone. At the grand piano sat Joseph Rumshinsky, playing his melodies for the same lyrics that Sholom had been given. Sholom recognized the dour-faced composer immediately from the photographs on the sheet music of Rumshinsky's songs that were prominently displayed in the music stores of the Lower East Side.

Madame Prager put a finger to her lips, and beckoned Sholom to sit down. When Rumshinsky finished playing, Madame Prager presented Sholom to him.

"This young man is studying music," she said, "and hopes to become a composer."

"I am honored to meet you," Sholom said nervously.

Rumshinsky grunted a response, kissed Madame Prager on the hand, and abruptly left. Madame Prager turned to Sholom, smiled, and said, "Now let's hear what a younger composer can do."

Sholom was numb with anxiety. Following Rumshinsky had turned his hands to lead. Sholom stumbled through his songs, apologizing for his mistakes, singing in a barely audible voice.

"That was fine," Madame Prager said softly. "Now, relax. I'm sure you can do better than that."

Sholom played the songs again, and this time Madame Prager sight-read the music. After they finished, she studied the music for several minutes.

"Rumshinsky's patriotic song works better," she said. "It captures the audience with the first bar. But I really like your version of 'Home Sweet Home.' It has tenderness and feeling. I'll use it."

Sholom grabbed her hand, as Rumshinsky had done, clumsily planted a kiss on it, and ran all the way home to rejoice with his family.

On opening night Abraham and Anna, his brothers and sisters and several neighbors from their building filled an entire row at the Odeon Theater. When Madame Prager finished singing "Home Sweet Home," they rose in unison, shouting "Bravo!" and stamping their feet. A noisier claque of *patriots* Sholom couldn't have imagined.

Sholom's song was published, and on the front cover of the sheet music was a large photograph of Madame Prager and a smaller one of Sholom. At home the music sat on the piano next to the music of Mozart and Beethoven.

On the strength of his success with "Home Sweet Home," Sholom was offered $25 weekly for the following season—1916-1917—to be conductor-composer of the Lyric Theater in Brooklyn. His job would include arranging music in the repertoire. In order to be able to accept the position, Sholom was required to join the Musicians' Union, the then Local 310 on 86th Street. That part was easy—he filled out an application, took an examination on the piano, and was accepted. What followed was Sholom's first taste of union politics.

In 1916 there were two satellite clubs (sub-locals) of the Yiddish theater Musicians' Union, one for the big theaters, one for vaudeville and smaller theaters. Only members of the two clubs could work in Yiddish theaters. The Lyric was under the jurisdiction of the smaller club. The managers of the Lyric—Hymie Wallerstein, a vaudevillian, and his brother, Saul—were told by the Union that although Sholom was a member of the Union, he was ineligible for membership in the sub-local. The satellite club, in order to protect its members, seldom took new members, and then only after an apprenticeship out of town (this was also true of the Actors' Union).

The Wallerstein brothers wanted Sholom not simply because of his talent, but also because composers who were members of the larger satellite club were vastly more expensive. The Wallersteins applied pressure on the smaller club to allow them to engage Sholom. The club agreed, only on condition that Sholom be fired in the event that one of its member-conductors, who were also violinists, needed the job.

On this tenuous—and confusing—basis, Sholom and the Lyric company began rehearsals for the coming season. Madame Frieda Zibel was engaged as prima donna. Sholom, to his astonishment, was not asked to compose new music that season. Madame Zibel, who had played in Gimpel's troupe in Galicia before it had come to the United States, performed roles from that company's repertoire. Sholom's function was to orchestrate operettas from the repertoire each week for the small orchestra—seven musicians. It was not easy. Each morning he went to classes at the Musical Institute. In the afternoon he conducted rehearsals at the theater, after which he continued giving piano lessons. Sandwiched in between these chores were his school projects and compositions.

Sholom had the enviable ability to compartmentalize the day's chores. He did his homework between numbers during the evening performances at the theater, he orchestrated other operettas, to be performed on a rotating basis, after the curtain, and slept and ate during whatever time was left.

Contributing to his pressures were political and artistic differences with his miniscule orchestra. His musicians were of uneven ability, and on one occasion he wrote a phrase for violin that an inferior musician was unable to play. The violinist screamed a string of epithets at Sholom. On another occasion Sholom was asked by the Wallersteins to call a rehearsal for the orchestra to accompany the cast. Sholom informed his musicians. The following day, everyone appeared at the theater—managers, performers, chorus members—everyone except the members of the orchestra.

"Hey, Sholom," Saul Wallerstein shouted impatiently, "where the hell are your musicians?"

"I don't know," Sholom replied. "I told them to be here."

The cast waited for an hour for the orchestra, and finally rehearsed without it, with Sholom accompanying them at the piano. That evening the musicians arrived shortly before the performance. Sholom walked up to the cornetist, who was a powerful member of the club.

"Where were you!" Sholom yelled. "I got into trouble because of you!"

"You little idiot," the cornetist hissed. "Who do you think you're talking to? Did you ask me when to call a rehearsal? What do you mean by calling a rehearsal and not consulting me? The next time you do a thing like that, I'll see to it that you don't work again."

Sholom knew that the man had the authority to carry out his threat. "I had no choice but to back off," Sholom recalled later. "I wasn't even their conductor. Sure, I waved my hands, but I had to follow them. If the cornetist found a certain passage too fast, because he wasn't much of a musician, then he played it a little slower. And so I would slow down the beat. During rehearsals this would confuse the actors, who would shout, 'Sholom, speed it up.' "

Cast and musicians alike contributed to Sholom's discomfort because he was a student. "Literat!" was a term of derision that was used most often. Many of the personnel had not even finished high school, and a few were illiterate, and were clearly threatened by Sholom's advanced schooling. To avoid insults, Sholom hid his books under his coat and tried to find a corner in the theater where he could study until he was needed in the orchestra pit.

By keeping a low profile, Sholom was able to finish out the season and complete his studies at the same time. He took his final examinations in May, 1917. In June, wearing formal evening clothes he had rented for $3 on Clinton Street, he received his degree at the graduation exercises at Aeolian Hall on 42nd Street.

The Secunda family had prospered modestly during the years of Sholom's study, and their increasing degree of domestic comfort mirrored that of other immigrant Jews in New York in the second decade of the 20th Century. Jews rarely wore dress from Europe, and prided themselves on wearing American fashions. Immigrant women replaced their babushkas with smart hats. As their English improved, so did their fortunes, and Jews began moving from the Lower East Side up to Harlem and out to Williamsburg, Brownsville and Queens. The Williamsburg Bridge had been opened in 1903, and in 1908 a new tendril of the subway system burrowed through the East River mud to Brooklyn, a borough of New York City only since 1898.[22]

In 1917 the Secundas moved to 256A Penn Street in Brooklyn.

"I've bought a house on *Hoizen* Street," Abraham announced one day.

"*'Hoizen'* Street?" Sholom replied. "There's no *'Hoizen'* Street in New York, Pa."

"*Hoizen* Street! *Hoizen* Street!" Abraham insisted. "In English, it's 'pants.'"

"*Hoizen*" was Abraham's translation into Yiddish of "Penn," or "Pants" Street.

Penn Street was in the heart of the Williamsburg section of Brooklyn, and one did not move there unless one was doing well. It was hard to get boarders in Brooklyn, and if you could afford to live in a house without them, well. . . .[23] But with Sholom and the other sons contributing to the family income, the Secundas were able to manage.

That year Sholom entered the United States Navy. He had been spared the draft, although America was involved in a World War, because his draft number had not been called. But by the time he was graduated from the Institute of Musical Art, he knew it was only a matter of weeks before he would be called up, and he assessed his military options. He chose the Navy, but feared rejection because of his height (he was 5'4'') and his feet (they were flat). The Navy found him acceptable, and he enlisted as a Seaman.

Sholom was stationed at the Brooklyn Navy Yard. For the first three weeks he received military training during the week. He was allowed to go home on weekends, as long as he returned to the Navy Yard by 5:30 on Monday morning. The fourth week he was sent, with other seamen, to the Naval Station on Ellis Island, where sailors waited to receive their assignments to ships bound for Europe and war.

He had not seen Ellis Island since 1908, nine years earlier, when he had been one of thousands of fresh arrivals from Russia, terrified of being sent back to his homeland. The irony of being sent back to Europe now, but under entirely different circumstances, was not lost on him. But Ellis Island had changed. Between 1917 and 1919, it served as a detention center for enemy aliens, a hospital for the Army, and a way station for Navy personnel (it would be used again as an immigration station from 1919 to 1954).

Sholom was classified as Mess Attendant, Fourth Class. When he received his assignment, he would be a cook at sea. Sholom killed time on Ellis Island exploring the Station.

One morning he heard music coming from one of the buildings, and discovered a military band in the middle of a rehearsal. At the end of the rehearsal Sholom went to the bandleader, saluted, and told him that he was a graduate of the Institute of Musical Art.

"I play piano, alto horn and cornet," Sholom said. "I'm also a professional arranger and orchestrator."

"What's your classification?" the bandmaster asked.

"Mess Attendant, Fourth Class."

"That can be changed. We need someone who can orchestrate the music for the shows we give here every week for the sailors."

Sholom was assigned to the band the following day and accorded certain privileges. He was permitted to work at home in the evenings, and to sleep at home, as long as he reported for duty on Ellis Island by 6 a.m. each day. When he told Anna that he would not have to go to Europe, she burst into tears. She readily agreed to wake her son at 4:30 every morning.

It was tight timing, getting from Penn Street in Brooklyn to Ellis Island, but Sholom was always there promptly. But he had one very close call.

Sholom took the elevated subway from Williamsburg to the Bowery, where he changed to the Third Avenue Elevated bound for South Ferry. One day, the Third Avenue El inched its way past repair work being done on the tracks, and when it finally arrived at South Ferry, Sholom could hear the whistle of the tender that would take him to Ellis.

When the subway doors opened, he ran down the stairs to the street and sprinted toward the moored Navy tender. The lines had already been cast off, and as Sholom raced along the pier, his lungs bursting, it was edging away from the dock. The sailors on board, watching the contest, had lined the railings and were leaning over them, stretching their arms toward Sholom, screaming at him to jump. Sholom leapt from the edge of the pier without thinking, and was caught by the jacket and hauled on board.

Sholom had his Naval music duties down to a few hours' work each week. Because he worked so quickly, he was able to make time to write an uplifting war tune, "Food Will Win the War," and to look for work in the theater. That season Sigmund Weintraub became the star and director of the Liberty Theater in Brownsville. Sholom joined the theater as composer and conductor. In the afternoons, following the band rehearsal at Ellis, he returned to New York, where he worked on original songs and orchestrations. In the evenings he conducted the orchestra, wearing his Navy uniform.

The bandmaster raised his rank to Musician, Second Class. "In this manner," Sholom wrote, "I continued to rout the Germans until the war ended."

Sholom was able to obtain an early release from the Navy, as were other servicemen, because he wanted to continue his studies. He asked Frank Damrosch to write to the Navy informing it that Sholom would attend graduate school at the Institute of Musical Art, and within a week, he was a civilian again. Sholom re-enrolled at the Institute, and continued his work on advanced forms of musical composition for two years.

As conductor at the Liberty Theater, Sholom knew that he could be replaced at any moment by an out-of-work violinist. Membership in the musicians' club gave every *klezmer* (hack musician) more authority than Sholom. Members of the orchestra needled Sholom and edited his music. "Everyone in the orchestra was my boss," Sholom wrote.

The jurisdiction of the musicians' club did not extend to Newark, New Jersey, where Sidney Hart and his wife, Bertha, directed the Metropolitan Theater on Montgomery Street. (In his youth, actor Paul Muni had worked at the Metropolitan as a bit player for $12 a week—his assignments included bringing sandwiches and beer for the other actors between acts.) Hart needed a composer-conductor, and had heard of Sholom's work. Sholom was engaged at Hart's theater.

His first operetta was "Children Come Home," text by Zolatarevski (which, with someone else's score, was playing on Second Avenue at that time). Sholom's second score was for "The Golden Time." Although critics from the New York press did not cover Newark theaters, Sholom's star was rising among the *au courant* of Second Avenue—he became a familiar figure at Yiddish theater hangouts such as the Cafe Royal and Stark's.

In 1919 the Weintraubs once again engaged the Liberty Theater, and Sholom was able to compose music for them but not allowed to conduct because of increased pressure from the union. Joseph Rumshinsky had forced the union to look for qualified musicians among non-members—he had the power to insist. By paying a bribe, these musicians were able to get work. The member-musicians, however, were entitled to jobs regardless of their musicianship, and one of them was hired to conduct the orchestra at the Liberty.

Rumshinsky, for all his tyrannical personality (and perhaps because of it), had fought for excellence in the Yiddish theater, thereby raising its operettas from *shund* to brilliant productions. Abetting his cause for better theater in the non-musical world was Maurice Schwartz, who rightly deserves credit for the best theater ever to be presented on Second Avenue—and, some say, on any stage in New York at that time.

In 1918 Maurice Schwartz found a home for his Yiddish Art Theater at the Irving Place Theater near Manhattan's Gramercy Park.[24] That year is considered the watershed of Yiddish theater, the beginning of its most glorious era, which was to last until the early 1930s. On Irving Place one could see Yiddish translations of Shaw, Moliere, Gorky. A London critic, reviewing a Schwartz production on tour in England, wrote, "The performance of these Yiddish players contains more great acting than I have ever seen on any stage in any place. . ."[25]

The great actors in Yiddish theater responsible for such assessments were Jacob P. Adler, David Kessler and Boris Thomashevsky. It was Thomashevsky who gave Sholom an opportunity which he was able to turn down.

Thomashevsky was then the star, producer, writer and director of the National Theater. His composer was Rumshinsky, and together they produced the best operettas on Second Avenue. Theirs was an unbeatable combination: Rumshinsky was the king of Yiddish musicals, Thomashevsky was Second Avenue's most popular star.

Boris Thomashevsky, the son and grandson of cantors, was born in the Kiev province of Russia. At the age of five he had created a sensation singing an entire synagogue service in the Asitnaitchka synagogue where his grandfather had been the cantor. Pinchas Thomashevsky, Boris' father, brought his family to America in 1881 when the boy was 15.[26] In New York Pinchas and his children appeared in amateur theatricals at Turn Hall on East 4th Street (where in 1884 the first professional New York Yiddish theater performance took place).

Boris began his career in New York playing women's roles. By 1902 he was

> . . .a young man, fat, with curling black hair, languorous eyes, and a rather effeminate voice, who is thought very beautiful by the girls of the Ghetto. Thomashevsky has a face with no mimic capacity, and a temperament absolutely impervious to mood or feeling. But he picturesquely stands in the middle of the stage and declaims phlegmatically the role of the hero, and satisfies the "romantic" demand of the audience. . .Girls and men from the sweatshops. . .are moved by a very crude attempt at beauty.[27]

Often Thomashevsky appeared wearing pink or yellow tights. His legs, *Forward* editor Abraham Cahan wrote, "were the finest in the Yiddish theater."[28]

For all his flamboyance, Thomashevsky was one of the earliest exponents of better Yiddish theater, insisting on regular and prompt rehearsals and, with Jacob Adler, attempting to offer artistic theater. But his niche was popular theater. While he was packing audiences into his theater with operettas, Kessler, Adler and Schwartz were struggling to support serious drama.

Thomashevsky and Rumshinsky parted professional company in 1919. Sholom speculates that Thomashevsky, as star-manager of the National Theater, "slowed Rumshinsky's attempts to scale even greater heights." Rumshinsky was negotiating with his one-time partner Josef Edelstein for the coming season at the Second Avenue Theater. Thomashevsky, aware of Rumshinsky's power and popularity, was anxious about the prospective competition. He realized that no one then on the scene could replace his prodigal composer.

Hanging around backstage at the National was a young, skinny, dark-haired musician by the name of George Gershwin. Gershwin had been brought to Thomashevsky's attention by his eldest son, Harry, who described Gershwin as a talented jazz pianist. Thomashevsky was hesitant to engage Gershwin as Rumshinsky's replacement because he was, as Sholom put it, "too much American and too little Jew." Still, Thomashevsky was interested.

Chaim Bas, a force in the Chorus Singers' Union, had befriended Sholom in the course of doing union business at the Liberty Theater. Bas told Thomashevsky about Sholom, and suggested to the star that by working together, Gershwin and Sholom could equal one Joseph Rumshinsky. Thomashevsky liked the idea and arranged for the two young composers to meet backstage in his dressing room during a matinee. As the actor applied his makeup for the afternoon performance, he introduced them, outlining for Gershwin Sholom's education and professional experience in the Yiddish theater.

Thomashevsky's dressing room had a piano which could not be heard onstage, and Sholom asked Gershwin to play some of his songs. Sholom admired Gershwin's virtuosity on the piano, but was less than appreciative of his obvious jazz orientation. Gershwin had started piano lessons at the age of 12. At 15 he had been the youngest song plugger on Tin Pan Alley—he had worked as a staff pianist at Remick's song-publishing company—and had written several songs, none published.[29] He had studied harmony, theory and orchestration, but could not match Sholom's academic credentials.

There was no hint that afternoon that Gershwin would go on to compose "Rhapsody in Blue," "Piano Concerto in F," "American in Paris," and "Porgy and Bess." Sholom at 23 (he was four years older than Gershwin) was already something of a musical snob. When Thomashevsky rejoined the two young men, Sholom informed him that his idea wouldn't work. "The two of us," he said, "are no pair. We have totally different approaches to music."

A year later, Gershwin would write his first Broadway score—"La La Lucille."

Sholom's recollection of his brief, disappointing encounter with Gershwin appeared numerous times in the American press over the years, told by Sholom himself in interviews. He repeated the event in his memoirs and added:

> Years later, when I had assumed my position in the Yiddish theater and Gershwin had become a composer of world standing,

we would often meet on Broadway or in a cafe. When he saw me, he would stretch out his hand with a big thank-you. No matter who was around, he would say, "Sholom's the one I owe my present position to in the musical world. If he had agreed to become my partner, I would now be a composer in the Yiddish theater."

Perhaps in his hyperbolic need to be associated somehow with Gershwin historically, Sholom sensed their true connection, which was their philosophical similarities. David Ewen cites the central conflict within Gershwin, his biographical subject: ". . .the struggle in Gershwin to reconcile his passion for jazz with his idea of writing serious music; his conflict of purpose in producing hits on the one hand and good art on the other."[30] Sholom's love of good Yiddish theater music, his pride in producing popular music, ran at odds with his need to be taken seriously as a classical composer. The conflict kept Sholom hard at work in both fields for most of his professional life, with measurable success in both.

In the last analysis, however, it was probably Sholom's artistic ego that precluded his working with Gershwin. Sholom was a solo act. He did not want to collaborate with anyone. A man of tact, it probably seemed simpler to say that he was the more classically trained musician and that he was not a jazz man, and let it go at that.

In the aftermath of his decision not to work with Gershwin, Sholom's career seemed to be at a dead end. He did not want to spend the rest of his days composing occasional songs for the smaller Yiddish theaters and teaching performers and chorus members their parts. His ambitions did not include giving piano lessons forever. Sholom began checking the English press for jobs in the theater. He also assembled, with other musicians, three times a week at Local 310 of the Musicians' Union in hopes of getting work.

He landed a job working for "Sliding" Billy Watson, star and manager of a burlesque company. Watson needed a conductor and pianist for a production he wanted to take on the road—to the "provinces," as it then was called.

"My mother didn't care too much for the idea," Sholom wrote. "Traveling around with naked girls—certainly not Jewish girls, for what kind of Jewish girl would undress, even half-way, in public?"

Sholom toured with Watson's company, playing in a different town every week, for which he was paid $45 weekly and $5 for hotel and food. He was able to send home $15 to his mother out of each paycheck.

He did not last in burlesque. The strain, he wrote prudishly, was too much: "On account of the girls in the chorus, I was forced to struggle with temptation every night. After a few months, I became convinced that my daily dealings and close relations with the frivolous chorus girls, all of whom were Christians, would not lead to any good."

Sholom pretended, he wrote, to be " a dangerously sick person," and Watson found a replacement for him. "I came home thin, pale, and worn out. My short career had given me a basic social education."

It is highly doubtful that Sholom, who had a reputation as a lady-killer in his bachelor days, resisted that temptation, although he would never boast about his conquests to his family because of the high morality of his parents and his later pristine view of himself. Sholom's prudery was the subject of hilarity with his sons in later years, and the closest he ever came to a locker-room exchange of confidences was in a letter to his eldest son who was then in the Army: "So how are you doing with the chicks? I was young once too, you know, and a father and son can talk about such things." Still, blue language used at home would offend him always, and the casual use of expletives by his sons would make him wince.

Sholom returned to the Liberty Theater and to his chores of writing occasional scores, of rehearsals and orchestra arranging. At the same time he continued his postgraduate studies at the Institute. The musicians in the orchestra continued to needle him, and more than once the violinist-conductor grabbed Sholom's music and tore it to shreds.

Weintraub, the director at the Liberty, wanted Sholom to put together some instrumental music for a certain scene. "You don't have to write any new music for this," he said, "just take something out of an opera or symphony. The other composers in the large theaters do it all the time."

Sholom selected an excerpt from Carl Maria von Weber's opera, "Oberon." He copied the music note for note on blank music sheets and brought them to orchestra rehearsal. After playing only a few bars, the violinist put aside his instrument and began, once again, to tear up the music. Weintraub, who witnessed the incident, ran over to the pit and yelled, "When you scream that Secunda can't write music, I don't say anything. Maybe you're right. But when you scream that *von Weber* can't write music, I must tell you that you're a bunch of cripples who can't play decent music!" Weintraub informed the startled violinist of the true origin of the music he was about to destroy. The musicians, mollified, didn't make any more trouble for Sholom.

Sholom completed his postgraduate courses at the Institute of Musical Art in 1919. Around this time he attended a concert at Carnegie Hall that was dedicated to the great Jewish composer, Ernest Bloch. Sholom was enchanted by Bloch's music and determined to study with him.

Born in Geneva, Switzerland, in 1880, Bloch came to the United States in 1916, where in later years he taught composition at the David Mannes Music School in New York, was director of the Cleveland Institute of Music and a professor of music at the University of California.[31] The *New York Times'* music critic Harold C. Schonberg has written,

> Until music took a right turn after World War II into the arms of serialism, Bloch was considered one of the most important composers of the century. . .such great conductors as Monteux and Stokowski rushed to present his new scores. . .he was the first great Jewish nationalist and most likely the only one of real importance. He was a nationalist in the sense that Ives, Smetana, Mussorgsky were nationalists. He did not have to quote Hebraic material; his music *was* Hebraic.[32]

When Sholom attended the Carnegie Hall concert, the pieces that moved him most were excerpts from Bloch's "Jewish Cycle," a body of work he wrote beginning in 1912 (it was completed in 1936). Of his "Jewish Cycle," Bloch wrote, "It was this Jewish heritage as a whole which stirred me, and the music was the result. To what extent the music is Jewish—to what extent it is just Ernest Bloch—of that I know nothing. The future will decide."[33]

The day after the concert, Sholom telephoned Bloch at his home on Lexington Avenue and made an appointment to see him. Bloch lived on the top floor of a three-story house. Sholom went to his house and told the composer about his music studies and theater experiences. He told him of his excitement about Bloch's music, and that he wanted to study with him.

Bloch, a shy, stocky man with the eyes of a cocker spaniel, said, "I charge $20 an hour. I don't have much time for students, because I compose most of the day. I know the price is high, but my compositions do not bring sufficient income to support a family."

Sholom was crushed. Bloch was his idol, but that sum of money was impossible for Sholom to manage, particularly since he was helping to support his family.

"I understand your situation," he said despondently, "but I can't afford it."

Bloch studied his anguished companion for a moment, sucking on a pipe. "Mr. Secunda," he said, "bring me your compositions in higher forms that you wrote at the Institute. I would like to examine them and give you my opinion."

The next day Sholom delivered a piano sonata, a string quartet, some preludes and fugues. Within a week, Sholom received a letter from Bloch, in which he said that he had studied the manuscripts carefully and that he would give Sholom a year's scholarship.

"The year opened new doors for me," Sholom wrote, "not only of knowledge, but of enthusiasm, inspiration, and new concepts of the inexhaustible sources of orchestral colors."

Sholom learned that Bloch had, in Switzerland, grown up in an environment that was "rich in finances and poor in Jewish spirit." With Bloch, Sholom analyzed the "Jewish Cycle," and wondered how a composer who had been raised in such an assimilated atmosphere could create such masterpieces of pure, Jewish spirit.

"I'll tell you," Bloch explained. "My grandfather, who was an observant Jew, once came to our house for a visit when I was a child. One morning I saw him dressed in a prayer shawl and phylacteries, standing in a corner, swaying back and forth, chanting prayers. I had never seen or heard such things. I never forgot the scene, especially the melody of my grandfather's praying. I never freed myself of that melody. When I began to study music seriously, I always found in my themes reminiscences of my grandfather's praying."

After their lessons, Sholom and Bloch would sit and discuss Jewish folklore and tradition. One statement by Bloch in particular lingered with Sholom, and accounts for his passion for composing serious, Jewish music: "A Jewish composer must aspire to write Jewish music, as his soul and heart feel. Only then can the music have true artistic value. Whatever an Italian composer writes will sound Italian. The same is true of a Russian or an American. It must also be that way for a Jew.''

Hearing his mentor verbalize that idea, which had been latent within Sholom's thinking, was similar to the moment when a patient in analysis hears his analyst phrase a concept which squares with the patient's willingness to hear it: something clicks in the head. So it was with Sholom. Bloch gave him a mandate for his unfocused musical ambition. Bloch gave Sholom his musical identity.

Sholom began writing serious music whenever he could. The ''Bloch influence'' haunted him. Although there was little market for art songs, he began leafing through the work of the best Yiddish poets and to write music that would reflect Bloch's style.

♫ EXILE TO PHILADELPHIA

In the evening of October 17, 1921, the Liberty Theater in Brooklyn was beginning to fill up. Curtain time was 8:30, and by 8:00, the theater's seats and standing room section were fully occupied. Members of the Yiddish and English press were scattered throughout the theater. Working-class Jews from Manhattan's Lower East Side had made the trek to Brooklyn, as had Jews who had graduated to New York's middle class. Stars of the Yiddish theater—whose official season was to begin the following week—were also among this evening's theater-goers: stars such as Michal Michalesko, Aaron Lebedeff, Lucy and her sister, Bella Finkel.

For this season at the Liberty, producer William Rolland had teamed up with co-directors Boaz and Clara Young. Boaz, an actor who came to New York via London from his native Poland, idolized Jacob Adler and wanted to present musical theater that was in the Adler-European tradition.[1] His young wife, Clara, had left America to appear in operettas in Europe, and had returned a star. Boaz had written an operetta for her called "Jakele Bluffer," and he had engaged Max Brot, a German operatic singer, to star with her.

Sholom had been engaged to write the score for "Bluffer," on the recommendation of Rolland. The more prominent Yiddish composers were committed to seasons in the big Manhattan theaters, and the Youngs wanted a composer able to write music of a more classical nature than the *shund* being offered on Second Avenue.

Sholom was the Young's choice but not, as usual, the Musicians' Club's. Rolland encountered the same resistance from the club he had in seasons past when it came to hiring Sholom—the club did not want him to conduct. Rolland decided to enlist the aid of Abraham Cahan, editor of the powerful *Forward,* the Yiddish daily newspaper

which, with a circulation of nearly a quar
newspaper of Lower East Side record. Cah
political and cultural life of Jewish immigra
the doings on Second Avenue, not because
was high art, but because it was so popular
The Downtown Jews: Portraits of an Imm

When Cahan began transforming the Forward into an instrument of mass appeal among the Jewish immigrants in New York, there was only one serious rival for the kind of influence he hoped to achieve: the Yiddish theater. If the Forward was becoming a kind of running Talmudic text for the secular cultural life of the Yiddish speaking masses, the theaters on the Bowery were serving as that culture's temple. In a sense, there could be no rival to the immediacy of the stage's appeal to a public which tended to adore its stars in a way that its ancestors had once adored their favorite cantors, and even Cahan's populist imagination could provide no match for the vulgarity of which Yiddish entertainers were sometimes capable. Cahan and his socialist intellectuals could never hope to displace the influence of the Yiddish theater—even though it was an influence that most of them had found questionable in its early days—and they did not try. Rather, what they hoped to do was to use their own growing influence in order to have some effect upon the standards of Yiddish drama. For they, as men of the written word—the secularized offspring of a rabbinical culture for which the written word was the holiest of human forms of expression—saw themselves as the guardians of Yiddish literary values, and they were determined to impose such values even upon the spoken culture of the stage. This is why the writing of drama criticism had an importance at the Forward second only to that of writing editorials, and why Cahan increasingly found himself taking on that job as part of his round of chores.[2]

Rolland informed Harry Lang, labor editor of the *Forward* of his difficulties vis à vis Sholom and the Union. Lang told Beryl Botvinik, who wrote a piece about Sholom's inability to get a job as a Yiddish theater conductor. Two members of the musicians' club protested to Cahan about Botvinik's article. Cahan's response was to write an even sharper piece about the situation. The club relented, and Sholom was _ed as composer-conductor for "Jakele Bluffer."

Although the Yiddish theater was at its zenith in 1921—there were approximately 72 Yiddish theaters around the globe, nearly 20 of them in New York—there was more than the usual interest in the October 17 performance at the Liberty[3]. Critics and fellow actors were curious about Clara Young, who was said to embody all that was required of a prima donna—youth, beauty, and a superb soprano ("She was a sex symbol," says Dinah Goldberg). They also wanted to see what the fuss was all about concerning the 27-year-old composer, Sholom Secunda.

Sholom had at his command the largest orchestra ever engaged at the Liberty. In addition to the stars, there was in the cast a comedian named Charlie Cohen, a well-known Yiddish vaudevillian. One of the show-stoppers of "Bluffer" was a song called, "Boy, Did I Run," during which Cohen ran across the stage, up and down the aisles, and back across the stage again, singing the satirical lyrics all the while. That opening night, as well as during subsequent performances, the audience clamored for more encores, as much to test Cohen's endurance as to delight in the hilarious performance of the song.

William Edlin reviewed the operetta the following day in *Tag* ("Day") newspaper, under the heading "The Elegance of Clara Young in 'Jakele Bluffer'":

> First of all, it must be said that the operetta is musically a very melodious and beautiful thing. For that, credit the young conductor, Sholom Secunda. There is so much of the light, flowing waltzing rhythm in almost all of the musical numbers that it can be said without exaggeration that one seldom hears better in the best Broadway operettas. . .The general impression of the music is that Mr. Secunda is a significant talent in the field of operetta and that a lot of good musical things can be expected of him.

That season Sholom wrote another operetta for Clara Young, "Berele Tremp," by Israel Rosenburg. At the end of the season Rolland brought "Bluffer" to Manhattan to Thomashevsky's People's Theater. Sholom conducted in a large New York theater—on the same podium from which Rumshinsky had conducted—for the first time.

One day, while having lunch at Stark's Cafe, Sholom was approached by Vatman Brash, and several other members of the Musicians' Club committee, who asked Sholom to meet with them at the Club headquaters. That afternoon at the Club's Bowery office, Vatman, speaking for the other members, invited Sholom to join the organization.

"There's only one catch," Vatman said. "We have older composers whose interests we must defend. They get first priority, understandably, in New York theaters. But we want to encourage new talent such as yours. So we've made arrangements with Anshel Shor at the Arch Street Theater in Philadelphia that you should work with him. The Arch Street is a very important theater—Jacob Adler, David Kessler and others have played there. In addition, Anshel Shor is a playwright and lyricist. The only stipulation is that you will not work for three years in New York. That will appease our older members."

Vatman's proposal was not without precedent. The Hebrew Actors Union, founded in 1900 (twenty years before Actors Equity), controlled Yiddish theaters in and out of New York, as well as Yiddish vaudeville and music halls.[4] It was the policy of the Hebrew Actors Union to send actors into the provinces for three or more years before they were permitted to even apply for membership in the union.[5]

Vatman arranged for Sholom to meet with Shor at the Musicians' Club. Shor, actor-director, and his wife, Dora Weissman, told Sholom that they had heard Sholom's operettas at the Liberty Theater, and that they looked forward to working with him in Philadelphia. Sholom was to be paid $125 a week, and would share the proceeds with the management for one benefit in his honor, a fee of $2,000 for Sholom.

Shor obtained a room for Sholom in the boarding house where he and his wife lived on Spruce Street. Sholom's three years in Philadelphia were a rite of passage not only professionally, but personally as well. As a man of 28, he lived away from his parents for the first time in his adult life (although he visited them on weekends).

Anna Teitelbaum (who was later married to Menashe Skulnik), a young actress who was born in France, was a prima donna in the Arch Street company. She describes Sholom as having been very shy, except when he laughed:

The first time I met him was on a blue Sunday, very quiet in town, and he was very quiet. And I said, "Let's talk." I am not in the habit of telling jokes, but I have a sense of humor, and he had a set of teeth. If I said "hello," he'd laugh. If I said "pillow," he'd laugh. And he laughed with a half-smile even when I criticized him.

Unlike many Yiddish theater actors, Anna Teitelbaum could read music and was literate in Yiddish ("Women actors didn't all read and write Yiddish," says Dinah Goldberg. "The director had to write out their dialogue phonetically—girls were not encouraged to be schooled in Yiddish"). In her childhood in France she had often attended the opera, and she loved classical music. She and Sholom spent many afternoons attending concerts in Philadelphia. They heard Sousa in the park, Stokowski with the Philadelphia Orchestra and, on one memorable occasion, saw Tchaikovsky conduct. Anna was then married, so their friendship, which lasted all Sholom's life, did not turn to romance.

Because of his respect for her intelligence, Anna could criticize Sholom where others could not. "In those days," she says, "we had every day another play, and on weekends five performances with one play. We 'baked' shows, not only musicals, but melodrama. He wrote me one song, and then, three weeks later, I was to sing the same song but with different lyrics. 'It's the same song,' I told him, and he looked at me with his half-smile.''

The first play for the 1922-1923 season was a melodrama, starring Dora Weissman, followed by William Siegel's "The American Rebbetsin" (rabbi's wife) with a score by Sholom. The musical was written for Dora, but she suddenly became ill. Anshel Shor went to New York and engaged Celia Adler, Jacob Adler's daughter, to replace Dora.

Celia Adler, who had performed with Maurice Schwartz's Art Theater, was one of the Yiddish theater's finest and most beautiful actresses. She was born in New York in 1890, one month after her mother's arrival from Europe (Jacob Adler was already in the United States). Her father was then the biggest dramatic star on Second Avenue. He and Celia's mother, Dinah, were divorced when Celia was six months old.

Celia's theatrical debut occurred when she was an infant. Dinah was appearing in a play in which she was to deposit her child on the steps of a foundling home because her husband had deserted her. "At that age," Celia said later, "the maid would always bring me backstage to be nursed, and when my mother saw her she said, 'Why should I take a rag baby on?' She put a shawl around me and took me on. And when she took me on, she had to cry to bid me goodby and beg my forgiveness for giving me away. So I raised my head to see what's wrong. And when the audience saw she was holding a live baby, which no one expected, they began to laugh. Mother said I turned my two big eyes in the direction of the audience. She couldn't finish her dramatic scene because I stole the show."

Celia and her mother, who had remarried, continued to play with Adler in his company for a brief time. Growing up, she saw little of her father owing, she said, to his wife's jealousy. "I used to stand on the corner of Grand Street and Chrystie Street, near the Grand Theater where my father played. And when he was approaching, the crowds gathered and I heard them say, 'Adler's coming! Adler's coming!' I used to watch from a distance. I was so proud."

Dinah's second husband was Siegmund Feinman. Because of her anger toward her remote father (who had married Sara Heine) and her love for her stepfather, Celia took Feinman's name for a few years. She later resumed her father's name and with it became, as Lulla Rosenfeld writes, "an important force in the Yiddish Art Theater movement. . .She had pathos and charm, she had an irresistible talent for comedy, she was frankly of the people and the people took her to their hearts. She is the only one of Adler's children who was to achieve stardom on the Yiddish stage."[6]

Celia was given a room in the boarding house where Sholom lived, and the two began a romantic attachment during rehearsals of "Rebbetsin." Celia was not a trained singer, so Sholom rewrote the music for her limited voice. She was charmed by Sholom, and would peer out at him through the curtain to watch him conduct in the orchestra pit. "If he saw me," she said, "he'd smile. He had the most beautiful smile. He was so happy to see that I watched him, and he would often take me home."

Sholom helped her with the articles she occasionally wrote for the Jewish press in Philadelphia, and coached her in her role in the operetta. "I was supposed to enter laughing," she said, "and I didn't feel like laughing. I said to Sholom, 'Tell me something funny,' which he did, and I began to laugh and couldn't stop."

Sholom's operetta was the first time Celia sang and danced on stage, a departure from her usual, tragic roles, which she welcomed. "I had top billing and dramatic parts in those days. Every play was a melodrama, a tear-jerker. I had to have hysterics in every act. And along comes 'The American Rebbetsin.' "

Celia played an American girl who falls in love with a Chasidic Jew and becomes very religious, blessing the Sabbath candles on Friday night. As she does so, she hears jazz music, presumably from the street, and she forgets about the ritual and begins to sing and dance. The play was so successful that at the end of the season, she took it on tour. By that time she and Sholom were no longer seeing one another, perhaps because Sholom's parents did not approve of actresses.

"When I got to Boston, I wanted him to know what a success he was," she said. "I didn't know where to get him on the phone. Finally I got him. I had to hear his voice or I would go crazy. I told him of the great success. I was in love with him, but he never asked me to marry him, and I regretted that."

During his Philadelphia years, Sholom wrote a song called "Vie Bist Du Yukele Meiner?" (Where are you, Yukel mine?) for the young soubrette, Yetta Zwerling. The song was recorded by RCA Victor and Columbia, and the then-new Roxy Theater orchestra in New York played an instrumental version of it. Sholom also wrote "Honor Thy Father," which was recorded by "Wee Willie" Robbins for RCA.

The Arch Street benefit for Sholom was his boldest undertaking. He chose Goldfaden's "Shulamis," the great Yiddish classic, which was performed originally in Russia, and was popular in the United States for the life of the Yiddish theater. Lucy Finkel, who suggested that Sholom do the operetta, played the title role. Michalesko, who had worked for Sholom's father in Nicholayev years before, played the role of Absalom. Sholom's old friend Hymie Jacobson played Tsingintang. They used Goldfaden's original music, except for Shulamis' desert scene in the third act, for which Sholom wrote new music.

While in Philadelphia, Sholom befriended a number of musicians who were in the Philadelphia Orchestra, and with their help he assembled an unusually large symphonic orchestra and chorus for "Shulamis." Anshel Shor took enormous advertisements in the press, and the benefit was sold out.

Sholom jumped into the mainstream of Philadelphia's cultural life and spent most of his free time with writers and musicians. Every Friday afternoon he went to the Academy of Music to hear Stokowski and the Philadelphia Orchestra. When he had a free Tuesday evening, he would hear the Metropolitan Opera Company's guest performances.

Sholom's prosperity continued with the receipt of two checks from RCA and Columbia totaling $2,000. He had never had so much money in his life, and while he sent most of his weekly salary home to his mother, he decided to use his windfall for a guest tour of Europe with Michalesko and his wife and Hymie Jacobson. There they would appear as guest performers at Yiddish theaters. In order to obtain a passport, Sholom instituted the paperwork for naturalization, and received a document proving his citizenship in 1923, prior to his leaving for Europe.

The four Yiddish theater friends booked passage on the United States Liner *Leviathan,* one of the most luxurious ships afloat (Sholom had painted the captain's stateroom while in the Navy). It was a far happier crossing for Sholom than the one he had made to America 16 years earlier. Postwar immigration restrictions had reduced the glut of steerage passengers—in part due to the new spirit of isolationism—and the term "steerage" was replaced in steamship advertisements by the term "tourist third cabin," or, simply, "tourist."[7]

Sholom traveled in this most modest class, but he had access to the public rooms on the upper decks. Part of the party atmosphere on board was attributed to easily obtained booze. Prohibition, begun in 1919, did not apply on the high seas, and trans-Atlantic passengers were lubricated by firewater unavailable at home. Many of the passengers who walked steadily onto a ship in New York were carried off in a stupor onto the English or French shore.[8] Sholom, never a big drinker, was doubtless upright as he disembarked with his friends, but it is certain that he had a high time at sea.

To be young and in Paris in the 1920s was a heady experience. Sholom's passions—for music, for books, for food—included women, for whom he always had a particular yen. His success with actresses and showgirls in the theater was no secret. Women found his smile and ebullience irresistible. But Paris had a particular naughtiness that Sholom relished. "At night girls went around openly pulling men by the sleeve—what little French I understood, I knew clearly what they wanted of me," he wrote. "I found the whole business pleasing."

He abandoned his normal frugality by going to dance halls to dance with scantily clad young women. "This luxury was really an expensive one," he wrote, "but for a young man of my age, it was worth it."

Sholom was the compleat tourist. He enjoyed spending afternoons in cafes, nursing a bottle of wine, and trying to eavesdrop on the conversations of Parisians, using his high-school French where possible. Walking the banks of the Seine, he was reminded of home. There were pushcarts, similar to those on Orchard Street, but French carts contained bargains in books and sheet music. Sholom bought many used manuscripts of symphonies, operas, sonatas and chamber music that remained in his personal library all his life.

The arrangements for Sholom's guest tour were incomplete when he, Jacobson and the Michaleskos arrived in Paris. Of inestimable help in nailing down engagements were Molly Picon and her husband, Jacob Kalich. Molly and Sholom knew each other slightly, but after renewing their friendship in Paris, their mutual esteem was cemented.

Molly had been on the stage since the age of 5, when she appeared at the Columbia (later called the Arch Street) Theater in Philadelphia. There she appeared with Adler, Kessler, Thomashevsky. In 1905 she appeared in a Yiddish translation of "Uncle Tom's Cabin," playing Topsy. Mike Thomashevsky, Boris' brother, played Uncle Tom.

Molly's early theater involvement, like that of many Yiddish actors, was linked to her family's poverty. Her mother, who was born in Odessa, was a dressmaker who made costumes for Yiddish theater actresses. Her father, an unemployed scholar of the Talmud, was seldom at home.

When Molly's mother went to the theater, she had to take along her two daughters, since she could not afford babysitters. Often Molly slept in a trunk at the theater, and when she did not, she would observe the great actors of the Yiddish stage. "I learned just from looking at them," she later said. "I never had a formal lesson of any kind because I didn't need it."

For fifty cents a night Molly would perform wherever there was a demand for a child performer—the Columbia, or the Chestnut Street

Opera House, or at the nickelodeons. Molly's mother, when Molly was performing at the Columbia, asked for a raise for her daughter. The management refused, so Molly went into vaudeville.

She appeared with three other teenage girls in an act called the "Four Seasons." "I was 'winter,' " she says, "because I could do a Russian dance." The act traveled all over the country for fifty-two weeks. Molly was paid $30 weekly, half of which she sent home. In 1918 the act arrived in Boston at about the same time as an epidemic of influenza broke out, which took thousands of lives. All the American theaters were closed down and Molly needed money to get back home. She found a company of Yiddish actors at the Grand Opera House that was headed by her future husband, Jacob (called "Yankele" by those who knew him). The Opera House had not been closed because the authorities were unaware that it was in business. Jacob offered Molly $35 a week to stay on and Molly, who was attracted to him, decided not to go home. Jacob saw that she had star qualities, and tried to arrange for her to appear on Second Avenue in New York, but was unable to penetrate the political quarantine of the New York Hebrew Actors Union. Jacob and Molly were married, and they decided to tour Europe, where Molly would establish a reputation resulting in her being brought to New York by popular demand.

Part of the Second Avenue resistance to Molly Picon was her size and type. She was five feet tall and weighed 100 pounds at a time when buxom, sensuous female figures were the vogue. Jacob guessed rightly that by expanding child-like parts for her, she would find her niche. With short curls and enormous, question-mark eyes, she was the consummate imp, and audiences loved her. During her three years in Europe, Jacob mounted several plays for her, the most famous of them being "Yankele," a sort of Peter Pan story. (In her 80s, a still-slight and fit Molly was still receiving requests for her to play that role. Over her long career she played the part over 3,000 times in theaters all over the world.) Molly returned with Jacob to New York in late 1923 with her repertoire of tailor-made roles, and she became a triumph on Second Avenue.

While they were in Paris, Molly and Jacob lived at the Hotel Moderne on the Rue de Rivoli, the Jewish quarter in Paris. Sholom, Hymie and the Michaleskos met often with them, and were given the names of Yiddish theater contacts in Paris and other European cities.

"Sholom was very handsome," Molly recalls, "and he was a flirt. A ladies' man. But everyone loved him."

After three weeks in Paris, Sholom and his little troupe went to Warsaw, where they appeared in Kaminska's Theater. There they befriended one of the most distinguished performers in Europe, Madame Esther Rokhl Kaminska, who had years before performed in America in "Mirele Efros" at David Kessler's Thalia Theater. Esther, her daughter Ida (who later achieved world fame in the film "The Shop on Main Street") and their families lived near the theater. Sholom spent all his free time with them, in part because the Kaminskas were legendary in the Yiddish theater, in part because he was captivated by the young and beautiful Ida.

Hymie was a great success with Warsaw audiences. His singing of wholly American topical-satirical songs, his eccentric New York dancing, enchanted the public. They loved one number in particular, a song in which, after each verse, he would do a dance à la George M. Cohan. At the end of each dance bit, he would take the straw hat he wore and pull it down over his ears, breaking the crown. The audiences yelled and stamped their feet for encores, and hat after hat would be punctured by Hymie's head. In time the management of the theater had difficulty keeping him—and the audience—in hats.

The Michaleskos remained in Warsaw to visit their son, who lived there, and Sholom and Hymie went on to Jassy, Romania. The high point of their trip, professionally, was appearing at the garden theater Famul Verde where Goldfaden and the Brody Singers had appeared in 1876, the first professional Yiddish theater production in the world. Playing with Sholom and Hymie were Chaim Tauber and his wife. Tauber, a lyricist, later came to the United States and worked on several operettas with Sholom.

From Jassy, Hymie and Sholom went to Berlin, where they were sightseers rather than performers. They caught up with the Michaleskos in Paris, and all sailed back to New York on the *Mauretania*. Cunard's most elegant ship, her marble fireplaces, titled and wealthy passenger list, and record-setting North Atlantic speed were a fitting conclusion to Sholom's European summer.

For his second season at the Arch Street Theater, Sholom's salary was raised to $150 a week. For a play by Moishe Rikhter, Josef Sheyngold, a superb dramatic actor and baritone singer, was engaged. In one scene Sheyngold was to sing a song based on the modes used for High Holy Days services. Sholom combined three pieces from synagogue repertoire—"Hineni Heoni Mimish," "Kol Nidre," and "Sosn Y'simkhe b'simkhes toyre," tying them together in a single song. It became known as "Dos Yiddishe Lied" ("The Jewish Song"), a staple in the repertoire of most cantors and Jewish concert artists, and was recorded by Cantor Mordkhe Hershman for Victor Records.

Sholom finished his third mandatory season at the Arch Street and was able, at last, to come out of exile and return professionally to New York. He signed with Nathan Goldberg, who had leased the Grand Theater. The 1924-1925 season opened with "Gypsy Prince" by William Siegel, music by Alexander Olshanetsky. Sholom, to his dismay, was hired as only the conductor. But at the end of the run of "Prince," Sholom wrote topical songs and duets, although he still was not given an assignment to do an entire score.

Impatient to write a full-length operetta, Sholom signed for the 1925-1926 season with Misha Gehrman at the Hopkinson Theater in Brooklyn. Gehrman's troupe included performers from Maurice Schwartz's Art Theater, such as Yidl Dubinski, Yitskhok Lipinski and Misha and his wife, Lucy. Gehrman promised Sholom a large orchestra and introduced him to Israel Rosenberg, who had written the libretto for the operetta "Moshka," for which Sholom was to write, at last, a full-length score. Gehrman gave the composer and lyricist this directive: "Write an operetta that will bring Jews to Brooklyn, for a change."

The summer before the season opened, Sholom worked at the Penn Street home of his parents. Getting Rosenberg to Brooklyn to work was not an easy matter. Rosenberg, known fondly as "The Little Tippler," would be goaded there by Sholom's promise of fine whiskey. The score they turned out was so pleasing to Gehrman that it ran all five performances of every weekend for the entire season—36 weeks. They brought the play to the National Theater in Manhattan for three weeks at the end of their season and took it to the provinces during the summer.

For the 1926-1927 season Gehrman asked Sholom to prepare a score for a new play, called "Margarita." In the spirit of Joseph Rumshinsky, Sholom suggested to Gehrman that "Margarita" include a classical ballet, not just a chorus line, and that trained ballet dancers be auditioned for the play. Gehrman liked the idea. It was a decision that would change the course of Sholom's life: among the dancers would be the woman he would marry.

♪ MARRIAGE

It is hard to imagine a woman better suited to Sholom Secunda than Betty Almer. Sholom was a man used to pampering—by his mother, his landladies, his girlfriends—and Betty was good at it. But she also understood the demands of the theater, as well as the artistic temperament, because she had grown up in the Yiddish theater.

If there was a key to Betty's personality and character, it was her mother, Katie.

Katie Almer, née Greenberg, was born in 1880 in Minsk, Russia, the granddaughter of a wealthy lumber exporter. Her father died before she was born, and she was brought up by governesses and tutors in her grandfather's immense house, where her mother was a remote presence. Her grandfather frequently made business trips to Europe and would return with toys from Germany and elsewhere. The gifts delighted Katie, but did little to assuage her loneliness. Although her youth was lacking in parental warmth, she had gaiety and wit and was often invited to parties.

Katie's grandfather lost his timber lands in a terrible fire in 1891—his assets literally went up in smoke. Katie's mother had remarried, but because the family became penniless in a sweep of flames and was in constant danger of pogroms, it was felt that Katie's future would be more promising if she were sent to the United States. Her family could not afford to go with her.

In 1892 at the age of 12, Katie was brought to America by a family who claimed to the authorities that she was one of their children, a ploy used frequently by Jews who were eager to have their children escape persecution in Eastern Europe. When she arrived in New York, Katie boarded a train to Chicago, where she was to live with one of her aunts who was already in this country.

Katie loved the theater, and at the Chicago World's Fair of 1893, she was hired to wear a Russian costume and march with one thousand other children at the Fair's opening. There she saw American Indians for the first time, performing traditional dances, and she began a lifelong affection for Indian culture and advocacy for their rights, long before it was fashionable. Indian and Russian slices of life were performed in cages around the fair grounds, a bit of symbolism that Katie would later recall with irony.

Katie had a beautiful singing voice and was asked by a minister in Chicago to sing in his church choir. Her aunt encouraged her to sing there, but Katie, even at 12, was a stubborn, fiercely Jewish girl.

"I won't sing with a cross over my head!" she shouted.

When she was 18, she moved to New York and fell in love with Sam Almer, a man who, Betty says, had matinee idol looks. Sam, born in Poland in 1875, came to the United States when he was 14. He began a career in the Yiddish theater as a costume designer. He designed costumes for Sarah Bernhardt and was Boris Thomashevsky's personal dresser, and then became an advance agent for touring Yiddish theater productions. Sam's mother, Clara, warned Katie that her son was not marriage material. "You're a good child," she said, "and my Sam is not for you." As usual, Katie knew her own mind, and in July of 1901 she married Sam.

In 1902 Betty was born, followed by Molly in 1905 and Lottie in 1909. It was fortunate that they were females, because Katie's bitterness toward men was acute. Sam Almer was a gambler who regularly lost money at the races. He was totally irresponsible, and Katie was forced by necessity to perform as a singer in the Yiddish theater.

Sam left his wife and daughters when Betty was seven, and Katie started working year-round in the Yiddish theater as an actress, occasionally in singing parts, and played minor roles opposite Jacob Adler and David Kessler.

Katie became something of an institution on Second Avenue. She worked with all the great stars and had a reputation for generosity, humor and candor. Performers respected her for her straight-forwardness and would ask her to critique their numbers.

But she had a sharp tongue. She had no patience for "private people"—people not in the theater—but she was also appalled by actors who fawned over the stars, producers and directors. Katie was extremely pretty, and Joseph Rumshinsky made one crude attempt at seducing her. She told him she wasn't interested.

"What are you saving it for?" Rumshinsky snarled.

"For the worms," Katie snapped, "not for you!"

Because she was preoccupied with her children until curtain time, she would rush to the theater minutes before her entrance, hastily applying her makeup. On one occasion an actress noted her smudged eyebrows, and said, "Look how sloppy your makeup is—you're a mess."

"A piece of soap can cleanse me," Katie retorted, "but you, the whole ocean won't cleanse."

Katie tried to be diplomatic at times. One evening Yetta Zwerling came to the theater, wearing a new hat. Katie hated the hat, but liked Zwerling. When Yetta asked Katie's opinion of the hat, she replied, "It's very nice." Henrietta Jacobson, another actress in the cast, drew Katie aside and said, "Come on, what do you really think of it?"

Katie replied, "Es pahst ihr vie a chazer, oirignlach (It suits her like earrings suit a pig)."

Katie had guts. She and her daughters lived in a walkup apartment on Eldridge Street, a coldwater flat near the theater district. She would take whatever theater work was available. At one time the only work she could get was in Newark, New Jersey. She had a bad case of flu, but could not afford to pass up the $5 fee for the performance. She fed her children, tucked them into bed, and started down the stairs with her tin makeup box under her arm. She caught her foot on a step and fell down the flight of stairs, her tin box bouncing behind her, and was badly bruised. A neighbor rushed out to help her to her feet and suggested that she go to bed.

"I have to feed my children," she said, and walked out the door.

When Katie went to work, she left her heart at home. When she was in a Second Avenue production, she could hear sirens of fire engines outside on the street, and wondered if they were going to her building, where her children might be trapped in a fire. Before leaving for the theater, she would say to her neighbors, "The door is unlocked. Remember, there are three fatherless children in there."

Katie instilled courage in her children. "Keep your head high," she would say firmly, "because if you bend it, someone will step on it." Or, "Never say 'never.' I can't stand the word." Put in charge of her children on the nights Katie worked was her nine-year-old daughter, Betty, who would sing her younger sisters to sleep before she went to bed.

None of the girls was able to go to college—there simply wasn't the money for it—and only Betty graduated from high school. Lottie was offered a scholarship to attend private high school, but had to turn it down because her income was needed, and she became a chorus girl on Second Avenue (Molly went into the line as well).

Betty became the family egghead. At the age of six she took a book on etiquette out of the public library so she could learn about table manners. As a little girl, she would buy newspapers and attempt reading them on her own. At dinner Katie would tease, "Look at Betty, she's putting her soup in her ear again. She's so busy reading that she forgets to put it in her mouth!" Later Betty took Lottie to her first opera—"Samson and Delilah"—at Madison Square Garden.

During World War I, while she was still in high school, Betty worked on weekends at a candy factory, Hawley and Hoops, on Great Jones Street in Manhattan, where she earned 83¢ a day. Katie made all of Betty's clothes, but because of her work in the theater, she occasionally fell behind on the sewing at home. One winter Betty went without winter coat until December. Still Katie did her best to provide the amenities for her daughters and bought a piano for $25 so the girls could take lessons.

Katie was afraid of nothing, and in 1911 she learned that her estranged husband was dying of Bright's Disease and diphtheria. Katie visited him daily in Willard Parker Hospital. She may have hated him for abandoning her, but she was essentially a woman of compassion.

"Katie, you're not afraid to visit me?" he said one day. "Aren't you afraid you'll catch what I've got?"

"Certainly not," she said.

"If I ever get out of this," he whispered, "I'll make it up to you for what I've done." Within hours, he was dead. He was 36.

"It's a wonder that we three sisters all got married," Lottie said later, "because mother hated men. She'd say, 'Men are pigs. Never give a husband a leg, only a foot.' She'd say, 'There are four old maids in this house. This is no-man's land.'"

Apparently, Katie kept her hostility under wraps when Betty's many beaux came to call. Betty was a beauty. She had been entered in a beauty contest sponsored by the *New York Daily Mirror* and was a finalist, but when the finals of the contest were held at an RKO movie theater, Betty was too terrified to go on stage and fled. The men who courted Betty adored Katie because she was hilarious and straight with them. But Katie had her sights on one man in particular for Betty—Sholom Secunda.

When Betty was 15, Katie had worked with Sholom, who was then in the Navy, at the Liberty Theater in Brooklyn. One evening after a performance, she came home and announced to Betty, "I hope you will marry someone like Sholom Secunda when you are older. He has *khain* (charm)."

Betty met Sholom eight years later, not through her mother, but because of a fluke. Her two sisters had become chorus girls in the Yiddish theater, but Betty was consumed by stage fright. "Literally," she said, "I couldn't walk across an empty stage." After high school she had gotten a job as a secretary at the Bishop Babcock Company, which manufactured soda fountain equipment.

One morning, en route to work, she was about to board a trolley that stopped directly across from her home. From the opposite direction, a horse and wagon rode by at a canter, and knocked her unconscious onto the street. A nearby policeman called an ambulance and she was taken to a hospital where she stayed under observation for several days. At her release, the doctor told her to stay home and rest for six weeks to recover from a concussion before going back to work. After three weeks, however, she felt too well to be idle and guilty that she was not bringing home an income.

Katie heard that the management of the Hopkinson Theater was readying a new production, an operetta called "Margarita," and suggested that Betty audition to be one of the dancers (because of persistent headaches, Betty was unable to work an eight-hour day). The salary would be $25, and Betty, who had taken ballet lessons for her own amusement, was qualified for the job. Guilt eclipsed her stage fright, and Betty tried out for the show.

Sholom was present at the auditions, because the dancers had to double as singers in the chorus. He asked Betty what kind of voice she had.

"I told him I was a contralto," she says, "so he asked me to sing scales as he played them on the piano. I just kept going up and up and up until I got to high E. Sholom said, 'You're no contralto, you're a soprano,' which I knew, but I was so terrified of the audition that I thought I'd play it safe so I wouldn't have to sing too high."

She was less nervous about the dance audition, and was accepted by the choreographer. Sholom hoped she would get the job because, he wrote, "I couldn't take my eyes off her."

"Margarita" went into rehearsals, which lasted for several hours during the day. Betty had not fully recovered her strength, and one afternoon, while Sholom was playing at the piano for the ballet rehearsal, he heard a scream. He ran over to the cluster of dancers and saw Betty, who had fainted, sprawled on the floor. With the balletmaster's help, Sholom lifted her onto a bench. The dancers were given a break and returned to their dressing room to rest. Sholom sat next to Betty and stroked her black hair until she regained consciousness. She said that she was feeling better and that the rehearsal could resume, but Sholom urged her to remain lying down a while longer. On impulse, he took her face in his hands and kissed her.

For the rest of the season, Betty and Sholom kept company. By this time Katie and her daughters had moved to Boston Road in the Bronx. From there to Penn Street, Brooklyn, where Sholom lived with his parents, was a very long trip. Sholom had a Nash—he was one of the few people in the theater who owned a car—so he drove Betty home in the evenings after the performances. (By his friends' standards, Sholom was a very rich man, because he always had a car. Those friends took advantage of his eye for pretty girls, and if they needed a lift to the country or to the mountains, they would promise him that their destination was overrun with nymphets. Sholom always obliged them.)

Sholom did not pamper his cars—benign neglect more accurately describes their fate. In 1925 he had purchased an Oakland automobile for $100, which he drove until it disintegrated. When he met Betty, his Nash was brand new, and after two years, the most he could get for it was $25.

But even with the convenience of a car, going out with Betty involved a lot of commuting, and from time to time, she would stay overnight at his parents' house on Penn Street.

Their romance escalated when "Margarita" went on the road. By the time it got to Boston, Sholom and Betty were inseparable. Sholom made no secret of his affection for her.

He knew that she was sending most of her salary home to her mother. One evening after a performance, he found her outside the women's dressing room in tears—someone had stolen her money from her purse. Sholom went into the dressing room and asked one of the chorus girls where the purses were kept. He was told that they were stashed behind the makeup mirror. Sholom found Betty's purse and, without telling here, put another week's salary into it.

That evening a group from the company that included Betty and Sholom went to a restaurant for a late dinner. At one point Israel Rosenberg, the "Little Tippler," rose from his seat, stood on the chair and said, "Ladies and gentlemen. As we all know, Betty and Sholom have been courting now for some time. I am pleased to announce that as soon as we get back to New York, they will be married, and we are all invited to the wedding."

No one was more surprised to hear this news than the principals. Sholom glared at his indiscreet lyricist, unamused by Rosenberg's little joke. Although he was deeply in love with Betty, marriage was not on Sholom's agenda. He was helping to support his parents, and he was not of a mind to relinquish his freedom or his latitude with the ladies.

After supper Betty went back to her hotel with the other chorus girls. Sholom spent a fitful night at his hotel. He did not want to lose Betty, but he was not prepared to commit to her just yet. The following day he said nothing about Rosenberg's impropriety. Betty and Sholom continued to spend time together, and, when they returned to New York in June, Sholom asked her to join him and his family for two summer months at his cottage in Loch Sheldrake, a bungalow colony in the Catskill Mountains.

Loch Sheldrake was a bucolic extension of Second Avenue. It was an inexpensive way to beat the city heat, and although bungalows were usually quite small—one or two tiny bedrooms—they were a semblance of rural ease. In July and August, when Yiddish theaters were dark, Loch Sheldrake was full of actors and musicians. Molly Picon and Jacob Kalich had a bungalow there, as did actor Aaron Lebedeff.

Sholom had bought his bungalow in 1924 so that his parents could escape the New York summers. The house had a small dining room, living room, and two bedrooms which were accessible from the front room. In the living room were a piano, so that Sholom could work, and a couch. Sholom's entire family was often there on weekends, sleeping three to a bed, and Sholom slept on the couch. Close quarters were not new to them, and they took it in stride. A chief attraction of Loch Sheldrake was the frequency of parties, at Molly's or Sholom's house, where gossip and chats could pick up where they had left off at the end of the theatrical season.

It was Betty's first taste of Sholom's home life. There could be no privacy in the Loch Sheldrake cottage, and Betty wondered how Sholom, whose work continued during the summer, could get any composing done. He could write scores in a room full of people, and his concentration flagged only when he was alone, a state that made him anxious.

Abraham, Anna, and Sholom's brothers and sisters were cordial to Betty. Winning over Anna Secunda was no easy matter. She had never approved of actresses, and said so to her son. (She was not alone in her disdain. In 1914 Abraham Cahan had written in the *Forward*, "An Open Letter to Jewish Actresses," enjoining them, as "honored ladies of the Yiddish stage, decent women and mothers," not to use foul language on the stage.)[1] Beyond that, no one was good enough for her son. Anna had in mind a nice Jewish girl with a hefty endowment. But Betty, who charmed everyone, won her over because of her loyalty to her family. Anna asked Betty to join the Secundas for Passover, and Betty demurred, saying that she had to spend it with her mother and sisters. "She respected me for that," Betty says.

The way to Anna's heart, however, was obeisance, and Betty not only knew who was boss, she knew that Sholom knew who was boss. "I never made waves," she says.

When Sholom finally proposed to Betty that summer, it was no surprise to either of their families. It was understood that Betty would give up dancing and become Sholom's full-time wife. Although a good Jewish wife and mother was expected to tend to hearth and home, she was relieved not to have to perform any longer.

Because of Sholom's new responsibilities in the theater, the wedding date depended on when he could be freed for a couple of days. Anshel Shor had left the Arch Street Theater in Philadelphia to take over the Liberty Theater in Brooklyn. He hired Sholom to be composer and musical director for the 1927–1928 season. The most convenient time for the wedding, Shor said, was Tuesday, October 25. The time was to be six o'clock in the evening, so that the actors and dancers attending the ceremony could get to their theaters for that evening's performance.

The wedding was held at a synagogue on Bedford Avenue, near the Williamsburg Bridge in Brooklyn, with Cantor Mordechai Hershman conducting the service. Five hundred people were invited, most of them colleagues in the Yiddish theater. The wedding was a fiasco.

Sholom wore formal attire—white tie, vest, cutaway and top hat. He had borrowed the suit from Pesach Burstein, an actor who needed the outfit for a performance in the theater that night. Betty wore a knee-length, sleeveless white taffeta dress, decorated with sequins, and a floor-length tulle veil. Lottie was her sister's maid of honor.

The trouble began before the ceremony even got underway. Flowers had been ordered for the bride and bridesmaid, but never arrived, and Betty had to borrow the photographer's artificial bouquet. Although Prohibition was still in effect (it was repealed in 1933), the *shammes* of the synagogue provided bootleg whiskey of unknown origin.

Sholom had engaged an orchestra of musicians who worked on Second Avenue to play after the ceremony at the reception in the synagogue. Some of them began sampling the booze prior to the ceremony. By the time Betty and Sholom walked back down the aisle as husband and wife, most of Sholom's hand-picked orchestra was passed out cold on benches.

The caterer, a cousin of Sholom's who was a maitre d' in Lakewood, New Jersey, never showed up. Some food had been prepared by Sholom's family. Jars and jars of pickled herring and fish had been brought to the synagogue, and hungry guests stabbed each other with forks as they speared large chunks of their free dinner. Sholom's brother, Jack, who was in the food business, had made hundreds of sandwiches.

After the ceremony, composer Alexander Olshanetsky, who was one of the invited guests, surveyed the inebriated musicians' bodies stretched along the walls and said, "Come on! Let's play ourselves!" He grabbed a violin that was laying on the piano and shouted, "Where's Rumshinsky?" Rumshinsky (with whom Sholom had a temporary truce) sat down at the piano and yelled, "Where's the groom? He can play drums."

And so the three foremost Yiddish theater composers, one of them the groom, provided the music for Sholom's wedding. Betty observed the spectacle from the other side of the room, fuming, as Lottie patted her shoulder. Finally the bride busied herself by serving herring to the guests.

Meantime, other guests were absorbing the uncertain contents of the *shammes'* refreshments. Sholom's niece, Florence Secunda Franzman, then 12, remembers the scene:

> The synagogue had an iron railing all around it. I walked outside and saw all these women hanging onto the railing, retching and crying. There must have been fifty women there who just adored Sholom and wanted to marry him. They were all weeping and very drunk. There were so many sad people and drunks and dancing and carrying on, and it was horrible.

Betty on her wedding: "It was horrible."

Sholom was given only two days off for his wedding and honeymoon. He and Betty spent their wedding night at the McAlpin Hotel on Broadway and 34th Street, and the next day they drove to Atlantic City for two days. Upon their return Betty was absorbed into Sholom's family. They moved into the house on Penn Street, a very full house indeed. Living there were Anna and Abraham, Jack, Aaron, Joseph and Thelma. Willie, Shirley and Meyer had married and moved away.

The house, an old brownstone, had four floors. On the ground floor was a dining room and an enormous kitchen with a coal stove. The second floor had a parlor, which was Sholom's music room, and a rear bedroom, which became Betty's and Sholom's room. On the walls of the music room, which housed Sholom's Mason-Hamlim grand piano, Sholom had had painted portraits of famous composers—Chopin, Rachmaninoff, Tchaikovsky, Paderewski—in the shape of a lyre. There was one quirk to the assemblage: Paderewski's portrait was upside-down because, Sholom said, the composer-pianist was an anti-Semite (Paderewski had headed the Polish government in 1919, but in later life he donated large amounts from his fortune to needy musicians and Jewish refugees).

The third floor had a bathroom and two bedrooms. The nine Secundas lived on the first three floors. The fourth floor was rented to a family.

Sholom and Betty were to live on Penn Street for the first six years of their marriage, until their firstborn son, Sheldon, was four years old. Anna's grip on Sholom was firm. The relationship was unquestioned by him, and was a source of constant grief for his bride. Until he married, Sholom always gave his unopened pay envelope to his mother—Anna would dole out his spending money. After their marriage, he gave the money to Betty, but a good percentage of his income was used to defray the expenses of the family.

Abraham was still manufacturing beds. He had a shop in Williamsburg where he, Aaron and Willie worked. Each day with horse and wagon Abraham would make the rounds of furniture stores in Brooklyn. Store owners looked forward to his calls, because of his endless supply of comic vulgarities. (Sample: "What leaks when you hold it in your hand and shake it?". . .pause. . ."A fountain pen.")

Anna was the cook for the family, a *baleboosteh* beyond measure. She made her own noodles which would dry on a white tablecloth on the dining room table. In the backyard she grew roses and would pick the petals and dry them in a closet before making them into wine or syrup for tea. The house was always spotless. But the kitchen was the gathering place, not only for family meals, but also for drop-ins from the Yiddish theater. Anna's cooking and Abraham's raunchy stories were a great draw for Sholom's friends.

Sholom's work took him away from his bride a good deal. At dinner on Penn Street, between rehearsals and evening performances, he would often sit, silently eating, and would suddenly disappear to the music room to jot down a few musical phrases. Most meals would be punctuated with these abrupt departures to the piano. He was also away from the house for long stretches, conducting the orchestra in whatever theater he was engaged at seven nights a week and two matinees on weekends. Rehearsals took up his afternoons. As a result, Betty was with Anna most of the time.

"I had a friend across the street who was a nurse, and I was very fond of her," Betty recalled. "I used to want to visit her in the evening, but Anna would always say, 'Don't go. I need someone to talk to.'" Betty would spend her evenings with her mother-in-law reading Yiddish newspapers or books aloud to her, or just talking. Sholom's sister, Thelma, who was friendly to Betty, was some relief to those long hours. A superb pianist, Thelma would occasionally play for Betty and Anna.

In April, 1928, Betty became pregnant. She began her entreaties to

Sholom to have their own apartment, but whenever the subject came up, Sholom would stall or refuse to discuss it. After the birth of Sheldon (from "Shmuel," Betty's father's Hebrew name)—who was always called "Shelly"—on January 5, 1929, Sholom was still unwilling to leave his parents. Finances were not yet an issue—he was making a sufficient living in the theater to help support his parents and still afford an apartment. Once the stock market crashed—in October—Sholom's income nosedived, and Betty dropped the subject. There were some weeks when he brought home only $8, and separate living quarters were out of the question (as part of management, Sholom and his partners would divide among them whatever monies were left over after paying the cast and other running expenses).

By 1931 he was earning a good living once more, and Betty was able to hire a maid, Mary, for $20 a month to help with Shelly and the household chores. Late in the afternoons Betty would tell Mary to sit in the backyard on warm days to rest a while. The kindness infuriated Abraham. "Why is Betty in the kitchen and the maid is outside?" he would roar. Mary inadvertently caused another brouhaha— the Sunday morning she took Shelly to church with her.

Betty and Sholom were never alone, even in their own bedroom. Shelly's crib was next to their double bed. Intimacy between them was a sometime and covert thing. During daylight hours Betty was never by herself, unless she went to her room, because Sholom's siblings always seemed to be around.

The strain of too much togetherness took its toll on Betty's health. She developed stomach problems and was tested by several doctors, all of whom attributed her troubles to stress. Once in desperation she asked her mother-in-law to intercede with Sholom on her behalf.

"Mama, talk to him," Betty pleaded. "I want a home of my own. We have a child. It's time we had a place of our own."

"Why should I talk to him?" Anna replied. "For me it's very comfortable having you living here. Why would I want you to move away?"

Betty confided in Clara Falk, another nurse who had become her friend, about her unhappiness. She told Clara that she had decided that if Sholom wanted to have another child, she would refuse, and threaten to divorce him. But Clara offered to mediate, and spoke to Sholom about his blindness about his wife's discontent. Apparently she was persuasive. In September, 1933, Sholom and Betty moved to a two-bedroom apartment on Schenectady Avenue in the Crown Heights section of Brooklyn. Betty became pregnant immediately, and on June 15, 1934, Eugene Secunda was born.

Sholom gave everyone in the family a nickname. Betty was "Kunya Basha," Shelly was "Meeley Peeley" (a variation of his Hebrew name) and Gene became "Ju-Ju." The origin of Gene's nickname reflects Sholom's occasional bawdiness, if not his Ashkenazi brand of machismo. Gene was one of those rare infant boys born already circumcised. Since the ritual of circumcision—a *bris*—had to be performed anyhow, this, in Sholom's eyes, made Gene a double Jew.

Upon his return from the hospital with Betty, Gene spent his first few days sleeping in an open dresser drawer (his parents were waiting for the arrival of a new crib). Shelly did not get to know his baby brother very well at first, because shortly after Gene's birth, Shelly, who was then 5, was shipped off to Camp Leonard in Kent, Connecticut. Given his parents' predilection for overprotection—bathing shoes, bathing caps, rubbers, mufflers, long underwear, hats with ear flaps and other safeguarding attire were in his wardrobe—it is strange that they would send their firstborn into the wilderness at such a tender age. Their justification was that Clara Falk was the camp nurse, and that Betty would have her hands full with a new baby in the house—a misjudgment, in the hindsight of Freudian analysis, that Betty now acknowledges.

Sholom's and Betty's first—and only—year on Schenectady Avenue was a horror. In September of 1934 Shelly fell off his tricycle and scraped his left knee. The knee became infected, then healed. Weeks later he developed a high fever that lingered for months, hopping between 99 degrees and 106. Betty and Sholom took their son from doctor to doctor, all of whom were unable to diagnose the malady. In December Shelly's illness was finally diagnosed—he had osteomyelitis, an infection of the bone and bone marrow, caused by his tricycle accident.

In the 1930s the illness was treated by surgery, often multiple operations, during which the infection would be scraped from the bone. Shelly was operated upon at Polyclinic Hospital with apparent success. (Osteomyelitis causes destruction of the bone, and amputations were often the only cure. The mortality rate in the 1930s from the disease was 30%. Those who recovered were often crippled for life.) No subsequent operations were necessary, and Shelly returned to his normal, active boyhood.

The relief of Shelly's parents on his recovery was soon interrupted. Within a month of his return from the hospital, his infant brother, Gene, contracted double pneumonia, and was himself rushed to the hospital. His prognosis was gloomy, but he recovered, thanks, Betty and Sholom believed, to the constant care of a friend, Ceil Harmetz, who was a nurse at the hospital.

A third tragedy drove the Secundas to break their apartment lease. One afternoon Sholom was driving home from a rehearsal. Across the street from his apartment a miniature merry-go-round was in operation. As Sholom approached in his car, a small boy, whom Sholom assumed was Shelly, darted across the street toward the merry-go-round and was struck by a car immediately preceding Sholom's. Sholom, leaving his car in gear and rolling (no one remembers what brought it to a stop), rushed to the blood-covered child on the ground and picked him up. A distraught woman, screaming "My son! My son!," snatched the boy from Sholom's arms. Dazed, Sholom parked his car and went up to the apartment, where he found Shelly happily playing, oblivious to the drama unfolding on the street below.

Believing that their apartment was jinxed, Betty and Sholom and their sons moved to a new, red brick apartment building at 66 Avenue A, between 3rd and 4th Streets, in Manhattan—change of place, change of luck. By then they had employed a young, thin, black woman named Savannah Saunders, who had just arrived from Asheville, North Carolina, to help Betty with the children and the housework. (Years later, when the family moved to Washington Heights, Gene came home one day in tears, claiming that some larger child had hit him. In a flash Savannah was out the door, wielding a baseball bat, in search of the bully whom, fortunately for him, she could not find. Savannah was very protective of her charges, and remained with the Secundas until Gene was 18.)

The new apartment was close to the Second Avenue theaters, where Sholom's career had finally taken him after years in Philadelphia and Brooklyn. He had paid his figurative and literal union dues, and was now in the mainstream of Yiddish theater in its heyday.

PRIME TIME
IN THE YIDDISH THEATER

While Betty was having her troubles with her in-laws and adjusting to marriage and motherhood, Sholom had his mind on his work. He finished the 1927–1928 season at the Liberty Theater in Brooklyn with Anshel Shor. During the run of "His Jewish Girl" a new theater in Brooklyn threatened the solidarity of the Liberty.

William Rolland was building a million-dollar theater on Eastern Parkway, one that was designed to rival any house anywhere. It had 1800 seats, and one of the first stages with an elevator, giving it capabilities of astonishing directorial effects. Shor said he could not take over the Liberty again against such competition.

Sholom had worked with Rolland in the past, and for the 1928–1929 season he was engaged to be musical director of Rolland's new theater. When Sholom signed his contract, he was given a *forshus* (advance) of $1,000, which was the custom when hiring stars, composers and other principal personnel.

On September 25, 1928, the Rolland Theater opened with Louis Freiman's "The Song of Love," starring Michal Michalesko, prima donna Lucy Levin, and comedian Jack Rechtseyt. At Sholom's suggestion, Rolland had engaged poet H. Gudelman as lyricist; a Russian-Jewish dance master, Krasnov (who had escaped from Russia via China the previous year), to stage a ballet; Benyomen Zemach to choreograph Chasidic dances. The Rolland Theater was barely complete—ticket-holders had to walk along wooden planks, over the unfinished sidewalk, to get to the lobby. But the theater created a sensation. New electrical equipment and the stage's elevator were used to stunning effect, and the quality of talent in the troupe, music and stars, eclipsed anything then on Second Avenue.

The smoothness of opening night belied the weeks of tormented ego struggles that preceded it, weeks during which Sholom's goals and those of the management were often at odds. Flaws in the Yiddish musical theater, and Sholom's disenchantment with art that fell below his sometimes rarified standards, emerged in sharp relief.

In his memoirs Sholom accurately appraised what has universally been cited as the touble with Yiddish theater: the star system. In the Yiddish theater the star was the director as well as principal actor and investor. Every aspect of a production spotlighted the star at the rest of the company's, and the play's, expense.

In the name of the star's glorification, great liberties were taken. Lulla Rosenfeld writes, "A well-known actress produced Romeo and Juliet, but since it was her theater, she advertised it as Juliet and Romeo."[1] Molly Picon recalls that when Jacob Adler made an entrance, a spotlight followed him through his scene and off into the wings, and that whatever actor made the next entrance did so in semi-darkness.

Michalesko, as Rolland's star, assessed plays with his star billing in mind. When plays were read to him, "he was not listening to the content of the play," Sholom wrote, "he was listening to his role, to whether he had enough lines to say, whether he had enough opportunities to change into different costumes, whether he had enough songs so that no one in the cast would be noticed except him—the star."

The playwrights knew that to have their plays performed, they had to showcase the star. And they knew, too, that the Yiddish audience, exhausted by horrors in the old country and poverty in the new, was not in the mood for serious drama. It wanted laughs. Thus, the expression *der oylem is a goylem* (the public is a fool) was the explanation by playwrights for plots with no logic. One explanation for the decline of the Yiddish theater is that it lost its audience through assimilation. Sholom's is this:

> The people had nothing to see that was new because they were familiar with the contents of the play even before they saw it. They knew by heart all the jokes and wisecracks that the comedian— especially if he was a star—was going to say, from plays they had seen in previous years.

Stock characters and scenes were recycled over 50 years of Yiddish theater: the stupid *goyim*, the incorruptable Jewish virgin, the long-suffering Jewish mother, the comic-buffoon, the chorus girls and—always a crowd-pleaser—a patriotic show-stopper with full cast, gigantic unfurled flag, red-white-blue lights, set to a rousing march.

Plots were predictable, so much so that a New York Times critic, covering an operetta by William Seigel and Sholom Secunda, delivered the following exasperated review:

> This time they call it ''A Night in Budapest,'' but the actors made such a good pretense of never having heard it before that the first-nighters believed them and enjoyed themselves. . .[2]

''You always had to have a wedding,'' says Fyvush Finkel, who began acting on Second Avenue in the 1930s when he was a child (and who later played on Broadway in ''Fiddler On the Roof,'' among other plays). ''Or the married couple has a problem,'' he continues, ''such as he finds out there is insanity on the wife's side of the family. Family was everything in those plots. The husband runs away, his business fails and he can't face life. They find him in a saloon toward the end of the show, build him back up again, and the last scene the entire ensemble is on the stage singing a song and he's back, dressed in a white suit.

''Patriotism could save a play. Especially during the Holocaust in World War II. If a scene was weak, all we had to say was 'Hitler should drop dead,' and the audience would applaud for 20 minutes.''

Yiddish theater had its defenders in the American press, who would cite Kessler or Adler or Maurice Schwartz for performing art and high drama while eschewing the star system—an arguable statement. No matter how lofty the dramatic intent, even these legendary figures had to dip into *shund* (to say nothing of scenery chewing) from time to time to meet expenses.

What drew actors and actresses to a career on Second Avenue was they they would be engaged for an entire 44-week season (36 weeks in New York, eight weeks on the road), in true repertory fashion, receiving a wage they could count on. Uptown, if they had landed a part in a Broadway show, they ran the risk of its folding and they would be out of work, having forfeited an entire season. On Second Avenue, if a show was a flop, another was flipped onto the boards in time for the curtain the following night.

Actors were so trained in repertory that often they went on stage with not a single rehersal, relying heavily on the omnipresent and very valued prompter to tell them where to stand and cue them on what to say. "The joke about bad prompters," Finkel says, "is, one actor says 'who says that line?' and another actor answers, 'the prompter says it first, then the audience hears it, then you say it.'"

The Yiddish actors who went on to play Broadway cite as the chief difference between the two brands of theater the sense of professionalism uptown and the sense of family downtown. Dinah Goldberg, who played Broadway and Second Avenue, says:

It was a great thing to attain a Broadway role, and there was more discipline on Broadway. A director takes you aside and whispers his notes. On Second Avenue it was one big family. The director or composer would yell and scream. Once Olshanetsky got angry with one of the actors. Olshanetsky's English, Yiddish and Russian were terrible, and sometimes the languages overlapped. So he yells at the actor, "You understand Russian?" The actor replies, "No, Mr. Olshanetsky."

"Good," says Olshanetsky and, thinking he was speaking Russian, he said, in English, "You son of a bitch, go fuck yourself!"

For all its informality, Yiddish theater provided experience for its actors that money could not buy. "Today," Finkel says, "young actors go to wonderful dramatic schools, and the road is shorter for them. They learn all the rudiments quickly. For us, we had to do it ourselves. What took us ten years would take an average student with talent today two years. Actors today do everything by reason. We did everything by instinct." Current historians of the theater, when assessing Yiddish acting of a half-century ago, refer to that instinct as "naturalism."

The star system was nourished by the benefit system. When an organization wanted to book a benefit, they would tell the management exactly what play or musical they wanted to see and it would be served up to them weeknights as though it had been ordered from a menu. If the star system worked, it was because the audience insisted on familiar types in familiar plays. Miriam Kressyn, a prima donna in

the Yiddish theater for three decades, describes the Yiddish theater
patriot:

> The Yiddish theater was a source of joy for him. It was the only
> public place for the immigrant to feel at home. He recognized
> himself on stage. He associated himself with the peddler who be-
> came a store-keeper, with a sweat shop boss who becomes a great
> cloak manufacturer. If it could happen to the character in the play,
> it could happen to him. He dreamed that his children would not
> have to go through what he did. His children would have every-
> thing. The daughter would play the piano and become a teacher or
> a bookkeeper, the son would become a doctor, because that is what
> he saw in the Yiddish theater. You didn't have to be a "greener"
> in America all your life. Americanization became a must, so even-
> tually the *patriot* would go to Broadway or to the movies, but he
> would always return to the Yiddish theater because it was always
> there for him—it was his experience. Yiddish theater became the
> back-street sweetheart.

The uneducated, often illiterate East European immigrant swallowed plots whole. Leon Liebgold, leading man on Second Avenue
for 25 years, recalls the time he played in Chicago in a show that
depicted a mother receiving news that her son had lost his life on a
battlefield. After the final curtain, several members of the audience
crowded around the stage door to find out the fate of the young man.
When the actor emerged from the theater unscrathed, the anxious *patriots* cried, "He's alive! He's alive!"

"The audience confused reality with on-stage death," Liebgold
says, "and they had to see if it really happened."

Only the most successful shows went on tour and, in fact, it's the
road that many Yiddish actors miss most.

"We always had our own railroad car when we toured," says Lottie
Almer Weintrop, a former Yiddish theater chorus girl (and Sholom's
sister-in-law). "The actors would get the lower berths, the musicians
and chorus girls had the upper berths. Joseph Rumshinsky, who was a
great gambler, would sit on the floor in the aisle, dressed in his
nightshirt and nightcap, dealing cards.

"We had so much fun on the road," Weintrop continues. "On
one tour to Chicago, we played a trick on Murray Rumshinsky,

Joseph's son. Murray went to sleep, and the chorus girls took all his clothes out of his berth while he was sleeping. The next morning when we pulled into Chicago, Murray had nothing to wear, so he pulled a sheet around himself and got off the train. I'll never forget seeing him walk through the Chicago railroad terminal, wearing nothing but a sheet."

For all its rough edges, Second Avenue theater was still the most passionate theater around. John Mason Brown, in a review of Maurice Schwartz's "Yoshe Kalb" for the *New York Evening Post* in 1933, wrote, "Instead of inviting spectators to forget that they are in a play, instead of pretending that 'the fourth wall' has been removed and that what is shown behind is merely a 'slice of life,' these Yiddish players glory in all that goes with their grease paint. And by doing so they manage to restore fervor to a make-believe world that stands sorely in need of it."

In 1932, Brooks Atkinson wrote in the *New York Times:*

If the Anglo-Saxon drama had that latitude and fever, the Anglo-Saxon stage might not seem so bloodless. For the realism that now hovers over our stage like a death's head has reduced the physical vigor and scope of the stage. But wishes do not change prevailing fashions. . .If "Yoshe Kalb" looks and sounds exhilarating at the Yiddish Art Theater, it is because Jewish actors understand that sort of mystical drama and Jewish audiences are enkindled by it. No matter how far as individuals they may be from the orthodox faith, something of that stormy emotion remains in the long, anguished poem of their blood inheritance. . .While the Anglo-Saxon stage is playing with attitudes and bright remarks, the Yiddish stage can still tell a full story and invigorate the scenes with pictorial figures and since the audiences believe in it, they can respond uncritically.

Audiences were given villains they loved to hate, and sob stories that were cathartic. Dinah Goldberg recalls singing a sad song in a production and when she took a curtain call, she was presented with a box of candy and no identifying card. After the show a young woman came backstage to visit the actress, saying that she was the giver of the candy and adding, "I cried so much, I didn't have such a good time since my father died!''

Yiddish theater was a cultural option for all New Yorkers, whether dressed in black tie and chauffeured from the Upper East Side, or Lower East Side Jews, dressed in work clothes and carrying a *nosh* (snack) to be eaten during the performance.

Sunday nights, according to Molly Picon, audiences were 30% non-Jewish, since Broadway on those nights was dark. People like Flo Ziegfeld, Irving Berlin, Theodore Dreiser, Al Jolson, Fanny Brice and others came to Second Avenue productions. "Even D. W. Griffith," Picon says. "He used to say that it was as much fun watching the audience as watching the stage. They were so much with you—they cried with you, they laughed with you.''

But it was one thing for an uptown audience to occasionally go ''slumming,'' as Yiddish actors called it, downtown to sample the exotic, innocent ethnicity of Yiddish theater. It was quite another to have to churn it out night after night.

Sheer professionalism on the part of the actors kept most performances fresh. It helped to be in a Sholom Secunda production, because of the composer's own enthusiasm. For all his interest in ''art,'' Sholom was the Yiddish theater's biggest *patriot*. He would laugh at the same joke night after night, no matter how corny or familiar. Lottie Weintrop recalls, ''When Sholom conducted, he would bend all the way over and all you could see were his hands and baton. His head would be bobbing up and down, he was giggling so hard.''

As overtly enthusiastic as he was, Sholom could not sustain his ardor or originality indefinitely. Miriam Kressyn, who had a classically trained voice, starred in many of Sholom's operettas. Kressyn occasionally sang rehashes of Sholom's music—a cantorial piece reworked for a jazz spot, a working girl's lament repeated the following season with new lyrics as a patriotic song. Submitting to time pressures, Sholom repeated himself, and hated himself for it.

''I had the same feeling about the shows as Sholom did,'' Kressyn says. ''They were not literary at all—or literate. I really disliked musical comedy. I always had a desire to play drama, no matter how good my operetta part was, because it rarely was that good. The male star got the good part, and the prima donna was always the sufferer. It was demeaning if you felt that you could do better. That's why I eventually left the musical field for a time and went with Maurice Schwartz.''

In working on "The Song of Love" in 1928, Sholom's only aesthetic choice was to write a score that satisfied the star. Rehearsals were strained, although Michalesko, the star, and Sholom had known each other since their childhoods in Nicholayev. At one dance rehearsal, a clash between Michalesko and choreographer Krasnov was barely averted. The number to be rehearsed that day was a *lezhinka*, a Russian folk dance that was Krasnov's specialty. The dance chorus, as was the fashion, was in the back line, and Michalesko was to be in front with the two best female dancers in the company. The women were able to master the steps easily, but Michalesko, who was not a dancer, had difficulty. Finally, Krasnov lost his Russian temper and screamed at the star, "You cannot dance! You go in the back row, and put a *real* dancer in the front row!"

Before Michalesko had a chance to respond, Sholom called a ten-minute break to explain to the outraged choreographer the facts of Yiddish theater life.

"You can't stage it that way," Sholom said. "Michalesko has to stay in the front line. If he can't do the dance, then change the steps so that he can manage them. It can't be any other way—he's the star."

Opening night was a spectacular success, as much due to Rolland's elaborate new theater as to the performance. The production was lavish—costumes, sets, lighting and special effects that rivaled anything in Manhattan. In the second act half the stage, holding the entire chorus, descended into the cellar on the stage elevator, followed by a ten-second blackout. When the lights came up again, the chorus was back on stage, continuing the production, as though by magic. The audience gasped at the effect.

For the first few weeks receipts were good, but began falling off. Because of the enormous expenses of the production, the play had to be replaced by a less ambitious production. Sholom wrote a score for Louis Freiman's "Senorita," which replaced "Song of Love." At season's end Rolland was in the black and began planning the 1929–1930 roster of plays. Misha Gehrman, who had just finished a season in Chicago, and who had had a great success at the Hopkinson with "Margarita," was asked by Rolland to form a partnership with him. Sholom was again engaged as composer-conductor.

It was to be more of the same. Yiddish theater was providing no challenges for Sholom. He had begun setting words of Yiddish poets to music, inserting these art songs where he could in his scores, but they did not satisfy his ambitions. Sholom's dissatisfaction with the star system and *shund* prompted him to set his sights elsewhere—toward Hollywood.

♫ NEW HORIZONS

During the summer months of 1929, Sholom made his first trip to California. "Talkies" were two years old. Composers and musicians whom Sholom knew were heading west. Muni Weisenfreund, whom Sholom had known when the actor was in the Yiddish theater, had become Paul Muni and a very successful film star.

Abe Sincoff and Peysache Burstein, Yiddish theater actors who also had Hollywood ambitions, accompanied Sholom on the five-day trip. With Betty and Shelly ensconced in Loch Sheldrake, together with Katie Almer and Sholom's parents, the three men left New York in later June aboard a train.

Sholom would be away for two months. There began a series of daily letters between Sholom and Betty, at Sholom's insistence. Betty, exhausted by caring for an infant and by back trouble and anemia, would have preferred a more leisurely correspondence. But Sholom required daily contact from his wife (as he would years later from his sons who, when away at camp or in college or the Army, would be required to write to their father every day—all hell broke loose when they did not).

When Sholom reached Chicago en route to the Coast, he wrote, "Twenty-four hours have passed since we parted. Hard, very hard hours have passed. It is my hope to better our future that gives me the courage to go on. I did not think it would be so hard to be away from you, from my sweet baby, and the folks."

From Chicago the train dipped down to Texas and from there went west to California. Sholom, who had never crossed the United States before, was astounded by its variety. On a stopover in El Paso, he sent some Mexican dresses and a table cloth to Betty. In Yuma, Arizona, the train stopped again, and Sholom bought some beads from the Indian women who sold their crafts on the station platform.

In Hollywood Sholom and his cohorts rented an apartment at 800 North Las Palmas Avenue. For $70 a month, they had a living room with a Murphy bed, a kitchen stocked with dishes and silverware, and a bedroom. The rent included linen service and a maid, electricity and gas. For $3.75 a month they had unlimited use of the telephone.

Sholom was the consummate tourist and registered each new impression in his letters to Betty:

July 4, 1929

The people here are very hospitable, far more than in the East. We met some Jewish families that are always ready to do most anything. They all have cars and are willing to show you around. The cottages, the palaces, the homes of the rich people in the hills and mountains are incredible. The tall palm trees stand in long rows and salute you all day. You can't imagine how beautiful it all is, no matter how rich your fantasy, unless you see it with your own eyes.

July 7, 1929

There are more Jewish performers in Hollywood than in New York. Everyone rushes to seek a livelihood here. It reminds one of the Gold Rush of 1849. However, there is no work here at the moment. The whole industry is paralyzed by a strike by Actors Equity Association.* It will take some time before this thing is settled. Until then, there is no chance for anyone, for there is very little activity in the studios.

July 8, 1929

The most curious thing about Hollywood is to see actors wearing beards and historic costumes walking down the streets or in restaurants. I was curious so I stared, but no one else paid any attention to them. It is such a commonplace that no one cares the least about it. I even saw a scene filmed at night on the street, and there was no crowd!

---

*Actors' Equity, founded in 1916, was trying to get a foothold in Hollywood. In 1929 it "launched a campaign. . .to have 80 per cent Equity representation in every movie cast," according to Robert H. Stanley in his book, *The Celluloid Empire: A History of the American Movie Industry.*[1]

July 10, 1929

We decided to take a little trip to Mexico. We went through Balboa Park which was the site for the World's Fair held there in recent years. A gorgeous park. We crossed the border and entered Mexico—out of a paradise, into a dump. No more of the magnificent roads and boulevards. No more of the cleanliness and masterpiece mansions. Just a little town which by the grace of Prohibition is the center of attraction for the richest American tourists. There we stopped and drank beer, real beer, which made the ordinary sandwiches taste better than turkey.

July 11, 1929

This week was the opening of the Hollywood Bowl. You surely read about it in *Musical America*. I could not attend the opening concert, but I didn't miss the second concert. It wasn't the symphony orchestra or the program that interested me. It was the Bowl. Think of it—a stadium, an open-air amphitheater constructed by nature. What a gigantic place. What acoustics! Natural acoustics—no wires, no engineering. You can't miss a tone of a muted string when you sit on the peak of a surrounding mountain. Mountains all around the Bowl, grass, and trees. Stars above in a blue sky, the moon on guard. God, what a bewildering scene. Last night enveloped me in its beauty. I felt that I loved you more than ever. What wouldn't I have given to feel your sweet breath and to kiss your tender skin. What wouldn't it be worth to me if you and I, as one, could cling to each other and listen. At times I've felt that I could be poor, as long as I could live in this glorious part of the country. So much beauty. I am bewitched by it.

July 15, 1929

Tomorrow I have an appointment with the chief musical director at the Fox Studios. I must try to meet everyone. The only way to get somewhere around here is to be stubborn and stick. I could surely get somewhere, but how? I am afraid I'll have to go back to New York, especially now that Equity has stopped most of its members from accepting positions and has demoralized the whole industry. Dear heart, don't worry. We will get there yet.

July 16, 1929

I had the appointment today at Fox, and I have encouraging news. I brought him my symphonic rhapsody and he was so enthused that after the first two pages, he stopped and said that I have no equal in these studios, etc., etc. He, however, is not the man who offers contracts. He only recommends. He said he will take it up with the Fox executives and will have a definite reply for me on Tuesday next.

July 19, 1929

Let me know, sweetheart, how you are enjoying the figs and preserved fruit I am sending you. My next parcel will be a package of avocados. I do not think you know what they are—a vegetable fruit. Very good for salads. They are very nourishing and fattening. Fortify your constitution so you'll be fit for motherhood.

July 21, 1929

Things do not run as smoothly as one might wish. I was waiting for this day, and while I wasn't disappointed, I wasn't gratified either. My Fox contact told me he recommended me to the board. The board, he said, was interested in his recommendation but they are too busy at present to negotiate with anyone new. He said he would call me as soon as he hears. You understand how I hope for that position.

Sholom was discouraged by the cool reception he was receiving at the film studios. The summer heat across the country reached record numbers, shortening tempers on both coasts. In Loch Sheldrake, Betty was trying to keep peace between her mother and mother-in-law, trying to regain weight she kept losing, trying to care for an infant son who seldom slept through the night.

Betty was no match for Anna Secunda and she tried to spare Sholom the details of the strained atmosphere at home, at the same time attempting to protect Katie from Anna's periodic testiness. Betty's frustration—no doubt provoked by the three-way stretch—erupted in this letter to Sholom:

About peace in the household, things came to a crisis today. I made my mother promise that she would go home Monday as I

couldn't stand Ma's (Anna's) constant fault-finding with everything she did. A number of times I heard my mother crying on the
porch in the dark, but she wouldn't admit she had cried. I
couldn't say anything to Ma, as I had promised you I wouldn't ag-
gravate her, but all this wasn't doing me much good. Today Ma
noticed how blue I looked and asked me the reason. Everything
spilled out of me and we had a thorough understanding between
all parties concerned. God, I hope there will be no repetition of
these incidents.

Sholom's reply was swift:

Why there should be any controversy between your mother and
mine I don't know. I pleaded with you before I left to consider my
mother's age and handle the situation with care and diplomacy
and I see that you have failed. I am not interested in what happened. I do know that if something happened, both are at fault.
Kiss my sweet son. Wait until he grows up. He will show you how
to handle intricate situations.

The domestic hostilities in Loch Sheldrake cooled off, and letters
East and West resumed their tenderness. Sholom wrote:

July 28, 1929
A group of wealthy Jews have offered to produce Yiddish musicals
every Sunday and want to hire me as musical director. They would
guarantee me $150 a week for 30 weeks. I haven't given them my
answer, but it is not for me. I left New York because I want to leave
the Jewish stage, and what happens? I go over 3,000 miles to join it
all over again, only on a smaller and cheaper scale. I want to find a
place for myself in the new sound industry. If I do not succeed
here, I will go back to New York and try Broadway.

August 1, 1929
This morning I had the long-expected appointment at Fox and it
proved to be unfavorable. The man explained to me that he cannot
offer me an assignment at present because I am not, he said, "A
man of reputation." He advised me to hang around the lot and he
will try to offer me some work until I get my chance to compose.

You understand that I cannot afford to take a chance like that. I am leaving Los Angeles next Tuesday and will probably be with you by Sunday. Now the days will be longer and more monotonous for me. Well, we will have to try our luck right in New York. The opportunity is here, but how can I afford to wait around for it? Gosh, it seems as if there is a hard time ahead for us. I depend on your moral support and we will land somewhere. I don't want you to worry though, because by the time you get this letter I will have forgotten all about it and be merry.

The timing for Sholom's trip to California could not have been more inauspicious. The transition from silent movies to sound had a devastating—although temporary—effect on the film industry. By 1930 there were 234 different types of sound equipment on the market, and sound systems throughout the network of movie theaters across the country were not yet uniform.[2] And, according to film historian Harry M. Geduld,

(The year) 1929 (was) a year of sound and fury, signifying that the silent cinema was doomed. . .The plight of many musicians was far worse than anything yet experienced by theater managers. In August 1931, the Monthly Labor Review of the U.S. Bureau of Labor Statistics revealed staggering information about the rise of unemployment among musicians as a result of technological changes in the film industry. . .'about 50% of the total number of musicians employed in theaters were displaced.'. . .Stunned, confused and angered, the musicians attempted to counteract the threat of sound movies by petitioning the studios, organizing public demonstrations, and placing pickets outside movie theaters. . .

By contrast with the theater musicians, composers—if they had any talent at all—suddenly found themselves riding the crest of the wave. In 1929 it looked as if Tin Pan Alley was moving to Hollywood. Every studio was making musicals, and theme songs were in constant demand for picture after picture. . .At the end of 1929, George and Ira Gershwin accepted a $100,000 contract from Fox to write the music and lyrics of their first sound picture. . .Aside from the Gershwins, handsome contracts also lured Irving Berlin,

Harold Arlen, Jerome Kern, Jimmy McHugh, Harry Warren, Vincent Youmans, Nacio Herb Brown, Harry Ruby, Buddy DeSylva, and a host of other song writers to the movie capital.[3]

Hollywood was flooded with songwriters of far greater "reputation" than Sholom, and against that competition his chances were small. His trip to California and his agonizing wait for a position in films was almost more than he could bear. He was utterly miserable without Betty and his son, and his homecoming was greeted with embraces and tears. But his professional troubles were only beginning.

For the season's opening at the Rolland Theater, Sholom wrote the score for William Seigel's new operetta, "Katya's Wedding," with lyrics by Israel Rosenberg. Starring were Misha and Lucy Gehrman with Betty Siminoff as the prima donna. The play, which was enthusiastically attended, seemed a promising beginning for the new season, and would have shown a profit, but for "Black Thursday." On October 29, 1929, the stock market crashed, and the shattered economy affected box office sales. Theater-goers could do without theater, but not without food. Receipts fell off sharply at the Rolland box office. Rolland's financial losses were reflected in Sholom's paycheck, and he began looking elsewhere for added income to help support Betty and their ten-month-old son.

Sholom took a second job—musical director of the Yiddish radio station WLTH in the Brooklyn Eagle Building. At the station, Sholom was allowed to hire and conduct a large orchestra. The station's owner, Sam Gellard, was eager to attract new listeners and advertisers and was banking on Sholom's reputation—on the Lower East Side, he had a "reputation"—to achieve both. Sholom played Jewish popular music, folk and art songs, and Jewish symphonic works. He hired Cantor Moishe Oysher and his sister, Freydele, to sing folk songs and cantorial music.

While at the station, Sholom wrote jingles for many products, including Manischevitz Matzohs. His most upiquitous jingle was for Joe and Paul's, a men's clothing store on the Lower East Side. "Joe and Paul's" became the basis of a comedy routine performed in the Catskills and on club dates by the Barton Brothers (who made a recording of it) and by Red Buttons. The ditty, in fact, was Buttons' trade mark until he achieved success in television and films.

Sholom also inaugurated a children's program called *"Feter* (Uncle) Sholom.*"* The station gave the program advance on-air promotion and asked parents of musically talented children to bring them for an audition and possible position on the program. At Sholom's suggestion, Nachem Stutchkof was hired to produce the program. Stutchkof and Sholom conducted the auditions. One of the children auditioned was Sam Rosenbaum, now Cantor at the Beth El Synagogue in Rochester, New York, who was to figure prominently in Sholom's career in later life.

Rosenbaum had studied and sung cantorial music at his Hebrew school in Williamsburg, but could not play piano well enough to accompany himself.

I would come to the station before the program and go over the music with Sholom. He said that I should rehearse at home, and since I couldn't sing and accompany myself at the same time, he offered to work with me at his home. Out of the blue. I was a little kid and very impressed. He lived on Penn Street, a ten-minute walk from where I lived. Every week he would work with me so that I could develop a repertoire of songs to use on the program. Manischewitz Matzohs sponsored the program, and Mr. Stutchkof wanted to pay me off in matzohs, but my father was in the grocery business, so I needed matzohs like an Eskimo needs ice.

The station was later moved to the Commodore Theater on Second Avenue between Sixth and Seventh Streets, and Sholom continued to do his radio program. Nachem Stutchkof left WLTH to join the staff of WEVD, New York's largest Yiddish radio station. His replacement, Victor Pecker, was also raided by WEVD. In 1932, Sholom would join their ranks.

The Yiddish theater limped along, in spite of unpredictable receipts and deepening economic depression. For the 1929–1930 season, Rolland engaged William Schwartz and Fanny Lubritski as his stars. He also signed a new comic, Menashe Skulnik, as the third star. The season opened with Frieman's operetta, "Sweet Moments," with a troupe including Hymie Jacobson's brother, Irving (who later played Sancho in "Man of La Mancha") and his wife, Mae Schoenfelt. Rolland's theater continued to be plagued by debt. One play after another was mounted, but business on Second Avenue—and, for that matter, Broadway—was bad.

Salaried employees of Rolland's theater were never sure what the size of their paychecks would be. Reuben Guskin, executive director of the Hebrew Actors Union, registered formal complaints against the theater owners who claimed, truthfully, that with poor attendance, the money for full payroll simply wasn't there. The solution to the financial dilemma was to make all the theater's personnel partners with the managers. If the week was a good one, everyone would be paid accordingly. If it was not, actors would get their share of the puny receipts (some weeks Sholom brought home $8—some weeks, he brought home nothing). Because he was still living with his parents, Sholom was in less desperate circumstances than most of his colleagues. But he began taking on music students to help pay the bills.

Theater managers did not quit. For the 1930–1931 season, Rolland hired Jennie Goldstein, then at the peak of her career as a prima donna, to star in "Stepsisters," a melodrama. In an effort to attract a wider audience, he planned to follow "Stepsisters" with a production of Sholom Aleichem's "The Grand Prize," re-titled "200,000." Headlining the cast would be Menachim Rubin, formerly of the Moscow Art Theater, who had starred in the play in Warsaw. Rolland had negotiated with Rubin by mail through the summer, and by August the European actor was in New York. He was met at the ship by Sholom, Rolland and Freiman, who escorted him to his hotel and then to the theater. Physically he was a disappointment to Sholom. With big ears and bad skin, he was no matinee idol. But the voice he displayed at the theater during rehearsal was brilliant. Rubin, as the star, was also the director of the operetta, and the opening was greeted with mixed reviews. The critics were unanimous, however, in their praise of Irving Jacobson, whom they were seeing for the first time in a dramatic role, that of Kopel (Paul Muni had distinguished himself in the same role in a Yiddish Art Theater production of the original I. F. Singer play).

But the public stayed away from "200,000," and by the summer of 1931, Rolland had incurred a large deficit and was behind in paying his employees' salaries. In order to turn his finances around, Rolland got rid of everyone at his theater—including Sholom—and engaged Rumshinsky and an entirely new troupe for the following season. Managers of Second Avenue theaters were not willing to risk an entire season with Sholom at the musical helm, although he was asked to contribute individual scores. Rather than take an assignment with a theater in the provinces, Sholom opted for waiting for one with more prestige in New York.

One evening in the spring of 1931, Sholom ran into two friends at the Cafe Royal, Yehuda Bleich and Zvee Scooler.

"Secunda!" shouted Scooler, as dramatic a personality off-stage as he was on. "We were just going to call you. You've saved us a nickel."

Scooler was, for the coming summer months, social director of Unzer Camp, a Labor Zionist camp for adults and children in Highland Mills, New York (the rest of the year he was a Yiddish theater actor). Bleich was to be dramatics director of the children's camp, called Kindervelt. They asked Sholom to join the staff, wearing two hats—to help Scooler by staging shows for the adults, and to teach the children Yiddish and Hebrew songs. They would pay Sholom $200 for the summer, which would include room and board for Sholom, Betty and Shelly. Sholom had sold his house in Loch Sheldrake, so he took the job.

A Socialist-Zionist milieu was new to Sholom. The camp population numbered approximately 400 adults and 500 children. Most of the adults were former Russian Socialist leaders or contemporaries and friends of such people as David Ben-Gurion and Golda Meir. Founded in 1925, it offered an opportunity for members of the working class to spend ten summer weeks—June 25 to Labor Day—in a recreational atmosphere, where they would have language (Yiddish and/or Hebrew) and background (European Jewish) in common.

In addition to summer sports, there were Yiddish and Jewish intellectual activities. On Saturdays musical programs and plays were presented, and on Sundays there were lectures. The staff of the camp over the years included sculptor Chaim Gross, who was arts and crafts counselor; actors Wolfe Barzell, Lily Liliana, and Leon Liebgold; film director Marty Ritt ("Sounder," "Hud"); composer Lazar Weiner, who played piano at camp; Baruch Lumet (whose son, Sidney, was a camper), drama director.

The adults who attended the camp were not all eggheads but were drawn to things educational and respected intellectual achievement. Most of them were unable to attend college, and they soaked up enlightenment about Jewish culture during those Sunday night lectures.

For the children it was different. They were first generation Americans. Most of the adults were from Eastern Europe and wanted to transmit their heritage and language to their children.

Emanuel Azenberg, now a Broadway producer, remembers 20 summers of Unzer Camp (his father, Charles, was camp director from 1931 until it closed in 1956).

It was not a religious camp. There was no religiousness at all. I suppose the food was what they would now call Kosher Style. You didn't eat ham or pork, but religious Jews would break pots over your head if they saw what you *did* eat. The camp was not the most magnificent accommodation. The facilities were not terrific—the basketball court had rocks in it. What kept everybody there was the camaraderie. You were there without fear. You came back to New York, and you were told that Roosevelt was a Jew. You heard that from the other guys on the block who beat the hell out of you. The city was complicated. Camp was not complicated. It was pure. The experience was clean.

As the boys and girls went to the dining room, they would all dance—dances to Hebrew and Yiddish songs that would be like walking dances. People who I talk to today remember the incredible innocence of the place and speak of it as the best time of their lives. We did things that were totally contrary to being in America. You didn't sing songs as boys in New York. But at camp boys sang, and with total joy.

That was because of Sholom Secunda. He taught you songs, Jewish melodies that you wouldn't sing on the street, songs that go back to the rabbinic period of Judaism. In the Bronx you ran away from Jewish accents, you fought the culture all day. But with Sholom, the culture was okay. Through his music he charmed you into learning the traditions. We all sang, and we liked it.

He was the most charming man imaginable. He gave you the Secunda smile, and you sang whatever he wanted. Do you know what it is to get eleven-year-old boys who want to play baseball to sing a song?

On the adult side of the camp, Sholom was able to create a kind of summer stock for Second Avenue. Many of the actors he had worked with came to the camp, either for specific Saturday night shows or for the entire summer. Sholom would be asked to put together pageants with Scooler, and for one of them, called "From Slavery to Freedom," Sholom hired Robert Merrill, who was still a music student, to sing. Poet I. J. Schwartz was a guest at the camp during Sholom's first summer there, and Sholom set his poetry to music.

Those summers were among the happiest of Sholom's life. He spent hours with Zionists for the first time. He learned new musical folk-motifs that fascinated him politically and artistically. In his spare moments he sat alone and worked on Palestinian folk melodies. He attempted to arrange them, develop them, write variations on them. After so many years in the Yiddish theater, Unzer Camp and Kindervelt provided cultural satisfaction in his work that heretofore had been missing.

The only unpleasant experience Sholom recalled about Unzer Camp involved Shelly, who was nearly three and far more assimilated a Jew than his father. Shelly spoke no Yiddish, and Yehuda Bleich's son, also nearly three, spoke only Yiddish. Shelly spent afternoons with his playmate, and during one of them Shelly suddenly hauled off and punched his companion in the face.

Mrs. Bleich, who witnessed the incident, rushed over to Betty and said, "There are enough anti-Semites in the world without your bringing one to camp!"

When he was told about his son's behavior, Sholom grabbed Shelly by the arm and said angrily, "What's this? Why did you hit him?"

"Because," Shelly cried, "he *talks funny!*"

In the fall, Sholom was asked by William Rolland to contribute several scores for the 1931–1932 season. One of them was "The Street Singer," by Abraham Blum, starring Menachim Rubin and Bella Meisel, which opened on December 25, 1931. Of the production, the theater critic for the *World-Telegram* wrote,

> . . .Boasting a score comprising twenty-two numbers, it is only logical and fair to report that Sholom Secunda, prolific composer, has done more than his share toward building up a musical production which, in other hands, might not have stood the test half

so well. Of course, the outstanding numbers were few and far between, but they sufficed in their combined efforts to carry out the
producer's main intent, the showing of Menachim Rubin's voice.

The book is a typical Yiddish creation and one which sadly lacks
the plot, business and artifices necessary to so capable (a singer) as
Mr. Rubin. . .The situations were as hackneyed as one might expect of any ordinary Yiddish musical story. Placed in the hands of
Menachim Rubin, the entire affair seemed like a pitiful lump of
putty in dextrous but sticky hands. . .

Max Karper, theater critic of the *New York Evening Journal,* was
more sanguine:

Here is a truly entertaining production. . .that will have tremendous appeal, not only to Jewish play-goers but to those who are
accustomed to seeing Broadway musicals. . .Secunda contributed a
snappy score of musical numbers that he can be well proud of. It is
the best he has done.

Sholom had no doubt that the former review was closer to the
truth. And he cannot have missed the splash caused by the opening,
the day after ''The Street Singer'' opened, of George Gershwin's
''Of Thee I Sing'' (the first musical comedy to win a Pulitzer Prize for
drama), and must have wondered how, if he had teamed up with
Gershwin, the course of his own career might have been altered.
One of Sholom's failings was that he had no nose for business,
which the following season, and its repercussions, would graphically
and noisily illustrate.

𝕊 "BEI MIR BIST DU SCHÖN"

By the summer of 1932, Sholom had been re-engaged by William Rolland to be resident composer at the Rolland Theater in Brooklyn. Rolland had signed stars Aaron Lebedeff, Leon Blank and Lucy Levin to star in the new Yiddish musical "I Would If I Could" by Abraham Blum, which would open the 1932–1933 season. Sholom was to write the score. Jacob Jacobs was hired as lyricist.

Sholom was also music director of the Yiddish radio station WEVD. He was lucky to have any work, let alone two jobs. The United States was three years into the Depression. Amelia Earhart had briefly lifted everyone's spirits when she became in May the first woman to fly solo across the Atlantic Ocean. One of the few signs of prosperity in New York was the elegant, 102-story Empire State Building, completed the year before. It contrasted sharply with men on the streets asking for handouts, some of them well-dressed, ruined Wall Street bankers.

With his livelihood assured, at least for the coming season, Sholom decided to rent a room in Far Rockaway for the summer months. Betty and Shelly would be spared the heat of their Brooklyn brownstone on Penn Street, and Sholom could write the music for his new production on a piano he had rented.

The evening before they left for the summer resort, while Betty was packing, the telephone rang. It was Jacobs.

"I have a title for the show's leitmotif," he said to Sholom eagerly. "Lebedeff loves it."

"What is it?" Sholom replied.

"'Bei Mir Bist Du Schön.' See what you can do with it. I'll call you in a couple of days."

The following morning, Sholom drove his wife and son to Far

Rockaway. That evening after dinner Sholom, Betty and Shelly took a stroll along the boardwalk to be cooled by the gentle breeze blowing in from the Atlantic Ocean. They walked slowly, the pace set by their three-year-old son, who clutched his father's hand. As Sholom and Shelly chatted, Betty watched the other strollers, noticing particularly the clothes and jewelry worn by the women.

"Sholom!" Betty said suddenly. "Did you see that woman? She's wearing a diamond ring as big as her knuckle!"

"I don't understand you," Sholom said with mock irritation. "While you're looking at the women, you seem to be unaware that everyone who passes us is admiring you. And it's not because of your jewelry. It's because of your beautiful face."

Sholom grabbed Betty's cheeks, pinching them with pleasure, an impulse he could seldom resist with those he loved, regardless of their size or sex. He kissed her lustily on the mouth and said, with a grin, "Bei mir bist du schön. To me you're beautiful."

He began to hum the melody that fit the meter of the title words, the tune developing idly as he and his family resumed their leisurely walk. As the sun set, they returned to their room and went to bed early.

Sholom got up before the rest of his family the next day and made himself breakfast in their tiny kitchen. The tune to "Bei Mir" had gestated overnight. He drew a music staff on a piece of paper and quickly jotted down the notes to the melody. After breakfast, he rewrote the tune at the piano and left for WEVD in Manhattan, taking the song with him.

Moishe Oysher, a celebrated cantor, was scheduled for an appearance on a program at the station that day. Sholom played "Bei Mir" for him to rehearse it before showing it to Lebedeff, who was to sing it with Lucy Levin in "I Would If I Could." Lebedeff's ego tended to roadblock his artistic approval of others, and Sholom wanted to minimize his criticism by polishing the tune.

"Very catchy, Sholom," Oysher said, humming the refrain as he left the studio.

Sholom phoned Jacobs and asked that he join him at the Secundas' house in Brooklyn so that Jacobs could set Yiddish lyrics to the melody. That afternoon they met, and within two hours the song was complete.

Sholom called Lebedeff, with whom he had never worked before, to tell him that the song was ready. Lebedeff invited them to come to his house on Second Avenue.

The songwriters sang the song for the broodingly handsome star who was known alternately as "the Yiddish Al Jolson" or "the Fred Astaire of the Yiddish stage."

"Not bad," Lebedeff said, examining his fingernails. "I just have a couple of minor suggestions." His "minor" suggestions included an entirely new bridge for the song, and he began to sing a substitute. The notes sounded familiar to Sholom. They were, in fact, from a Russian folk melody that Sholom had learned as a child in the Ukraine.

Sholom took a deep breath and said, "That is a beautiful tune, Lebedeff, but every Russian remembers it from Europe. I have written an entirely new song. That's what I want you to sing in the show."

Jacobs looked at the two men nervously.

"We'll see," Lebedeff said airily. "The chorus is good. But something's missing. Don't worry, we still have time to make changes before the opening."

As they left, Jacobs grabbed Sholom's arm. "It's a good sign!" he said optimistically. "At least he likes *part* of it. You'll have to get used to Lebedeff, Sholom. It's the way he works—he changes everybody's tunes. So you'll give in a little here or there, and we'll all get along."

Sholom steamed all the way back to Far Rockaway. He could foresee trouble with Lebedeff on every song in the show. He was tired of the stranglehold of the star system on the Yiddish theater. He was tired of the egomania of star-managers who often had an investment in the theaters in which they starred, and who threw their artistic weight around. And he was tired of being thwarted in his efforts to write original show tunes and of being asked to rehash old ones.

For the rest of the summer, Sholom churned out tunes for duets, satirical numbers, ensembles and ballads, which he took to Jacobs, who then wrote lyrics appropriate to the action in the play. Jacobs, Sholom and Lebedeff met frequently during the passing weeks. At the end of August, Sholom and his family returned to Brooklyn, and the play went into rehearsals. Lucy Levin, as likable a woman as she was beautiful, loved "Bei Mir." Lebedeff, however, insisted that the song was unsatisfactory. He kept suggesting new melodic inserts, which Sholom continued to reject. At last, a dress rehearsal was called with full orchestra. The run-through of the score went smoothly—until they got to "Bei Mir Bist Du Schön."

"I will not sing it the way it is," Lebedeff announced, and walked off the stage to his dressing room.

Sholom, who was conducting the orchestra, rehearsed the number with Lucy Levin alone. Then he slowly put down his baton and gave the orchestra a ten-minute break. William Rolland, the producer, beckoned Sholom into the wings, and said in Yiddish, "Sholom. Lebedeff says he won't sing your song because he doesn't like it. You tell me you won't change a note. He wants to sing a song he wrote. The situation is already strained, so do what he wants. For me, do it. You'll use 'Bei Mir' in another show."

Sholom's face turned crimson. He shouted in English, "Over my dead body! Over my dead body!" and stalked into Lebedeff's dressing room.

"Listen to me!" he yelled at the astonished star. "Even if this theater has to close, that number will stay in! Let the audience decide who's right, you or me. At the opening tomorrow, you'll sing the song my way. If the audience doesn't ask for an encore, we'll do your song the next day."

Lebedeff was not accustomed to being contradicted. Startled, he agreed to the terms of the agitated composer.

The following evening the Rolland theater was sold out, and rows of standees lined the back of the house. During the performance, the audience applauded each number enthusiastically. Toward the middle of the first act, the orchestra began to play the introduction to "Bei Mir." As he conducted in the pit, Sholom managed to conceal his anxiety. Lebedeff looked down at Sholom from the stage with an irritating grin. He sang the verse alone, then with Levin the refrain. The cast stood in clusters in the wings, watching the duel of artistic egos as though it were a tennis match.

At the end of the number, the audience thundered its approval. They gave the song a standing ovation and yelled for an encore. Lebedeff and Levin were forced to sing the song three more times for the cheering audience.

At intermission Sholom went to Lebedeff's dressing room, savoring his victory.

"Well, Lebedeff, what's it going to be? My song or yours?"

Lebedeff looked up at Sholom from his chair in front of the

makeup mirror and said, wearily, "You're as stubborn as a mule, Sholom. You win."

"I Would If I Could" was the first profitable run the Rolland had had in several seasons. Lebedeff and Sholom developed a grudging mutual esteem based on respect for each other's talents. Lebedeff was impressed by Sholom's classical training. ("None of the composers of the Yiddish theater had Sholom's academic background," says Dinah Goldberg. "They couldn't even *say* 'Walter Damrosch.'") Lebedeff, as Sholom put it, "had an extraordinary, natural talent as an actor. He was so realistic that, even though I had seen the play dozens of times, I forgot that he was playing a role."

In 1933 "Bei Mir" was copyrighted, and Sholom and Jacobs published 10,000 copies of the Yiddish version of the song at their own expense, a common practice among Yiddish theater songwriters. The sheet music was sold in the lobby of the Rolland Theater and in music stores around the Lower East Side. Within weeks it became a staple of orchestras playing at weddings and bar mitzvahs in New York and at Jewish resorts in the Catskill Mountains.

Of even greater box office appeal than "I Would If I Could" was the next Rolland production, "The Rabbi's Temptation." "Temptation" had the same cast as "I Would"—Lebedeff, Levin and Blank. Of the production Max Karper wrote,

> One of the funniest and most entertaining Yiddish musicals ever shown at the Brooklyn Rolland Theater arrived there during the weekend (and) scored an immediate hit. The production, in two acts and six colorful scenes, has everything in it in the line of novel and diversified entertainment; a tuneful score of catchy music from Sholom Secunda, an interesting book with genuine laugh-provoking situations by Samuel Steinberg and, above all, it provides both Lebedeff and Blank with unusually fine roles. . .

The operetta, a triangle between an old rabbi (Blank) and his son (Lebedeff) and a young girl whom they both want to marry (Levin) was an improvement on ordinary *shund.*

During the play Sholom and Blank became close friends. They shared similar backgrounds—Russian poverty, synagogue choir-singing, cantorial work. Blank, who was a superb dramatic actor, had performed in Yiddish theater in Russia during the 1870s, and had starred in the plays of Jacob Gordin in turn-of-the-century New York.[1] By the time he and Sholom worked together, he was no longer young.

At the end of the season, the troupe took "I Would If I Could" on the road—a week in Chicago, a week in Cleveland and Detroit, one-night stands in smaller cities—ending with a week in Philadelphia, where the run ended in tragedy.

Leon Blank began to complain to Sholom that he did not feel well. Their rooms in the Philadelphia hotel were adjoining, and they spent much of their time together, dining at William and Rose Siegel's home. One evening after dinner, Blank sat silently, which was uncharacteristic of him. He looked pale, and Rose called a doctor, who came to the house. He took Blank into the bedroom to examine him. When he emerged, he told Sholom that the actor was gravely ill and should be taken to a hospital immediately in New York. Blank was unaware of their conversation.

"Listen, Blank," Sholom said cheerfully, "maybe it would be a good idea for you to see your own doctor in New York."

"Are you crazy?" Blank said, "We've got three more days left in our run here. How can I leave?"

Blank's "the show must go on" attitude was typical of Yiddish theater stars. For one thing they did not have understudies. In addition, their *patriots* would not accept a substitute, and more than one performance was held up while the audience waited for an indisposed actor to get out of his sick bed and appear on stage. (Molly Picon recalls an appearance by Madame Regina Prager who played an entire performance with her face grotesquely swollen, due to an abscessed tooth, as though nothing were amiss. "Would she let somebody go on in her part?" Picon asks rhetorically. "Only if she were dead.")

Blank refused to go to New York until the end of the week. Each day his condition worsened. The crisis occurred Saturday night. Sholom watched Blank from the pit during the first act, and although the audience was unaware of the actor's condition, it was obvious to the cast that he was in trouble.

At intermission Sholom rushed to Blank's dressing room. Lebedeff stood next to Blank and said gently, "We'll finish the play without you. You must go straight to New York."

"All right," Blank said weakly, "but Secunda has to go with me." The first violinist was told to conduct the remainder of the performance. Blank was still in costume and Sholom was wearing black tie. They got into a taxi and went to the railroad station, leaving their belongings to be packed up by the company manager.

On the train Blank appeared to be slightly improved. He poked Sholom and, with a wink, pointed out the pretty girls passing up the aisle. At Penn Station in New York, the two men hailed a cab and Sholom dropped Blank off at his home. When Sholom got home, he called Blank's wife, who had already summoned a doctor. The doctor confined Blank to bed.

The following day, with his friend Sam Kestin, Sholom went to visit Blank. When the bedridden actor saw his two friends, he began to weep. "My friends," he said, "it doesn't look good."

"Don't talk nonsense," Sholom said. "You'll be fine after you have a few weeks' rest." Privately Sholom knew the accuracy of Blank's remark.

In two days Blank was dead.

The Cafe Royal on 12th Street and Second Avenue was the Sardi's of the Yiddish theater. In the 1930s it was open 24 hours a day. Cafes on the Lower East Side were gathering places for immigrants to socialize together before going home to their dreary flats. It was an extension of cafe life in Europe, and each cafe had its special identity: poets went to Goodman and Levine's, radicals went to the Monopole (even Leon Trotsky, when he was still called Lev Davidovich Bronstein).[2]

But the most glamorous cafe of all was the Cafe Royal, where actors, writers, producers, composers, the intelligentsia of immigrant Europeans gathered. It is said that Marc Chagall sold his paintings there for $25 in the 1930s. Yiddish theater stars, dressed as though for a Hollywood opening, would make a grand entrance—Lebedeff usually showed up wearing a belted cashmere coat with a carnation in the lapel, a white fedora and spats.

"Ninety per cent of business of the theater was conducted at the Royal," one actor recalls. "The fighting, the politics of the theater, everything went on there. You would walk in, someone would come over and wish you good luck in your new engagement, which you didn't know about yet, but he did. People from uptown came there to look at the actors."

Like Sardi's, the Royal had its territorial imperatives. The actors sat in the right front corner, the writers on the left, the musicians in back. A long corridor led to a rear room where card players congregated—pinochle was a favorite game. If an actor wanted to talk to a writer, he did so in the writers' corner. Union officials sat near the telephones, which rang incessantly through the night. An actor might not have a phone at home, but you could probably reach him at the Royal—even if the caller were the maitre d', who was frequently paid by the actor to have the actor paged.

One evening Sholom sat at a table with three other composers—Olshanetsky, Rumshinsky and Harry Lubin. He overheard a conversation at the next table.

"I hear Rolland wants to leave his million-dollar theater."

"I know, but I can't believe he's leaving the theater altogether."

"He's probably going to take a big house on Second Avenue—I wonder which one?"

"It won't be the Second Avenue Theater—Edelstein is making piles of gold there."

During this speculation about Rolland's plans, the man himself walked into the Royal. Sholom watched people rush over to Rolland saying "Mazel tov!" Rolland had, he said, engaged the Public Theater on Second Avenue. He had finally become a manager of a big Manhattan theater.

Everyone watched Rolland, wondering where he would sit. Slowly he threaded his way past the small tables. As he walked by each one, the curious actors quickly buried themselves in quiet conversation, feigning disinterest.

Rolland sat down at Reuben Guskin's table, next to the composers' table. Guskin was the dynamic and powerful head of the Hebrew Actors Union, and it was then clear to everyone that Guskin had known all about Rolland's move.

Sholom made a mental note of Rolland's new plans and returned to the conversation at hand which, that night, outweighed even a change in theatrical management. That evening, at the composers' table, was the birthdate of the Society of Jewish Composers.

Olshanetsky pitched the idea. He had opened an office on Broadway where he booked orchestras for banquets, weddings and bar mitzvahs. He wasn't making enough money as a composer alone, and the booking business was very profitable for him.

"Look," Olshanetsky said, "ASCAP (American Society of Composers, Artists and Publishers) collects royalties for the performance of its members' work. But our music is performed on Yiddish radio stations and all over the Catskills, and we don't collect a penny.''

The other composers agreed that they were being robbed, and made plans to form their own organization. They agreed to hire two lawyers who knew corporate law and were familiar with the structure of ASCAP—Messrs. Seginberg and Moscowitz (who later changed his name to A. Edward Masters). They were retained and asked to draw up a constitution for the Jewish Society and to register it under the name "Society of Jewish Composers, Publishers and Songwriters.''

In subsequent weeks Yiddish music publishers Joseph and Jerry Kammen and Henry Lefkowitz were asked to join the organization. Also invited were lyricists Isadore Lillian and Jacob Jacobs, and composers Michel Gelbart and Pinchos Jassinowsky. The fledgling Society wrote letters to all the radio stations that used Yiddish music, to all the hotel owners in the Catskills, and to the halls where weddings and bar mitzvahs were celebrated with Jewish music. Of those who responded to the letters, a few said that they were already affiliated with ASCAP.

A more direct approach was required, but the Jewish Society did not have funds to pay for a representative to do the muscling for them. The members were already paying for stationery, postage and phone calls out of their own pockets. The members agreed that Sholom and Moskowitz would personally approach the stations and halls. They went to every Yiddish radio station in Manhattan, Brooklyn and the Bronx, and acquired some contracts. They drove to the Catskills where hotel owners often refused to see them or were gruff—there, too, they got contracts. Little by little, the Society began to accrue a small income.

On the strength of their growing ranks, the Jewish Society wrote again to the resisting stations and hotels and wedding halls, putting pressure on them to pay the Society for their use of its music. Within a year the Society was meeting its expenses and showing a profit.

In the meantime Rolland was gearing up for his first season in Manhattan. His theater, the Public, was two blocks away from the Second Avenue Theater, where Molly Picon was the reigning star. Molly, a tiny bundle of sass and talent, could out-sing and out-dance anyone in the Yiddish theater. Her gift for comedy was cosmic. Any theater boasting her name on its marquee enjoyed a box office bonanza.

Rolland had his work cut out for him. To compete with Picon, he engaged five ranking Yiddish theater stars: Aaron Lebedeff, Menachim Rubin, Lucy Levin, Itsik Feld, and Yetta Zwerling. Because of his success the previous season, Sholom was engaged as composer. He was a Second Avenue composer at last (a term he grew to despise), after 15 years of bucking the union and the provinces.

Hiring five important stars to compete with Molly Picon had its price. It was a matter of properties. Any play chosen would have to have five juicy parts for the principals. Willie Siegel, once again, came up with a play that seemed to solve management's problem of too many cooks: "A Happy Family." Chaim Tauber was engaged as lyricist. Rolland spent thousands of dollars on new sets and on publicity for the opening. He implored Sholom to write songs that would please the five stars. Lebedeff, as top star, had to be satisfied above all.

For Menachem Rubin, Sholom wrote an aria called "Shadows." For Lucy Levin, he wrote coloratura arias to showcase her spendid voice. For Feld and Zwerling, he wrote, "Scrape, Fiddler, Scrape."

"A Happy Family," which opened on September 21, 1934, was a box office success. Reviews were mixed, the best from the ever-faithful Max Karper of the *New York American:*

The production is tastefully staged and contains one of the finest musical scores Sholom Secunda has yet contributed to the Yiddish operetta field. William Siegel, who authored the piece, gave each of the stars a role calling for the specific talents of each; thus all are artistically effective.

Walter Hartman wrote in the *News:*

Leading woman and featured player in Yiddish musical shows for several years, Lucy Levin reaches the heights of stardom in Sholom Secunda's new operetta. . .Miss Levin reaps the benefit of the gems of the composer's score which, incidentally, is as sparkling as any that has graced a Jewish musical in many seasons.

The New York Times kept its enthusiasm in check:

"A Happy Family". . .while having its full share of the usual faults of the Yiddish musical comedy, is nevertheless good entertainment of its simple kind. It would take hard searching to discover the plot William Siegel and his associates have provided. . . The score by Sholom Secunda is not especially original, although he does conduct it with refinement; and the sets are quite tawdry. For all that, "A Happy Family" has its attractive members. For one thing, it brings to town Menachim Rubin, who has been knocking around unhappily since his arrival in this country some years ago. He is an excellent actor, though he has no role to speak of unblushingly in this show; and he also is a glorious baritone. Mr. Secunda has written one dramatic number for him in which he demonstrates it superbly. Then there is Itsik Feld, who almost stopped the show with a patter song, "I Don't Understand," and he is also a graceful gnome of a dancer. For handsome innocence there is Lucy Levin. . .Finally, there is Aaron Lebedeff, who directed the play and who manages to be genial and sing, even though he has a hoarse, choked voice. He went over well, especially in a song entitled, "If You Gots 'Em, Then You Gets 'Em," reputedly a bit of American folklore. . .

The title of the operetta in no way mirrored the backstage mood. Lucy Levin alone was pleasant about line changes and cuts. The other stars griped over who got the best lines or the biggest laughs. Sholom kept a low profile during their squabbles.

Sholom managed one particularly inventive number for the show that set a precedent. A Spanish dance called the Carioca was popular as a result of the 1933 Fred Astaire-Ginger Rogers musical film, "Flying Down to Rio," which included Vincent Youmans' tune, "The Carioca." Sholom borrowed the melody for a comic duet (in Yiddish) for Feld and Zwerling. Other composers used the gimmick and it became standard in the Yiddish musical theater for the comic couple to sing a duet purloined from, or at least strongly imitative of, Hollywood or Broadway musicals.

For all its mixed reactions and backstage feuds, "A Happy Family" had an unusually long run—it was the mainstay for the Public for that season.

Rolland retained his roster of stars and his composer for the

1935–1936 season, to which list he added Gertie Bulman and Leon Gold. The season opened with "Heaven on Earth," in which Sholom wrote a quartet for the stars that resembled an operatic ensemble piece. The season was financially successful and personally painful for Sholom. His two sons had become critically ill—Sheldon with osteomyelitis and Gene, an infant, with double pneumonia—over a period of a few months.

Sholom wrote the score for "Heaven on Earth," but was unable to conduct during its run, which began on October 8, because of the necessity of helping Betty with his sons and visiting them at the hospital. During those long weeks he had not been able to earn an income. One afternoon Rolland and Lebedeff visited Sholom at home and told him that if he could not continue at the theater, they would have to engage another composer. Sholom promised to be there the following day.

The combination of family troubles and of Sholom's frustration with his work finally affected his own health. The strain of his children's illnesses was compounded by his work load: between 1935 and 1937 he wrote the scores for "East Side Wedding," "Itche Mayer of Warsaw," "Two Hearts," "Oh, You Girls!," "Pinye of Pinchev," and "Night in Budapest," as well as "Heaven on Earth"—seven operettas in two years. In that time he had also continued working for WEVD and for the East Midwood Jewish Center in Brooklyn as music director of each. The pressure became too much.

One night on the way home from the theater, while walking to his home, he fainted on the sidewalk. He went to see a doctor the next day and was told that his blood pressure was abnormally low. "I was in a bind," Sholom later wrote. "In the Yiddish theater, I was a big, unhappy fish, and I knew that if I left it, I would have to start all over again with something else."

Sholom went to see Reuben Guskin of the Hebrew Actors Union for counsel. Guskin was sympathetic, but urged him to stay in the Yiddish theater.

"How can you leave a career you've been working in for so long?" Guskin asked. He thought for a moment and said, "I have an idea. Next season Maurice Schwartz is putting on a new play by I.J. Singer called 'The Brothers Ashkenazi.' I know he'll need music. The Yiddish Art Theater will be playing uptown this season, at the Jolson Theater on Seventh Avenue and 59th Street. It will be a complete change of pace for you. If you like, I'll sound him out about engaging you."

Later that afternoon Guskin ran into Sholom at the Cafe Royal and told him that he had set up an appointment for Schwartz for the next day.

Sholom slept poorly that night. Rolland had always put Sholom's name above the title of his productions, and he knew that Schwartz would not give him top billing. Sholom was concerned also about loss of income, knowing that Schwartz, who performed the most prestigious theater on Second Avenue, paid the price for artistry with small but loyal receipts at the box office.

Guskin, Schwartz and Sholom met the following day at the Hebrew Actors Union office on Seventh Street. Schwartz offered Sholom $75 a week—less than half what he had been earning with Rolland.

"I can't afford the luxury of hiring a composer who will only compose and conduct," Schwartz said. "You would have to play in the orchestra as well. My theater depends not so much on music as on the play, and the music you would write for me would be incidental music ("accidental music," Sholom called it privately)."

Sholom reviewed his options which, because of his physician's warning to slow down, were few. He accepted Schwartz's offer.

Schwartz told Sholom that he would be traveling to Europe and Palestine that summer, and that they would begin working on "The Brothers Ashkenazi" upon his return.

During the summer months, at the end of the forty-four-week season, Yiddish theaters were dark, and actors and musicians had to forage for other employment. With Schwartz out of the country, Sholom was without work for the summer of 1937. He posed the idea of a second California visit to Betty, this time as the guest of Jacques Renard, musical director of the Eddie Cantor Radio Show.

"You have nothing to lose," Betty said. "The timing is perfect. Take your music out there and see what happens."

The Depression years were lean for everyone, including the Secundas. They had two small children and their income in the fall would be halved. It was financially impossible for Betty to accompany Sholom. To keep expenses down, Sholom took a bus. Across America, people were on the move—Okies in dilapidated pickup trucks, unemployed factory workers from the East hitchhiking, hoboes riding the rods and Sholom Secunda, a New York composer hoping to change his luck in California. On his arrival in Los Angeles five days later, Renard met him at the bus depot.

Jacques Renard had been a fan of Sholom's ever since they had met backstage at a Secunda operetta in New York. Renard's orchestra had played a Secunda tune, "Minuet," on the Cantor show, giving the composer his first wide exposure to other than a strictly Jewish audience. Secunda had written a note of thanks, and in reply Renard had invited him to California to try to get on the musical staff of a Hollywood film studio.

On his first evening in California Renard and his wife took Sholom to dinner at a restaurant frequented by radio and film performers. Renard introduced Sholom to everyone as the "famous Jewish composer." Some diners hadn't heard of him; others recognized his name, saying, "I like to see a Jewish show when I come to New York," or, "Oh yes. When I was a child, my parents used to take me to the Yiddish theater."

The following morning Renard took Sholom to a rehearsal of the Eddie Cantor Show, a run-through of songs that would be performed on that week's program. Sholom was impressed with the differences between a Hollywood rehearsal and those of Yiddish productions. In New York Sholom accompanied the singers himself at the piano during rehearsals. In Hollywood Renard stood next to the piano while a pianist rehearsed the numbers, and an orchestrator took notes. On Second Avenue Sholom orchestrated and arranged his own music and conducted the orchestra, less than half the size of Cantor's. In Hollywood conductors, orchestrators, arrangers and rehearsal accompanists divided up these functions. It was all a matter of economics. The money was in Hollywood.

After the rehearsal Renard and Sholom went to Warner Brothers Film Studios to keep an appointment with its music director, Leo Forbstein. Sholom's name was familiar to Forbstein, a heavy-set, elegantly dressed man, who had heard "Bei Mir Bist Du Schön" performed by Jewish singers in a Los Angeles night club. He asked to see a copy of the song. Sholom played it on a grand piano that stood in a corner of the spacious office as Forbstein gazed impassively through his pince-nez.

"A beautiful melody," Forbstein said, "and quite a lively rhythm. But I doubt that the song has possibilities here, even if it had an English lyric. It is too obviously a Jewish song."

Renard argued the point and suggested that Sholom play some of his other songs.

"Look," Forbstein said, "I'm going to level with you. You are too steeped in Jewish melodies to write for another language or style." He rose from his chair, signaling the end of the meeting, and held out his hand. "I'm sorry," he said.

"One man's opinion!" Renard said encouragingly in the parking lot. "Tomorrow we'll go to the other studios."

For several days, they went from studio to studio and the response to Sholom's music was the same: too Jewish.

Sholom was unaware of a bias against things "too Jewish" on the part of many of Hollywood's Jewish executives. Just two years prior to Sholom's 1929 California trip, when Warner Brothers searched for a property with which to introduce sound to motion pictures, Darryl F. Zanuck, a non-Jew, suggested "The Jazz Singer." According to Zanuck biographer Leo Guild,

> Harry Warner threw up his hands. He refused to buy it. "No," he said, "it's too strongly Jewish. Therefore it limits its appeal."

> Zanuck argued, "Look Harry, you've seen 'Nanook of the North.' Well, when that Eskimo woman loses her child on the ice cap do the audiences stop to ask what religion she is? No, they just burst out crying."[3]

Unfortunately Sholom never met Darryl Zanuck.

After a month of frustrating interviews, Sholom had had enough. Constant rejection convinced him that he lacked whatever it took to make it in the non-Jewish field. He decided to return to the Yiddish theater and to concentrate increasingly on composing classical and liturgical music.

His mind made up, Sholom informed Renard of his plans. But Renard had saved what he thought to be the best interview for last. He had arranged a meeting for Sholom with his boss, Eddie Cantor, whom Sholom had known slightly in New York. Sholom hoped that Cantor, whose real name was Edward Israel Iskowitz, would have a more enlightened attitude toward him and his music. He agreed to one more meeting.

Cantor was cordial and listened attentively as Sholom played and sang his songs. Sholom concluded his demonstration with "Bei Mir," the song he felt offered his best hope of crossing over into the world of American popular music. But Cantor's reaction echoed all the others, albeit more gently expressed. "Sholom," he said, "I love your music. But I can't use it. It's too Jewish."

Sholom's heart sank. He could see from Cantor's dour expression that the entire trip to California had been a waste of time and money. In 1929 he had been told that he was not marketable at a Hollywood film studio because he was not a "man of reputation." Now he was, but, it appeared, in the wrong field.

Trapped with his disappointment on the long bus trip back to New York, Sholom determined to abandon his Hollywood fantasies. He would continue working for the Yiddish stage, and in his free time he would concentrate on his real ambition, which was to write serious Jewish music.

Sholom took up his duties as musical director for the Yiddish Art Theater. One afternoon in September, after Sholom had returned from a rehearsal at the theater, Betty gave him a message to call Joseph Kammen of the J. & J. Kammen Music Company (owned jointly with his identical twin, Jerry) in Brooklyn. Kammen had published several of Sholom's songs, and had sold many of those Sholom had published privately. Sholom returned his call.

"It's time we printed more of your songs," Kammen said. "Your printing of 'Bei Mir' is sold out. Why don't you let us publish a new edition of it?"

"I Would If I Could" was no longer running, and sales of the sheet music had dropped off. Sholom could think of no reason to hang onto the rights, so he agreed to Kammen's terms, as he had for so many other songs: $30, to be shared with Jacobs. Believing that he had given "Bei Mir" his best effort, on September 28, 1937, he signed a contract giving J. & J. Kammen the copyright to the song. In spite of his earning additional money as music director of WEVD, every penny counted. "In these hard times," he told Betty, "fifteen dollars is better than nothing."

Sholom thought no more about the matter. The truth of what happened next to "Bei Mir Bist Du Schön" is a little like *Roshomon*—it depends on the source.

Sammy Cahn, who wrote the English lyrics to "Bei Mir," says he first heard the song in 1935, when he was a contract lyricist with Warner Bros. Inc., parent company of Harms Inc. He and his songwriting partner, Saul Chaplin, had written songs for Ella Fitzgerald and Jimmy Lunceford, modest hits such as "If You Ever Should Leave" and "Until the Real Thing Comes Along."[4]

Cahn, a short, skinny man who wore a slim moustache and wire glasses, was aggressively in love with the music business and New York's night life. According to Cahn, he, his manager Lou Levy and Chaplin went to the Apollo Theater in Harlem one evening to hear two black singers, Johnny and George. To the astonishment of the three Jewish men, Johnny and George began to sing "Bei Mir" in Yiddish. (Johnny and George had learned the song from Jennie Grossinger, proprietor of Grossinger's Hotel, a large Jewish resort in Liberty, New York, in the Catskill Mountains. The Catskills were then known as the "Yiddish Alps" or the "borscht belt," terms that today annoy hotel owners in the area.)

"The theater absolutely began to undulate," Cahn says. "The beat absolutely caught hold of you. I turned to Levy and said, 'Can you imagine this? Do you know what language they're singing?'"

The audience, he says, roared for more.

A few days later Cahn ran into Tommy Dorsey, "the sentimental gentleman of swing," who was performing with his orchestra at the Paramount Theater in Manhattan. Cahn suggested that Dorsey perform "Bei Mir," adding that it had "broken the building down" in Harlem.

"You want me to take a Jewish song to the Paramount?" Dorsey asked incredulously.

"There are a few Jews up in Harlem," Cahn replied, "and at the Paramount, you get one or two."

"You're crazy," Dorsey said.

Cahn was not easily put off. He went to a music store, bought the sheet music to the song, and took it to Dorsey. Dorsey threw him out.

Two years elapsed. In 1937 Cahn had an apartment, he says, on 57th Street and Sixth Avenue in Manhattan, which he shared with Lou Levy. Levy had discovered a trio of singers—Patti, LaVerne and Maxene Andrews—whom he brought to the apartment. As Cahn remembers their first meeting, "They saw the sheet music for 'Bei Mir' and said, 'Is that a Greek song?' I said, 'No, it sounds Greek but it's not.' I played it for them and immediately they started to sing

along. They asked me for a copy of the song and I gave it to them."
(Maxene says the conversation never took place.)

The Andrews Sisters were in New York trying to break into big-time show business. The daughters of Greek-Norwegian parentage, they were born in Minnesota and had begun singing in 1927 at the urging of their mother. As long as they were singing, she had said, they wouldn't bicker. The group eventually split up in the 1950s not, Maxene says, because of internecine rivalry, but because Patti wanted to be a solo act. Harmonically, the three voices were a magic blend. Patti, the lead singer, was 16; Maxene, who sang the soprano line, was 18; and LaVerne, alto, was 20.

In order to attract professional attention, the Andrews Sisters imitated the Boswell Sisters of New Orleans, so much so that they sounded not so much midwestern as southern. "On 'Bei Mir Bist Du Schön,' we sound like shrimp trawlers," Patti later said. They landed a job singing with a band at the Hotel Edison, receiving $15 per radio broadcast. David Kapp, Artists and Repertoire man at Decca Records, heard the trio sing "Sleepy Time Down South" on the radio while riding in a cab. The announcer said that the music was being broadcast from the Edison. Later Kapp directed Lou Levy to go to the Edison to talk to the Andrews Sisters. Levy found two of them sitting in the lobby, talking to the musicians, and he introduced himself. He asked them to come to Decca the following morning so that they could sing for Dave Kapp's brother, Jack, who was president of the company. Jack Kapp signed them with Decca.

The first Decca 78 rpm record for the Andrews Sisters was "Why Talk About Love" by Sidney Mitchell and Lew Pollack, and "Just A Simple Melody" by Sammy Cahn and Saul Chaplin. For their second record, they were slated for a session to record "Nice Work If You Can Get It" by George and Ira Gershwin, for the A side. They had not yet found a song for the B side.

According to Maxene, it was Lou Levy, and not Sammy Cahn, who told the Andrews Sisters about "Bei Mir," a song, he said, that was a lullaby sung to him when he was a child. He wrote out the Yiddish lyrics phonetically for them, she says, and they took it to Decca to record it for the B side at the session. The Andrews Sisters believed Levy's story, and assumed that "Bei Mir" was in the public domain. It wasn't until several months later that they discovered that the song had a living composer—Sholom Secunda.

Abraham Secunda

Anna Secunda

Clockwise from upper right: Abraham, Meyer, Sholom, Jack, Joe, Aaron, Willie. In Russia, 1901.

Sholom, age 11, in Russia

בזמירות נריע

דער פרינץ פֿן דיא יונגע חזנים
דער קלײנער 14 יעהריגער חזן

שלום
סעקונדא

וועלכער האט איבעראשט מיט
זיין דאווענען דיא גרעסטע מבינים
אין חזנות וועט דאוונען
אין בענטשען ראש חדש
דיזען שבת בראשית
דען 24 אקטאבער, 1908
אין דער צווייטער
רומענישער קאנגרין.
בית יעקב
58-60 ריווינגטאן סט.
מיט א כאהר.

קומט פריינדע וועט איהר זעהען נאטטעס וואונדער וועלכעס קיינער האט נאך
אזעלבעס נישט געהערט אין געזעהען. אללע מעננים אין אללע גרויסע חזנים זאגען דאס
אזעלבעס הירד איינמאהל אין טויזינד יאהר געבוירען. דאהער פריינדע וועט עם וויל
האבען א וואהרעם פערגיניגען זאל זיך וואס פריהער מיט א איינלאס-טיקעט בעזארגען.

טיקעטס זינד צו בעקומען: ביים שמש אין בית המדרש, אין ביי מר.
מארקעוויץ אין ביער סאלאן 75 סטענטאן סט.

פ־־יע דער טיקעטס זינד: פיר מעננער, דאן סטעירס 15ס. באלקאני 10ס.

ייאהרנגע פֿן דעם 14 יעהריגען חזן שלום סעקונדע איז 144 קארומביא סט., רום 17, ניו יארק.

Feuer Bros., Printers, 178 Stanton St., N.Y.

Flyer promoting Sholom, the little cantor, on Lower East Side in 1909.

Sholom at 19

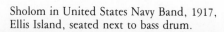

Sholom in United States Navy Band, 1917, Ellis Island, seated next to bass drum.

Celia Adler and Sholom, Philadelphia, 1923

Sholom, Michel Michalesko and Hymie Jacobson en route to Europe, 1923.

Betty and Sholom on their wedding day, Oct. 25, 1927

Betty Almer, 1926

"Senorita" cast at Rolland Theater in Brooklyn, 1929. Sholom is fifth from left, front row.

Family seder, Brooklyn, 1927. Seated, left to right: Shirley Davis (son Stanley on lap), Jack Secunda, Ida Secunda (son Edwin on lap), Thelma Secunda, Joseph Secunda, Anna Secunda, Abraham Secunda, Anna Secunda (daughter Florence on lap), Frieda Secunda (daughter Roslyn on lap), Meyer (son Ezra on lap). Standing, left to right: Louis Davis, unidentified woman, Sholom, Aaron Secunda, Willie Secunda.

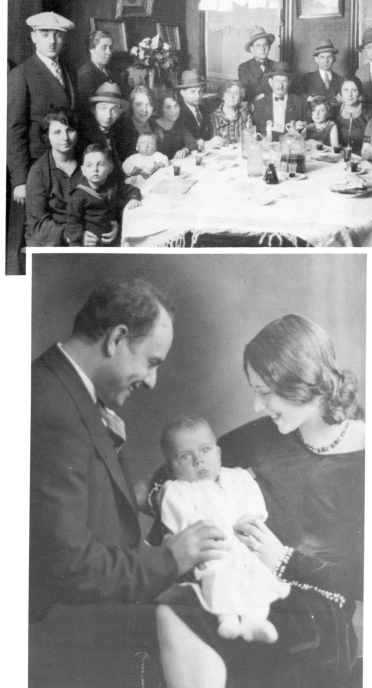

Sholom, Betty and
Sheldon, 1929

Sholom with Mr. and Mrs. Boris Thomashevsky, 1920s

Michel Michalesko, Hymie Jacobson, Aaron Lebedeff

Executive board of Society of Jewish Composers, Publishers and Songwriters. Standing, left to right: Abraham Ellstein, Joseph Broder, unidentified man, Harry Lubin, A. Edward Masters. Seated, left to right: Alexander Olshanetsky, Joseph Rumshinsky, Sholom.

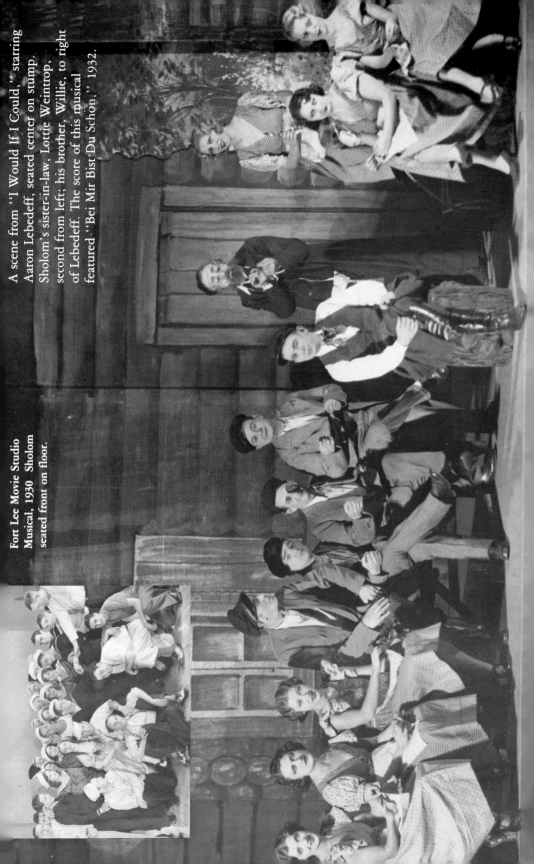

Fort Lee Movie Studio Musical, 1930 Sholom seated front on floor.

A scene from "I Would If I Could," starring Aaron Lebedeff, seated center on stump. Sholom's sister-in-law, Lottie Weintrop, second from left; his brother, Willie, to right of Lebedeff. The score of this musical featured "Bei Mir Bist Du Schön," 1932.

Bei Mir Bistu Shein

בייַ מיר ביזטו שעהן

געזונגען פֿון

אהרן לעבעדעוו און לוסי לעווין

אין שלום סעקונדא'ס רייע מוזיקאַלישע קאָמעדיע

מ'קען לעבן נאר מ'לאָט ניט

פֿון אברהם בלום זיכערטער פֿון הושייקאָב הושייקאבט

I WOULD IF I COULD

Now playing at the
ROLLAND THEATRE
Eastern Parkway at St. John's Place
Tel. Dickens 2-6600, 6601

WILLIAM ROLLAND, Gen'l Manager

איצט געשפילט אין

ראלענד טעאטער
איסטערן פּאַרקװיי און סיינט דזשאנס פּלייס
װיליאם ראָלענד, דזשענעראל מענעדזשער

Published by I. KALMUS, Brooklyn, N. Y.

Patti, LaVerne, Maxene Andrews with Sholom in Chicago, 1938.

Sholom signing autographs at Cafe Royal, 1938. To left of him, Aaron Lebedeff; to right, Joseph Rumshinsky.

Eddie Cantor radio program, 1938. Front row, left to right: Bert Gordon, Eddie Cantor, Bobby Breen, Deanna Durbin, Gloria Swanson, Stanley Field, Sholom, Fifi, Jacques Reynard, conducting.

Shelly, Sholom, Betty
and Gene, 1939

Clockwise from top: Jacob Kalich, Lily Liliana, Sholom, Molly Picon, at
Workman's Circle, Hopewell Junction, New York, 1941.

Sholom conducting orchestra and Richard Tucker, Concord Hotel, 1960s.

Richard Tucker, Sholom and Joseph Garnett at recording rehearsal.

"Bei Mir Bist Du Schön" rights revert to Sholom, 1961. Left to right: William Starr (Harms Music), Sholom, Betty

Sholom and Pablo Casals, Puerto Rico, 1967

Sholom, Gene and granddaughter Ruthanne, Fire Island, 1967

In his office Jack Kapp had speakers over which he could monitor any recording session in Decca's studios. When he heard the Andrews Sisters singing "Bei Mir" in Yiddish, he punched the intercom button and said, "What are you doing, a 'race record'?"

The term "race record" would have unpleasant political overtones today, but in the 1930s it was an accepted term for foreign language songs and for rhythm and blues.

Maxene says that Sammy Cahn and Saul Chaplin were in the recording studio that day. Kapp came down to the studio which was two floors below his office. He turned to Cahn and Chaplin and said, "Could you write an English lyric?" Two days later, she says, the English lyric was set.

Cahn's recollection is quite different. He says that Lou Levy asked him to write the English lyric, which he refused to do for ten days because he was, he says, "offended. I told him I don't do translations." One afternoon, alone in his apartment, Cahn reversed himself and decided to do the lyric. Two songs were popular in 1937—"Umbrella Man," which had the words "bella, bella" in it, and Al Jolson's show tune, "Voonderbar." Cahn knew Yiddish, having been taken to Second Avenue productions by his parents when he was a child.

A literal English translation of the Yiddish lyrics did not fit the melody. "Bei Mir Bist Du Schön" means "you're beautiful to me," but "beautiful" was two syllables too many, so Cahn changed the word to "grand." He wrote down these words, he says:

Verse: Of all the girls I've known, and I've known some,
        Until I first met you I was lonesome,
        And when you came in sight, dear, my heart grew light,
        And this old world seemed new to me.
        You're really swell I have to admit, you
        Deserve expressions that really fit you,
        And so I've racked my brain, hoping to
        Explain all the things you do to me:

Chorus: "Bei Mir Bist Du Schön," please let me explain,
        "Bei Mir Bist Du Schön" means that you're grand.
        "Bei Mir Bist Du Schön" again I'll explain

It means you're the fairest in the land.
I could say "Bella, bella," even say "Voonderbar,"
Each language only helps me tell you how grand you are,
I've tried to explain "Bei Mir Bist Du Schön,"
So kiss me and say you understand.*

"It didn't take, I promise you, maybe ten minutes," Cahn says. "I have a theory that you can write a song as badly in a month as you can in thirty minutes." (Saul Chaplin says that he participated in writing the lyrics.)

On November 24, 1937, the Andrews Sisters recorded the English version for a flat fee of $50. The studio musicians backing the trio were Bobby Hackett and Vic Schoen (who did the arrangement) on trumpet, Al Philburn on trombone, Don Watt on clarinet, Frank Froeba on piano, Dave Barbour on guitar, Haig Stephens on bass and Stan King on drums. When Jack Kapp heard the record, he said, "You'll either be the biggest hit or the biggest flop." Saul Chaplin was equally dubious—he says that he and Cahn wanted Ella Fitzgerald, rather than an unknown trio, to record the tune.

In the meantime the Yiddish version was beginning to attract a wider audience on its own. Before the Andrews Sisters' record was released, Guy Lombardo and his Royal Canadians performed an instrumental version at the Roosevelt Hotel. One witness recalls that when the song was played, the dancers stopped dancing and just listened, the ultimate accolade in a dance-crazed era. Lombardo later performed the song over the CBS Radio Network, and cut the first recording of the song, also an instrumental version.

Sholom knew nothing of the Andrews Sisters' or the English version of the song. Neither, according to Cahn, did J. & J. Kammen, who owned the song. He admits that when he wrote his lyric, he did not have permission from Kammen to do so, nor did the Andrews Sisters, who say they first heard the song the month Sholom sold it, have permission to record it. They were unaware that the rights had not been obtained to do either.

As Cahn explains it, "We have taken a property which doesn't belong to us, and without a by-your-leave, we've just changed it, have we not? And you just can't do that, can you?" One evening, en route

*©1937 (renewed) Warner Bros. Inc. All Rights Reserved. Used by Permission.

to Peter Luger's Steakhouse in Brooklyn, he dropped in on the Kammens at their store on Roebling Street.

"And I say to them—you can call it cunning or just downright lying—I say, 'I think I have an idea that I could take a song of Sholom Secunda's and write an American lyric. Where can I find him?'

"'He has nothing to do with it,' they say. 'You have permission to do the song,' they say. You understand, all this time the record is finished. Total, unquestioned *chutzpah*."

Three days later, Cahn called the Kammens to say he had written an English lyric and added, "I think I can get a record at Decca Records." He suggested that they sell the rights to Warner Bros. (Harms) to publish the English version, from whom they would collect a royalty. The Kammen twins agreed.

On November 30, 1937, just two months after acquiring the song from Secunda and Jacobs, J. & J. Kammen sold the American rights of "Bei Mir" to Harms, Inc. The record, recorded six days earlier, was released a couple of weeks later.

The Andrews Sisters were living in a small apartment on the West Side with their parents. The three young women slept in one bed, and their parents in another. On Christmas morning, 1937, their father woke them up, saying excitedly, "Get up and come down to Times Square—they're playing your record!" Patti, Maxene and LaVerne dressed quickly and, with their father, went to Broadway. Patti describes the scene:

"The crowds were lined up all over the street with police keeping them back and over this loud-speaker they were playing our song and hundreds of people kept shouting, 'Play it again!' and we were telling everybody, 'That's us!'"⁵

The song was, in the current argot of the record business, a "monster hit." In the first month, 75,000 copies of the record were sold, and by the end of January, 1938, a quarter of a million records, as well as 200,000 copies of the sheet music. It outsold "The Music Goes Round and Round," which until then had held the record for being the all-time biggest American hit record. Business was so good at the Gaiety Music Shop on Broadway that people crowded in front of the store's clerk, gave him 50 cents, and he handed them a rolled-up copy of the sheet music to "Bei Mir," all without exchanging a word.

People unfamiliar with Yiddish would ask for copies of "Buy a Beer, Mr. Shane," or "My Mere Bits of Shame." It won the ASCAP

(American Society of Composers, Authors and Publishers) award for most popular song of 1938. "Bei Mir" made its film debut in Warner Bros.' "Love, Honor and Behave," starring Priscilla Lane (who sang the song) and Wayne Morris. Nelson Eddy announced plans to perform the song in its original Yiddish at his concerts. Every major artist gave it a new treatment. Ella Fitzgerald's was "hot," the orchestras of Tommy Dorsey (who had changed his mind) and Jimmy Lunceford made it "swing." Over the years it was recorded by Ziggy Elman's Orchestra, the Crew Cuts, June Christy, the Milt Hirth Trio (with Willie "the Lion" Smith on piano), Arthur "the street singer" Tracy, Glen Gray and his Casa Loma Orchestra, Rudy Vallee, Judy Garland, Russ Morgan, Kate Smith, Keely Smith and Louis Prima, the Adrian Rollini Quintet (Bobby Hackett on trumpet, Buddy Rich on drums), Si Zentner, the Ramsey Lewis Trio, Steve Lawrence and Eydie Gorme—and Seymour and his Heartbeat Trumpet.

The best-known "swing" version was Benny Goodman's. On January 16, 1938, Goodman and his orchestra brought down the venerable roof of Carnegie Hall at the most famous "jam session"—as it was called—in the history of jazz. The highlight of the evening was "Bei Mir," as described in a United Press syndicated story:

> . . .At one point. . .the audience—which included scores of standees—almost took over the performance from Benny Goodman and his swinging orchestra. During the playing of Sholom Secunda's "Bei Mir Bist Du Schön," the audience burst into rhythmic shouts and handclaps, which momentarily produced more decibels than the instruments on the stage. The orchestra met the challenge, however, with a tremendous fanfare that made the clappers give up.

Even Leo Forbstein, the Warner Bros.' music director who had turned down the song in Hollywood, performed the song with his orchestra.

The song was translated into dozens of foreign languages, including Japanese. During World War II, it was a favorite of Hitler's Nazis, until it was discovered that its composer and lyricists were Jewish, after which it was banned in Germany. Inmates of Nazi concentration camps in the war years learned and loved the song, in spite of its official disfavor.

The Russians made it into an anti-Germany propaganda song during the war, calling it "Baron von der Shpik." It was recorded by the State Jazz Orchestra of the U.S.S.R., featuring Leonid Utesov as lead singer. O. Kandat and Fidrovsky were credited with authorship. The lyrics told of the disgraceful cowardliness of a titled German soldier.

The song was even fodder for a 1938 political cartoon which showed Adolf Hitler on one knee singing "Bei Mir Bist Du Schön" to a coy diplomat identified, in letters across his portly belly, as "(The) Hague."

Why does a song become a hit? In 1938, certainly, it was not force-fed to the American public through a glut of media advertisements. The song was a hit because of its merits: the tempo was "up," perfect for fox trot or jitterbug. Its singable melody, requiring a range of less than an octave, was set in a bittersweet, minor key, reflecting the mood of a world on the cusp of crushing economic depression and World War.

In 1938 the New York World's Fair of the following year was in the works, which would cost $150,000,000, despite depression (as had the World's Fairs of Philadelphia 1876, Chicago 1893, St. Louis 1904 and Chicago 1933). The Fair, heralding "Building of Tomorrow," transformed a swampy, former city dump in Flushing Meadow, Long Island, nine miles from Times Square, into a surprisingly accurate set of shiny predictions.

Life under Hitler was being revealed in America for the first time in news footage brought out of Nazi Germany by the March of Time. The film, called "Inside Nazi Germany—1938" had been banned by the Chicago police board of censors on "the ground that it might offend a friendly nation," but the ban was lifted because of press protests.[6]

President Franklin D. Roosevelt, then in his second term, was being called a dictator because of his efforts to augment the power of the Executive branch of the Federal government. Former President Herbert Hoover told the Women's National Republican Club in California that "the world is in an emotional stew."[7] Americans were tired of being poor and frightened, and women's fashions reflected the need for glitter. A record amount of fake jewelry was being sold, and designers Chanel and Schiaparelli were showing "jewelry dresses'' in their collections, although they probably did not have rhinestones in mind.[8]

Internationalism was in the air. So a Yiddish title to a song containing Italian and German had a cosmopolitanism not reserved solely for the upper classes. ''Bei Mir'' had the universal appeal of a lovesong that ignored politics and poverty, very unlike Depression songs such as ''Brother, Can You Spare a Dime.''

But a song is only as good as its singers, and the Andrews Sisters' imprimatur was never topped. The energetic, young women sang with eagerness, optimism and perfect vocal harmony. To a world full of dread and anticipation, it simply cheered people up.

''Bei Mir'' had an alchemic effect on the careers of its writers and original performers. The Andrews Sisters' weekly salary shot from nearly nothing to $500 overnight. They were engaged in early 1938 for a job in Boston, and had not yet built a large repertoire of songs. It didn't matter. Every time they sang ''Bei Mir'' during that engagement, the audience screamed for more.

''All we did,'' Patti later said, ''was sing that song and we got $500 a week.''[9] Soon they were getting $650 weekly, and a year after the record was released, they received a royalty of 5 cents per record sold (among recording artists, they were the second to receive record royalties—the first was Bing Crosby). They went on to record other hits—''Three Little Fishes,'' ''Rum and Coca-Cola,'' ''Apple Blossom Time,'' and ''Beer Barrel Polka''—and to make a string of Hollywood films.

''It was 'Bei Mir' that really floated our careers,'' Maxene says, and the Andrews Sisters were always to be identified by that song. In 1974 Patti and Maxene starred in a Broadway musical, ''Over Here'' (LaVerne died of cancer in 1967), and as an encore at the end of the show, they would do fifteen minutes of their old songs. ''The minute Patti would start the first few notes of the verse to 'Bei Mir,''' Maxene says, ''the people would go crazy.''

Bobby Hackett, the legendary trumpet player, had been a little-known musician when he was hired to play backup for the Andrews Sisters' recording. After it was released, his salary jumped to $300 weekly.

Lou Levy, the Andrews Sisters' manager (later married to and divorced from Maxene), founded the Leeds Music Publishing Company which he later sold to MCA for $3,000,000.[10]

Although the song did not make the Sammy Cahn-Saul Chaplin team rich, Louis Sobol, in his column "The Voice of Broadway" in the *New York Evening Journal*, reported that "Chaplin's father, who is a dress operator, is unemployed because the dress establishments won't hire him on the theory that his son is a millionaire." Together and separately—they broke up as a writing team in 1941—they became success stories in the music business, richly deserved because of their enormous talents. Chaplin was the music coordinator for such films as "Singin' in the Rain," "The Sound of Music," "West Side Story," and "Seven Brides for Seven Brothers." Sammy Cahn wrote lyrics to giant hits such as "I've Heard That Song Before," "Guess I'll Hang My Tears Out to Dry," "Day by Day," "The Tender Trap," "Come Fly With Me," "High Hopes," and "My Kind of Town," many of them recorded by Frank Sinatra.

At the 1955 Academy Awards in Hollywood, both men collected Oscars—Chaplin for "Seven Brides" and Cahn for "Three Coins in the Fountain."

For Sholom Secunda, "Bei Mir" was a mixed blessing. He became an international celebrity as the press had a field day chronicling the million-dollar song that slipped through his fingers. *Life Magazine* devoted a full page to pictures and text about the history of the song.[11] Anecdotes about "Bei Mir" surfaced in the newspaper columns of Leonard Lyons and Ed Sullivan, as well as in headlines in the *Jewish Daily Forward*. In his column Walter Winchell rubbed it in by writing, "The current air sensation is a swing version of an old Yiddish chant named 'Bei Mir Bist Du Schön' which means 'By Me You're Pretty,' to most of the radio translators. . .The composer sold it for practically nothing, and now is biting his nails over his poor judgment."

Sholom was publicly good-natured about having sold the number one hit song of 1938 for a paltry $30, as evidenced by this article in the January 13, 1938 edition of the *New York Post*:

Mr. Secunda. . .isn't worried about his share of the profits. He's a gentle musical soul, free of greed and overweening ambition. He's glad he has a steady job, that he and Mrs. Secunda and their two boys have their health. Besides, he hasn't time to worry. He is too busy denying that he's dead. On an average of twice a week, acquaintances on Broadway and on Second Avenue (the Broadway of the East Side) put themselves in his place and spread the rumor that he has killed himself.

"Only the other day," he said, "a customer rushes into the Metro Music Store at 60 Second Avenue. They sell a lot of my songs there. The customer is all out of breath. 'Have you heard?' he asks Mrs. Lefkowitch, who runs the place. 'Sholom Secunda is dead. Jumped from the window.'
"'Omygawd!' screams Mrs. Lefkowitch. Right away she calls up my house. I wasn't home that day. I was uptown presiding at a meeting of the Jewish Composers' Society.

"As luck would have it, Mrs. Lefkowitch uses her brains. She doesn't ask my wife: 'Did Sholom jump from the window?'

"Like a smart woman, she asks; 'Is Sholom there?'

"My wife tells her no, I'm uptown presiding at the society.

"So Mrs. Lefkowitch calls up the society. I come to the phone. 'Are you there?' she says. 'Yes,' I say. 'How are you feeling?' she says. 'Fine,' I say. 'That's grand,' she says and hangs up.

"Then all of a sudden Mrs. Lefkowitch does NOT use her brains. She phones my wife and tells her the whole story. So I'm called again. My oldest boy: 'Papa, come home—Mama has fainted!'"

In a piece he wrote for the *New York Journal-American*, Sholom said, "I was a pretty poor businessman, that's all. . ."[12]
But privately he was despondent. On New Year's Eve, 1937, Betty and Sholom spent the evening alone with their two sons. Depressed over the endless reminders of his loss, they decided not to turn on the radio, which seemed constantly to be playing the Andrews Sisters' recording of "Bei Mir" on every station, not even to hear the stroke of midnight. They could not, however, shut out the noises from the revelers on the street below, who sang the song at the tops of their lungs. It was not, Betty recalls, a happy night.
Sholom's colleagues at Maurice Schwartz's Yiddish Art Theater teased him mercilessly. That "Bei Mir" was the first Yiddish song

ever to become an international hit only fueled their fun at his expense.* Schwartz, never a reticent man, did his share of second-guessing, but nevertheless he tried to help his musical director. Schwartz arranged for Sholom to meet Lou Ervin, agent for a number of famous Broadway and Hollywood stars. Ervin wrote to his powerful contacts in Hollywood on Sholom's behalf, but the response echoed that given Sholom in 1937: too Jewish.

Prodded by the publicity surrounding the Andrews Sisters, their manager Lou Levy, Sammy Cahn, Saul Chaplin and Harms executives, Sholom wrote letters to all of them offering to show them other songs—another "Bei Mir" perhaps—he had written. He did not receive a single reply. His public protestations to the contrary, he never got over the rejections. He wrote in his memoirs, "Before the song, no one had heard of them. None of them. How could they totally ignore me?"

Of all the mortifications of "Bei Mir," none wounded Sholom more than the recriminations of his mother, Anna Secunda. When the Andrews Sisters' recording became a hit, the newspapers reported, Anna fasted for a week in a synagogue, praying for the expiation of her sins. Why else, she told a reporter, would God have punished her by having a son commit so expensive—and public—an error? According to a United Press story, "'. . .it is your song,' Mrs. Anna Secunda said, over and over again to her son in Yiddish. 'What is a contract? You wrote it, and I know you wrote it, and my friends say to me, Sholom should have a million dollars soon for that song. And I want you to have a million dollars.'" Privately she complained to her son of daily visits from neighbors in Brooklyn who embarrassed her with questions about the soundness of Sholom's mind.

Sholom saw the humor in certain aspects of his celebrity. On March 16, 1938, he was, with Gloria Swanson, a guest on the Eddie Cantor "Texaco Hour." Deanna Durbin and Bobby Breen were regulars on the radio show. Breen claimed during the broadcast that Sholom had taught him "Bei Mir" when he was four years old, giving him the pretext to sing the song in its original Yiddish. Cantor, who had rejected the song the year before, sent Sholom a gold watch to com-

---

*Cahn and Chaplin tried to make "Joseph, Joseph" the second in 1938 by writing English lyrics to the Yiddish song "Yussele, Yussele," originally written by Nellie Casman and Samuel Steinberg. The English version, published by Harms, was a modest hit.

memorate the broadcast. The watch had this inscription: "To Sholom—a man with a soul."

On April 6, Sholom appeared with the Andrews Sisters on "The Wrigley Chewing Gum Hour" radio program on CBS in Chicago while he was on tour with "The Brothers Ashkenazi." During the broadcast, he was interviewed about his importunate sale of the song. The trio then introduced a new Secunda tune, "Dream of Me," as he conducted the orchestra. In addition to his fee for that appearance, the advertising agency handling the Wrigley account paid him for posing with the Andrews Sisters for Wrigley Gum advertisements. "How ironic," Sholom wrote in a letter to his wife, "that I am getting a lot more money for letting myself be photographed than I am for composing the song."

His celebrity generated more advertising revenue in New York. For an ad in the English-language newspapers, he was photographed and quoted for an endorsement of Buchman-Silberman kosher wines. In the Yiddish press he smilingly endorsed Swee Touch Nee Tea.

Another by-product of his fame was the genesis of his career as a lecturer. Various organizations in and around New York invited him to speak, for a modest fee, about the saga of "Bei Mir." At times these affable confrontations, which Sholom encouraged—any publicity was good publicity—made him wince. On one occasion, following a lecture in Philadelphia, Sholom was approached by a woman who had been in the audience.

"You know, Mr. Secunda," she said wryly, "I've earned more from your song than you have."

"How?" he replied.

"Well," she continued, "as soon as the record with the Andrews Sisters came out, I ran to a record store to buy a copy. There was a big crowd there and people were pushing each other until someone gave me a shove, and I fell down and broke my leg. I brought a claim against the owner of the store, and I settled with him for $100. So who made more? You or me?"

As it happens, Sholom was not entirely bereft of profits the Kammen brothers were earning from "Bei Mir." On December 3, 1937, they agreed to give Sholom 20% of their share of the roylaties they collected from Harms.

Jacobs complained to Sholom that he had received virtually nothing for his participation in the song. (According to copyright law, composer and lyricist own their song jointly and neither can sell his contribution alone. Sholom could not sell the melody to "Bei Mir" without Jacobs' permission, which the latter had in fact given at the time of the original sale to Kammen). On December 28, Kammen drew up a new agreement with Sholom, voiding that of December 3. The new contract stated that Kammen would give to Sholom 50% of the royalties received from Harms for recordings and 40% from publication and sale and all other uses. The agreement contained a clause that in the event of a lawsuit by Jacobs, any resulting payment to Jacobs would be made 60% by Kammen and 40% by Sholom.

Jacobs did sue Sholom, Kammen and Harms. According to the complaint, "during the month of September 1937, the defendants, except the defendant Harms, Inc., conspired together for the purpose of unlawfully depriving plaintiff of his interest in said musical composition so that the defendants may obtain plaintiff's interest in said musical composition for a nominal consideration, knowing very well that the said musical composition had a great monetary value and that plaintiff's interest therein was worth a large sum of money." Jacobs claimed that he had signed but not read the contract selling "Bei Mir" to Kammen, believing that the $30 was payment for authorizing Kammen to publish 1,000 copies of the Yiddish song. He had done so "reposing confidence and trust in the said defendant Secunda." Harms was a co-defendant because it published the English-language version of the song without, Jacobs alleged, his consent and in violation of his rights.

The case never went to court. On August 25, 1938, the co-defendants paid Jacobs a total of $850 as an out-of-court settlement, releasing them from any future indemnity. Throughout he received and would continue to receive half of whatever revenues the song earned in royalties for Sholom. In any case, Jacobs' confidence and trust in Sholom were apparently not shattered. They were to continue working together in the Yiddish theater for many years.

Although Sholom was, as a colleague put it, the "laughingstock of Tin Pan Alley," he could have reversed his losses. Sholom expected unquestioned loyalty from his friends. He gave no less of himself. That loyalty often eclipsed his professional judgment. It got squarely in the way of his legally earning a good chunk of the proceeds from "Bei Mir." The reason: he refused to join ASCAP, which collects fees for the radio, television and film performance of its members' music.

In 1941, Sholom was the president of the Society of Jewish Composers, which he had founded in 1932 with Alexander Olshanetsky, Joseph Rumshinsky and Harry Lubin. The Society, for a variety of technical reasons, was ineligible for membership in ASCAP, as were many performers and songwriters. In 1940, Broadcast Music, Inc. (BMI) was founded in competition with ASCAP, which had virtually monopolized the music business. Because its requirements for membership were less restrictive than ASCAP's, and because the fledgling organization was eager for members, the Jewish Society signed with BMI. BMI agreed to pay the Society $5,000 minimum annually, to be distributed among the Society's members, in return for taking over its collections. They were principally interested in the Society because of the popularity and financial potential of Sholom's songs. BMI's contract with the Society, renewable every three years, depended on Sholom's continuing participation. Although revenue for "Bei Mir" was not collected by BMI but by ASCAP (of which Harms Music was a member), others of Sholom's songs did produce an income for the Jewish Society: "Mein Yiddishe Meidele (My Jewish Girl)," "Zug Far Vus (Tell Me Why)," "Die Fehlst Mir (I Miss You)."

Sholom's dilemma was not simply a matter of disappointing members of the Jewish Society or of depriving them of BMI's collections, however small. It was a matter of morality. Yiddish music had been an integral part of his childhood; it had given him and his family a livelihood in America since their arrival from Russia in 1908. He had worked on Second Avenue as a chorus boy, conductor and composer. He had become the pride of his Russian immigrant family (as well as his countrymen on the Lower East Side)—and was able to help support it—because of his fidelity to Jewish life and culture. To allow the Jewish Society to go under represented to him the crassest kind of greed.

He was well aware of the consequences of not joining ASCAP: 50% of the performance royalties of "Bei Mir" (which the songwriters retain even if they sell the publishing rights but are unable to collect unless they belong to ASCAP or BMI), a fortune of money in 1941, would be lost. Betty, acutely aware of Sholom's professional disappointments, and aware also of how much her family could benefit from their increased income after years of Depression struggle, would not have tolerated his loyalty to the Society had she known of his alternative.

Sholom met with the general manager of ASCAP, who told him that he could join the organization, providing he resigned his Jewish Society (and BMI) affiliation. Sholom then called a meeting of the officers of the Society: Olshanetsky, Rumshinsky, Abraham Ellstein, Michel Gelbart, Pinchos Jassinowsky, and Henry Lefkowitch. Sholom told his coleagues of his dilemma.

Gelbart and Jassinowsky responded by citing principle, and wondered how Sholom could crush the Society he had helped to build. Olshanetsky said, "Everyone must think of himself. If I had to deal with this situation, I would join ASCAP in a minute." Ellstein (also an alumnus of Juilliard, and, among Yiddish composers, Sholom's closest friend) ever the diplomat, said, "The Society would suffer if Sholom left us. But we can't ask him to sacrifice his family because of us. I don't have the heart to say to him, 'Sholom, stay with us and lose so much money.'"

Rumshinsky remained silent through much of the debate. He had long been a rival of Sholom's in the Yiddish theater, and had made plain his dislike of having to share his position of prominence on Second Avenue with the younger composer. Rumshinsky also enjoyed a reputation for being the most unpleasant man in Yiddish theater.

At last Rumshinsky spoke. "Why are you begging him to stay?" he shouted. "Let him go! Besides 'Bei Mir Bist Du Schön,' he hasn't written anything in his life. If the Society has to depend on an eight-bar composer, it's in real trouble!"

Sholom left the emotional meeting filled with doubt. "In spite of Rumshinsky's vitriol," he wrote, "my conscience plagued me over dealing against my colleagues, who sorely needed my participation." Without informing his wife, he decided not to join ASCAP.

♌ YIDDISH ART THEATER

When Sholom returned from his trip to California in the summer of 1937, he was 43 years old and in a frame of mind that today would be diagnosed as a mid-life crisis. It was during this contemplative period, prior to taking up his duties as musical director for Maurice Schwartz's Yiddish Art Theater, that he made the most enduring and professionally catalytic friendship of his life, a relationship that would give him the imprimatur of serious composer that he had longed for.

Gene Secunda, Sholom's three-year-old son, liked playing under the piano more than anywhere else in the house. Sholom could spend hours at that piano composing while Gene hummed and hammered and generally made the playful noises of a little, curious boy.

One afternoon Sholom joined his son under the Mason-Hamlin grand piano, laughing and roughhousing. Betty walked into the room, peered under the piano, and said to Sholom, "Someone is here to see you." Sholom crawled out and stood to face a somber-looking young man. Without identifying himself, the visitor said, "I have a letter for you from Jan Peerce," which he handed to Sholom.

Peerce in 1937 was an internationally known tenor who was a regular headliner at the Radio City Music Hall (his Metropolitan Opera debut lay four years ahead). He had begun his career as a violinist, and had played with Alexander Olshanetsky in the Catskill Mountains. In addition, he was a cantor.

"I always wanted to learn from the experts," Peerce says, "and Sholom was an expert in cantorial music. I went to him to pick his brains—he was wonderful in *nusach* (cantillation)." Peerce had sung Sholom's theater songs long before they met, and the friendship that began with cantorial coaching lasted until Sholom's death.

Sholom opened the letter from his old friend:

My dear Sholom:

I am sending you this note with my brother-in-law, Reuben Tucker, who recently married my sister, Sarah. He is currently a salesman of linings in the garment center and also is a cantor in a synagogue in Passaic, New Jersey. He wants to become a professional singer. Since you are connected with WEVD, perhaps you could get him on "The Forward Hour" or some other program. He's really good. See what you can do for him—I would be very grateful.

With warmest regards,
Pinky

(Jan Peerce was known as "Pinky" before he started singing at Radio City Music Hall in the 1930s. Born Jacob Pincus Perelmuth, he had changed his name to Pinky Pearl when he played the Catskills as a dance band leader and singer. After he began performing classical tenor repertoire, Samuel L. "Roxy" Rothafel suggested he change it —again—to John Pierce. "I gave the spelling of that name a six-month life," Peerce said in his memoirs, explaining the devolvement of his name to Jan Peerce.)[1]

Listening to an unknown musician was torture for Sholom. He was constantly besieged by mothers who were convinced that their children were incipient Misha Elmans or Carusos. But he could hardly refuse Peerce's brother-in-law.

Sholom sat down at the piano and said, "What would you like to sing?"

"Dos Yiddishe Lied", Tucker said, handing him a copy of the song Sholom had written several years before. Sholom smiled at the flattery of the selection, and began the introduction. Under ordinary circumstances, Sholom would have listened to perhaps eight bars of singing, enough time to evaluate a voice. But Tucker's voice had such brilliance and control that Sholom accompanied him through the entire song. When he finished, he asked Tucker to sit down.

"It's been a long time since I've heard a voice like yours," Sholom said. "What are you doing with such an incredible instrument?"

Tucker said that he was studying with Paul Althause, a former tenor with the Metropolitan Opera and a highly regarded voice teacher. He added that he was working in the garment district to augment his synagogue salary in order to pay for music lessons.

"My advice to you," Sholom said, "is that on no account should you give up singing, because you possess a rare gift. I predict that you will have an extraordinary career in opera."

Sholom assured Ruby—as his friends called him—that he would get in touch with B. Charney Vladek at WEVD to arrange for Tucker to sing on the "Forward Hour." Tucker did not have any songs arranged for orchestra, so Sholom gave him one of his own songs, "Sand and Stars," with the orchestral parts.

"When you learn the song, come back again and I'll teach you how to sing an art song," Sholom said. He made good on his promise —Tucker was booked for the Sunday broadcast soon after their appointment—and he worked with Tucker on the song.

"After that," Sholom wrote, "he no longer needed my help. His future in the music world was soon assured. The friendship that began with music grew into a bond between our families."

Sholom looked forward to Maurice Schwartz's return from Europe in the fall of 1937 with mixed emotions. On the negative side, Sholom would not be given top billing, and he would not be writing musicals, only incidental music. Moreover, his income would be half of what he had been earning in the large Second Avenue theaters.

But to many people, Maurice Schwartz *was* the Yiddish theater, and when theater historians recall the great days of Yiddish theater, they write of him. Born in 1890 in the Russian Ukraine, Avrom Moishe Schwartz came to the United States in his early teens and began his theatrical career at the Delancy Street Dramatic Club. His first directorial work occurred at the Auditorium Theater in Cincinnati, where he graduated from minor roles to stage manager to director. David Kessler brought Schwartz to New York in 1912 from Philadelphia, where he had seen Schwartz at the behest of Esther Kaminska, in "Madame X." Six years later, Schwartz founded the Yiddish Art Theater in New York.[2]

Irving Howe writes of Schwartz:

Idealistic and crafty, imaginative and gross, pure in heart and a bruising "go-getter," Schwartz was simultaneously leading actor, stage director, play doctor, and manager. To keep his theater alive over so many years was itself a triumph of will: he exploited actors, pilfered ideas from gentile directors, courted financial backers, entangled creditors in promises, used every device of modern publicity to win the Yiddish (and American) public, wrote, adapted, and butchered plays. . .A man of Rabelaisian energies and appetites, Schwartz wanted to put everything into theater, loading his stage with the whole jumble of Yiddish cultural aspiration. He wanted to please the East Side intelligentsia while wooing the *alrightniks* from the outlying neighborhoods. . .But eclecticism. . .was in the very nature of the Yiddish theater. Ill-educated as he was, and therefore especially susceptible to the lures of alien culture, Schwartz understood in his bones that, finally, the kind of theater he wanted to create could flourish only if it were rooted in Yiddish culture, in its deep if narrow soil, in the native, the indigenous, even the provincial.[3]

Howe's assessment, written in 1976, was the long view, a hindsight appraisal when Yiddish theater had become nearly a relic of an era long gone. But in the 1920s and 1930s, Schwartz-watchers and the American press were downright rhapsodic about the man and his repertory theater. Dr. S.M. Melamed, in an article for the *World,* wrote in 1925:

The man who modernized and Americanized Yiddish theater, placing it on a sound basis from the point of view of technique and artistry, is Maurice Schwartz, founder of the Yiddish Art Theater. Maurice Schwartz is not only a powerful and able organizer. He first conceived and organized the ensemble in the Yiddish theater. . .Instead of Adler, Mogulesko, Thomashefsky and Kessler, there are today men like Maurice Schwartz. . .able and well trained artists not only interested in deriving a personal benefit from their work but also seriously concerned with the fate and the future of Yiddish theater. . .

Whitney Bolton wrote in the *Herald Tribune* in 1928:

. . .What has this Schwartz produced in his eleven years that makes him sufficiently impressive, apart from his direction, playwriting, and advanced stage designing? He was the first person to

produce "The Dybbuk" in America. . .nine years ago in the old
Madison Square Theater in Madison Square Garden. He produced
plays by Leonid Andreyev some years before the Theater Guild
bought and produced the same man's "He Who Gets Slapped."
. . .Schwartz is doing "Kiddush Hashem" in three acts and seven-
teen scenes on a revolving stage, the only successful and thought-
fully carpentered revolving stage in the United States. . .

Does everyone know that Ludwig Satz, Muni Weisenfreund and
Jacob Ben-Ami were student players in the Schwartz company before they came to impress Broadway theater-goers? Has it ever been
recorded that Schwartz utilizes sixty 1,000-watt spotlights, each in-
dividually moveable and dimmable, something mechanistically
not possible uptown? Do the theater records show that his theater
on Fourteenth Street holds 1,983 seats, not counting the last balcony, which is not used, and that it is therefore the largest repertory house in the world? Finally, do the astute theater people know
that Schwartz has eight productions for this season, each artistically
equal in scope and authorship to the exact same number by the
Theater Guild?

Sholom knew both sides of Maurice Schwartz—the commendable
and the crummy. The latter quality characterized the beginning of
their professional relationship.

When Schwartz returned from Europe, he summoned Sholom to
his house on 59th Street, near the Jolson Theater that housed the
Yiddish Art Theater for that season.

"I've saved you a lot of work," Schwartz said magnanimously, inviting Sholom into his sitting room. "I met a woman in Paris to
whom I spoke of my new production of 'The Brothers Ashkenazi.'
She became so excited about it that she volunteered to compose music
for it." Schwartz handed Sholom the woman's score, adding, "Don't
be disconsolate, Sholom. You will write enough music for the Yiddish Art Theater."

Although his ego was bruised, Sholom admired the woman's
work. The trouble was, it was too good. The music required for
Schwartz's plays was incidental, or background, music, designed to
enhance the action on stage. This woman's music distracted from the
action. Schwartz cornered Sholom during rehearsals of "Ashkenazi"

and said, "Some of the music will have to be cut and I want you to write new music." By the time the play opened, almost all of the original music had been replaced by Sholom's.

In his three years with Schwartz, Sholom wrote the music for "Salvation," "Three Cities," "If I Were Rothschild," "Esterke," "Sender Blank," "Street Singers," and "Who is Who?" These productions were not always well received by the press, but the critics made an effort to mete out criticism that would, at least, be constructive. Consider, for example, these reactions to "Salvation," which opened September 29, 1939, a two-act play with 18 scenes by Sholom Asch and music by Sholom Secunda:

. . .Most of the actors wear highly impressive beards. . .beards do have a way of making actors look curiously alike. I think it would be of considerable help to us outsiders if Mr. Schwartz would place numbers on his actors' backs. . ."Salvation" is considerably helped for the alien by excellent settings of Alex Chertov, the interesting musical accompaniment devised by Sholom Secunda and the picturesque folk dances. . .Its acting, too, is effective in the florid manner of the Yiddish stage. . .It is my grave suspicion that "Salvation," despite its picturesque background of Poland of Napoleonic War days, will not have the great interest for outside audiences that many of Mr. Schwartz's early productions possessed. . .I found its rather studious mysticism curiously aimless and undramatic and completely lacking in the theatrical effectiveness of ("The Brothers Ashkenazi").
  —Richard Watts, *New York Herald Tribune*.

The audience which greeted. . ."Salvation". . .was. . .enthusiastic. I mean, of course, the more fortunate members of that audience who had some mastery of Yiddish. The rest of us, the ones who had spent the day reading and re-reading the English synopsis and who even then could not follow it with any surety, were not so happy. . .We were able to respond to the eerie quality of Mr. Secunda's musical accompaniment. . .We could. . .realize the sincerity of the performance. . .Yet the truth is we could not pretend to do justice to Mr. Schwartz or to Mr. Asch. . .We (the compact minority, mind you) might as well have been Martians seeing a talkie for which H.G.Wells had forgotten to write explanatory captions. . .I do wish Mr. Schwartz would consider having one press preview. . .in English. . .What he has done in "Salvation". . . .is much too much to be dismissed lightly by someone who does not speak Yiddish. . .

—John Mason Brown, *The New York Post.*

These criticisms, although ascribed to only one production, were the tip of the iceberg of Yiddish theater trouble. By 1939, the children of its *patriots* were too young to be nostalgic about their roots but old enough to call themselves Americans rather than Europeans. Maurice Schwartz, in an interview for *Theater Guild Magazine,* had predicted his own theatrical doom in 1930: "The Yiddish Art Theater," he said, ". . .has served only as a sort of night school for the better Jewish audiences. As soon as they learn sufficient English, they graduate to Miss Le Gallienne's Repertory Theater, where they avidly absorb the culture of the dominant language."

If not in music and equal billing, Sholom found in Maurice Schwartz a kindred spirit in the pursuit of feasible excellence. Sholom later treasured his seasons with Schwartz because he knew he had been associated with the best that Yiddish theater had to offer.

Sholom was also associated with Schwartz in the making of several Yiddish films. The Yiddish film industry had a brief life—from 1931 to 1941—during which about 100 films were made, but less than half of which survive (thanks to the Rutenberg and Everett Yiddish Film Library of the American Jewish Historical Society at Brandeis University, and the American Film Institute and the Library of Congress). Schwartz, who had spent eight months under contract in Hollywood and who appeared in only one English-language film, starred in many Yiddish films, as did many great Second Avenue stars. The films were shot on a shoestring—with a budget of around $3,000 (Hollywood was spending an average of $500,000)—and in a scant five days. Most of them had plots of the most melodramatic (and overacted) soap opera.[4]

A handful were powerful stuff. Maurice Schwartz's portrayal of "Tevye," considered by some to be the greatest Tevye of them all, was filmed in 1939. Sholom Secunda wrote the score for the film. (Years later, Zero Mostel, who played Tevye on Broadway in "Fiddler on the Roof," said to Sholom's son Sheldon, "Your old man should have done the music for the show." Indeed, Sholom—who felt that "Fiddler's" score was more Russian than Jewish—thought so too.) Any "outsider" who has seen the film is astonished at the forceful performance by Schwartz and, in fact, films like "Tevye" are perhaps the only proof extant of the superb abilities of the best actors on Second Avenue

In Schwartz, too, Sholom found a mischievous playmate. Sholom loved to play tricks on actors, and that bent revealed a streak of cruelty that, at times, strained the patience of even his closest friends and associates.

"Many times I'd say to him that I expected a call from Bellevue Hospital because somebody had beaten the hell out of him," Betty Secunda recalls. "He'd say to one actor that another actor said this about you, then go back to the other actor and say the first one said this about you, and the two actors would want to kill each other. Another time, there was a star in the theater, Kurt Katch, who talked about some day going into the movies. Sholom sent a letter to a crony of his in Hollywood, asking the Hollywood friend to post a letter back to Katch telling him he was being considered for a starring role in a film. Of course, Sholom had written the letter. Katch got the letter and showed it to everyone. And Sholom and Maurice Schwartz, who was in on the prank, stood off in a corner and laughed."

Miriam Kressyn, who by this time was a member of Schwartz's troupe, remembers "an actor whom Sholom disliked intensely. So he got another actor to jab the man with his elbow every time he delivered a line during a performance. The audience laughed, of course, and the actor never knew it was Sholom who engineered the jabs. But Schwartz was the greatest degrader who ever came into a theater. There was a young performer who had a peculiar speaking voice, and Schwartz would say to him, 'What kind of language is that? How can you speak like that?' And he would always punch the boy. People laughed at it. I thought it was dreadful. It was like slapping a clown."

"Sholom was also the fall guy for any practical joke," Dinah Goldberg says. "One summer we were staying near Sholom's bungalow at Loch Sheldrake. One day my husband, Irving Grossman, and Hymie Jacobson went over to visit, but Betty and Sholom were out. So they walked into the house and rearranged all the furniture—they put the bedroom furniture into the living room, and the living room furniture into the kitchen—and left without leaving a note. When Sholom returned, he surveyed the redecoration and said to Betty, 'It looks like Irving and Hymie were here.'''

Sholom's occasionally heavy-handed humor was offset by his loyalty to friends that went beyond the ordinary gesture of affection. In 1939 Schwartz persuaded the Polish Yidishe Bande to appear at his theater in New York. The troupe performed musical revues of political satire and folklore. In the company were a young, attractive and gifted couple, Lily Liliana and Leon Liebgold. The Yidishe Bande arrived on the *Ile de France* on February 22, the same night that Sholom was to be given a testimonial dinner commemorating his 25 years in the Yiddish theater, in the ballroom of the Central Plaza on Second Avenue.

Schwartz, who was touring Europe with "The Brothers Ashkenazi," had seen the troupe and engaged them through impresario Sol Hurok. The company of nine actors was invited to attend Sholom's dinner.

"Everyone was there," Liebgold says, "Rumshinsky, Olshanetsky, Ellstein, Molly Picon—about 700 people. It was a wonderful opportunity for us to meet them all. We understood their conversation because everyone spoke Yiddish. I was 25 at the time, and I was astonished that Sholom was so young—45. To me he was some sort of giant, and I thought he would be very, very old."

Under Sholom's musical direction, the Yidishe Bande put on Sholom Aleichem's "200,000," which ran in New York for eight weeks, and then toured the provinces. "By then we were very close friends," Liebgold says, "and on the road I was practically his valet. As competent as he was in the theater, he was a lost soul without Betty, and I promised her I'd take care of him."

The Bande toured Milwaukee, Detroit, Chicago, Cleveland, Philadelphia and Canada. When it returned to New York, several members of the company appeared in "Tevye," Schwartz's film, including the Liebgolds. At the end of three months, when their contract expired, half the troupe returned to Poland. At Sholom's insistence, the Liebgolds remained in New York to do some sightseeing.

The Liebgolds and others had had their troubles in Poland. Most Jews were not permitted to go to Polish schools, so Yiddish culture and literature and theater filled in the intellectual gaps. Though Polish anti-Semitism was rampant, no one anticipated, in early 1939,

Hitler's invading Poland (which, in fact, his troops did on September 1, precipitating World War II).

"Lily wanted to go back because she missed her mother and sisters," Liebgold says, "but Sholom persuaded her to stay." The Liebgolds went to the pier to say goodby to their friends in the Yidishe Bande. With the exception of one person, it was the last time they ever saw them. By the time the ship had returned them to their homeland, Hitler had invaded Poland—theirs was the last boat under Polish flag to sail from the United States.

One actor, fearing the Nazis, hanged himself. The others were sent to concentration camps. Lily lost her entire family, as did her husband (with the exception of one brother, who managed to escape from a concentration camp).

"When the war broke out," Liebgold says, "we didn't have anywhere to go. At that time it was impossible for Polish citizens to obtain permanent stay in the United States because of the quota of the Immigration Service. But because of the war, the government allowed us to stay temporarily, provided we obtain a sponsor and put up a bond of $2,500 each—that meant $5,000. If we disappeared, we would be subject to prosecution and we would forfeit the money. Of course, we didn't have that kind of money."

Sholom had a life insurance policy in the amount of $5,000, which he cashed in. He gave the money to the Liebgolds, and they were able to stay in the United States.

When the United States entered the war, Liebgold joined the Army and worked in counter-intelligence behind enemy lines in Germany. Within 90 days of his release from the Army, he became an American citizen. Lily attained citizenship in 1943. After they became U.S. citizens, the Treasury Department returned their bond, and the Liebgolds were able to repay Sholom. Sholom does not mention the life-saving loan in his memoirs.

In the fall of 1939, Maurice Schwartz was forced by heart trouble to take a sabbatical. Leon Fuchs was engaged to take Schwartz's role in "If I Were Rothschild," and Schwartz went to Florida to recuperate. The comedy was not a success. As the critic for *Variety* wrote, ". . .Illness forced out the star during the rehearsal period, but it's questionable as to whether his performance would be sufficient to give the play greater verve."

"Schwartz's health improved," Sholom wrote, "but not the condition of the Art Theater, which was beginning its long decline. Though Maurice Schwartz continued with his activities and produced a number of plays, each year in a different New York theater, the essence of the Art Theater grew weaker with each season."

The Yiddish Art Theater was not alone in its box office doldrums. All along Second Avenue, theaters were in trouble. Contributing factors included not only the increasing seediness of the Yiddish theater district, but also a World War that was draining the United States of revenues and manpower, two essential commodities to a theater in search of an audience. The audience that wasn't eaten up by the draft or assimilation spent its money at the movies, where the evils of Hitler outdrew the threat of the *goyim** as an entertaining issue.

In 1940 Schwartz teamed up with William Rolland. It was a mutually satisfying partnership. Rolland had always longed to produce artistic theater, and Schwartz needed a home for his troupe without the headaches and pressure of management and overhead. They took over the Public Theater where Schwartz continued as director and star, and Rolland served as general manager.

The Rolland-Schwartz combination mounted, among other productions, "Esterke," with a company that included the cream of Yiddish theater: Schwartz, Samuel Goldenburg, Misha and Lucy Gehrman, Lazar Fried, Anna Appel and Abraham Teitelbaum. Sholom wrote a particularly lyrical score for "Esterke," including a song called "Dona, Dona, Dona." The song would surface 25 years later and become an English-language folk standard.

That season Sholom also wrote the score for "Mazel Tov Rabbi," starring Menashe Skulnik, at the McKinley Square Theater in the Bronx.

During the summer months of the years 1940 to 1945, Sholom was director of entertainment at Workman's Circle Camp in Hopewell Junction, New York (sharing the premises was *Kinder Ring,* the Workman's Circle children's camp, but Sholom's activities were confined primarily to the adults).

The Camp was a division of The Workman's Circle, a socialist organization founded in 1892 whose aim was the education of its members in philosophy, science, literature and social reform. It

*Non-Jews

operated as a fraternal organization by providing sick care and burial services.[5] As a haven for immigrant Jewish workers, it transmitted secular Jewish ideas and labor ideals. At its height in the 1930s, it had nearly 80,000 members. Workman's Circle Camp provided rural ease in a socialist and cultural atmosphere.

Sholom repeated many of the duties he had performed at Unzer Camp, but on a bigger scale. He was given a large enough budget to pay for a band and a variety of Jewish actors, singers, dancers and instrumentalists. He provided a broad spectrum of entertainment, from comedy sketches in Yiddish to excerpts from grand opera. As he had at Unzer Camp, he gave lectures every Sunday night about Jewish music, or about the structure of the orchestra, using his musicians to illustrate his points (a precursor to Leonard Bernstein's Young People's Concerts). He acquainted his audiences with the music of Verdi, Beethoven, Mozart, Mendelssohn. He gave talks explaining the differences between an art song, a popular song and a folk song. All these talks provided fodder for his appearances later on the lecture circuit.

Sholom's lectures at Workman's Circle Camp were always in English. By the mid-1940s the younger members of the Camp had formed an English-speaking division. They were growing in numbers and began to clamor for more entertainment in English. To placate them, Sholom supplemented his staff with a visiting troupe of English-speaking actors, but it wasn't enough.

By 1945 his differences with the English-speaking division had become irreconcilable, so he spent that summer traveling with Betty and Gene, and the Camp hired a completely new social staff.

Apparently Sholom's *patriots* still had some clout, for he was rehired by Workman's Circle Camp for the summers of 1946 and 1947, before switching his allegiance, in 1948, back to Unzer Camp, where Yiddish culture was still predominant.

Unzer Camp was less realistic in its purism about Yiddish customs and culture, and eventually, because of a dearth of patrons, it went out of business. Workman's Circle Camp, on the other hand, due to its acceptance of assimilation, is as of this writing still in business, still stressing Jewish culture and heritage, but spanning the interests of the grandchildren of its early adherents.

Sholom could see the English handwriting on the wall. His mother-in-law, Katie Almer, would say it best to her grandchildren.

When one of them bought a new bike or car or boat, Katie would nod knowingly and say, "*Your* America." America of the 1940s for Jews bore scant resemblance to the nation of immigrants two, three and four generations earlier.

Sholom's America was transitional. He would be the last of the great Yiddish theater composers and one of the first to acknowledge that Yiddish theater had begun to outlive its *patriots*. It was for him an uneasy awareness.

♫ FAMILY LIFE

In 1938 Sholom, Betty, Shelly and Eugene moved to 590 Fort Washington Avenue in upper Manhattan between 186th and 187th Streets, an area known as Washington Heights. The neighborhood of their Avenue A apartment was no longer a suitable milieu for two young boys—Shelly was nine, Gene was four. Around the corner street gangs congregated, and tenements in the area grew more dilapidated. Washington Heights, where the Secundas would live for 36 years until Sholom's death, provided a solid, Jewish middle class atmosphere and education for the boys. Over the years residents would boast of the famous men and women who lived in the neighborhood: Henry Kissinger, Neil Simon, Abbe Lane, Don Kirschner—and Sholom Secunda.

After the grimness of Avenue A, Fort Washington Avenue looked like a Paris boulevard. It was lined with stately American elm trees, one of which seemed to be growing into the boys' bedroom window, from which at night they could observe the aircraft warning light rotating atop the George Washington Bridge.

Most of Sholom's theater friends had never been north of 14th Street and were, on their visits, impressed by the area. Each apartment house was surrounded by trees stretching up from undeveloped lots. Unlike most city boys, Shelly and Gene spent much of their youths climbing trees and playing in caves. The Secundas' building was built on a steep hill which plunged on one side down to Bennett Avenue. The caves were reached by clambering down a wooden staircase—later rebuilt with stone—that led from Ft. Washington Avenue down to Bennett.

When friends and relatives came to visit, Sholom delighted in taking them on the "Grand *Shpatsir* (stroll)" up Fort Washington

Avenue to nearby Fort Tryon Park, 66 acres of trees and meadows that seemed, to Lower East Siders, exotic indeed.

The Secunda apartment had three bedrooms—one for the boys, one for Betty and Sholom, and one which was converted to a music room housing Sholom's grand piano, music library, and a convertible couch (which was by night the bed for Savannah, their housekeeper). The living room and small kitchen rounded out what was, if not spacious, at least a comfortable, compact home.

As parents, Sholom and Betty were unequaled in their belief that their sons were without peer. When the boys were small, Betty, in an effort to squeeze one more mouthful of nutrition into unwilling mouths, would leap around the kitchen and make faces. Sholom, trying to entertain his sons into open-mouthed (and therefore feedable) awe, would tell stories about how he had in the Navy singlehandedly sunk a German submarine while stranded in a rowboat on the high seas (only later did he confess that he spent his entire Navy stint on Ellis Island).

Discipline in the Secunda home was—except when it came to music—in short supply. If Shelly was late with a report for school, Betty would write a note saying that he had been sick. If the boys requested a new, expensive toy, Sholom would provide it. Any accomplishment, however small, was greeted with huzzahs.

Gene and Shelly were, in a word, spoiled. But Sholom, in the very human tradition of generational turnabout, wanted to lavish the attention on his children that he, due to the sheer numbers of his siblings, had been denied in his childhood. It is doubtful that he consciously considered the effect of his fame in the Yiddish world as the cause of his overly indulging his sons. (He was not a believer in psychiatry. "See a psychiatrist?" he would ask rhetorically. "You gotta be crazy.") Rather, his spoiling of them is traceable to his need to be loved. All the time. What easier route with one's children than to deny them nothing?

Gene and Shelly were, to be sure, proud of the fact that their father was a celebrity among their friends and neighbors. Still, Shelly recalls the embarrassment of being asked in the eighth grade where his father's office was. Sholom's "office" was either the music room of their apartment on Fort Washington Avenue or the theater at which he was signed for a given season. But "office" in the sense of corporation did not apply and Shelly was humiliated to have to report that his father had none. By the time Gene was an adolescent, he felt the same chagrin:

> I had this "thing" where I wanted him to be like everybody else's father in the neighborhood. And I didn't know at that time what a difficult economic period it was for him because he was trying to make the transition out of Yiddish theater into other areas of endeavor. So there were times when he just wasn't working. Obviously, where the hell is he going to be but at home? He would be scoring or composing, but he'd be doing it at home.

The beneficial side of Sholom's nonconformist work life was that he was on deck for ballgames and school concerts or whatever daytime school function of his sons that did not conflict with rehearsals or matinees in the theater. He took Shelly to his first professional baseball game at Ebbetts Field and, although he had no real interest in sports, he became, because of his son, an ardent Giants fan.

Nevertheless Gene and Shelly were not altogether spared the second-banana aspect of having a famous father, which Shelly's Bar Mitzvah epitomized.

The ceremony was held in January of 1942, a month after Pearl Harbor. Out of deference to Abraham and Anna Secunda (Orthodox Jews are forbidden to drive or be driven on the Sabbath), Betty and Sholom chose a synagogue within walking distance of their Penn Street, Brooklyn, home—the Talmud Torah Pride of Israel Anshe Brisk d'Litah, better known as the Keap Street Synagogue. One month before the event, a huge, hand-lettered sign was erected over the entrance to the synagogue with the following message:

COMING, IN JANUARY
CANTOR MOISHE OYSHER
WILL OFFICIATE AT THE BAR MITZVAH OF THE SON OF
SHOLOM SECUNDA,
Sheldon Secunda

"The sign marked my earliest awareness that I was the son of a famous man," Shelly says. "My father never made me consciously aware of it. He was always affectionate and supportive—perhaps too much so. It would take me a long time to discover that not everyone in the world adored me.''

Sholom was a sucker for the latest gimmickry of American technology. A born consumer, in the late 1930s he had purchased a Wilcox-Gay home disc recorder, which occupied a large portion of his living room. Shelly's rehearsal of his "Today, I am a man" speech was memorialized on a steel disc.

Following the Bar Mitzvah ceremony, a reception was held in the synagogue's basement, catered by Uncle Jack who had made hundreds of sandwiches which disappeared into shopping bags that miraculously appeared in the hands of the guests, many of them uninvited members of the congregation. Shelly collected numerous fountain pens to commemorate his coming of Jewish age, but he remembers the pickings as being lean. ("My brother," Shelly says, "had the good sense to become a man five years later, in a period of post-Depression and post-War affluence.")

Sholom, although he observed religious holidays and traditions, was not a particularly religious man. It was his father, Abraham, who taught Shelly how to use the *t'filin* (philacteries), the very ones he had used as a child, which he gave to Shelly as a Bar Mitzvah gift.

The family seldom went to synagogue services, save for those during which Sholom later conducted at the Concord Hotel when he became musical director there. The cuisine at home was not kosher, although Betty was unable to eat pork because as a child she had once surreptitiously consumed some bacon and had immediately thrown it up. "Probably guilt," she explained.

Nevertheless the boys were aware of having a special ethnic identity, and of the often anguished history of Jewry. When Shelly was in the Army, Sholom encouraged him to attend High Holy Days services. In a letter to Shelly he wrote, "I am concerned with the traditional effect of any holiday. I feel it is important as a Jew to observe the High Holidays, not necessarily because of their religious value, but because of their spiritual influence. Pray your own way—that carries more weight with me than all the prayers some people read and do not understand. Such prayers to me are meaningless."

Sholom at 49 was still a dutiful son. Frequently he, Betty and the boys went to dinner at his parents' Brooklyn house. He called every day on the phone, and Betty visited often. Every religious holiday was observed with Anna and Abraham until their advanced age made it impossible for them to host large family gatherings.

The *Pesach* seder in the spring of 1941 was held at the home of Sholom's older brother Meyer and his wife Frieda. Abraham sat at the head of the table, conducting the service as always. He complained of not feeling well, which was the first time in family memory that Abraham complained of any sort of discomfiting symptom. That night he awakened Anna with his moans, and a doctor was summoned. Abraham was rushed to the Israel-Zion (now Maimonides) Hospital where it was diagnosed that he had had a heart attack.

Abraham, although he was 81, still manufactured and sold beds. After his heart attack, the doctor forbade his working. Abraham obeyed his doctor's orders, saying that it was better for him to be on hand to help take care of Anna, herself in fragile health. But Abraham's condition deteriorated to the degree that the family felt he could only receive proper care in a nursing home. There he died, on June 28, 1943.

Sholom received the news at Workman's Circle Camp. His friend Leon Liebgold drove him and Betty to New York and, after the funeral the next day, back to Camp.

Anna was not told of her husband's death. She was bedridden and, now 83, had lost many of her faculties. Still she wanted to see her husband and her children's excuses as to why she could not finally made her suspicious. In the fall all her children gathered together and told her that Abraham was dead. Upon hearing the news, she fainted, and was taken to a nearby hospital.

On October 7 Sholom was rehearsing a new production on Second Avenue. During a break, he was called to the telephone. Betty, sobbing, told Sholom that his mother had died—four months after his father's death. His parents had been born the same year, and they died the same year.

Sholom returned to the orchestra pit and continued the rehearsal. The funeral could not be held the next day because it was the eve of Yom Kippur. That night and the following day, Sholom conducted services at the East Midwood Jewish Center in Brooklyn. Only the Rabbi knew of Sholom's loss.

On Sunday morning Sholom attended his mother's funeral. He drove from the cemetery to the Second Avenue Theater to conduct the afternoon and evening performances of his new operetta.

"I sat on my chair between musical numbers," Sholom wrote.

"The audience burst into laughter at Menashe Skulnik on the stage, and I thought of the incongruity of a fresh grave for my mother and the songs and dances before me. But I couldn't weep. I felt as though I had turned to stone." That evening at home, when he returned from the theater, he fell apart.

"He was a totally broken man," Shelly says. "He was reduced to terrifying sobs. I had never seen him like that before, and never did again." For weeks Sholom was unable to accept the fact that both his parents were dead, and he would drive past the house where they had lived for nearly 30 years.

As so often happens, their deaths were oddly liberating. From then on Sholom turned his professional efforts more and more to liturgical composition and symphonic pieces. His powerful capacity for concentration and work kept him functioning through his grief.

At home Sholom was a blithe spirit with his sons. "He had an extremely high threshold for public embarrassment," Gene recalls. Unlike their father, Gene and Shelly were as embarrassable as any image-conscious kid has a right to be.

"He would do anything on a dare," Gene says. "One day, when I was around 15 years old, we were walking down Broadway and I said, 'I dare you to start skipping.' And off he went, skipping, wildly humming to himself and swinging his arms, oblivious to the people staring at him. Buddy Hackett, the comedian, was walking toward us—Sholom knew Hackett and was his biggest fan—and he started doing one of those crazy dances in front of Sholom. And the two of them were breaking up each other while I was cringing in a doorway, mortified by the whole scene."

Sholom, from his first trip to California in 1929, had been wildly in love with the United States, and for a week or two each summer, he would pack his family into the current car and make a trip north or south or, in 1949, due west.

"We visited Boulder Dam," Shelly says, "and we got into an elevator to go down to the bottom of the Dam. The elevator was jammed with midwestern, all-American types. My father had a jibberish language he used to use on all the children in the family—he'd tell us it was Turkish. I was 19 years old, had pimples and a crew cut and was terribly awkward. There, backed against the wall of the elevator, Sholom managed to get a hand free. He reached up, grabbed my cheek, and at the top of his lungs started yelling this made-up language at me. Every head in the elevator turned to see this chubby little man clutching at my cheek and babbling at me. I wanted to die. Every time we were in an elevator, anywhere, he'd do that. It didn't bother him at all.''

On their way home from that particular trip, his sons got their revenge. During a stopover in Chicago, they discovered that Sholom had an atavistic fear of being tickled. ''When I learned that,'' Gene says, ''all my sadistic impulses came out. I chased him down a long hotel corridor, Sholom backing away from me holding his hands up in front of him, saying, 'Now son. Now son. Let's discuss this.' And I kept coming at him. Finally he was backed up against a wall and he fell onto the floor in a fetal position, exposing as little of his body as possible. I tickled him mercilessly, getting even with him for all those years of embarrassment. From then on, whenever he would start pinching our cheeks in public and begin talking 'Turkish,' I would threaten to tickle him and he'd stop.''

Sholom had a single-mindedness that was awesome. He would utilize time spent on the subway from Washington Heights to lower Manhattan to get work done. He would pull out blank sheet music from his briefcase, balance a small bottle of ink and the music on the briefcase, and do his orchestrations en route to the theater, unmindful of the curious passengers and the careening subway car.

His single-mindedness rendered him totally unaware of his attire. Betty had to lay out his clothes every morning to make sure that there would be some uniformity of color. Once she was not at home to do so before he left the apartment to give a lecture. When he got home that night, he was wearing a navy blue jacket, brown pants and green socks. On another occasion he wore two left shoes—one brown, one black—and was ignorant of the gaffe until Betty pointed it out.

''My father's sensitivities did not extend to his feet,'' Shelly says.

Sholom's ability to tune out trivia was the source of giggles on the part of his family and friends, but it was also the key to his character. That he was able to work in the midst of noise or crowds or pain has been demonstrated. His talent for compartmentalizing also describes the way in which his private life functioned.

Sholom divided people into two categories: family and all the rest. For family, he would go out in the middle of the night putting out domestic fires (one niece threatened to marry a non-Jew and he was summoned to talk her out of it, which he did), answering distress signals, lending money which was seldom repaid. Friends were kept at an affectionate distance and few were allowed intimacy. Once a friend had been tested and accepted, he or she saw the tender or silly side of him. Those intimates all thought themselves to be his best friend.

Within the family Sholom set the tone and the rules. He was the breadwinner and cheerleader. Betty was the bill-payer and reluctant disciplinarian. "Women were categorized by Sholom," Gene says. "The actresses and performers were not what he considered to be the models of a Jewish woman. Betty was. She was his idea of what a woman is supposed to be: beautiful, smart, homely skills. I think it was an enormous frustration for her, and we'll never know what she might have done had Betty Friedan been around fifty years ago.

"I don't ever remember having had a serious conversation with my mother until my father died," Gene continues. "If you were in a room with Betty and Sholom, you didn't talk to Betty. The main thrust of any conversation was always with Sholom. He had a charismatic quality that overpowered people who were less assertive."

Nevertheless Betty made her presence felt within the family, and especially in private with her husband. She and Sholom developed a jesting repartee along the lines of a Henny Youngman "Take my wife" routine, wherein Sholom was cast as the browbeaten husband and Betty the loudmouthed Yenta. These exchanges made for hilarious copy in Sholom's letters to his sons, as this one, written to Shelly in 1954, illustrates:

> Last night we went to a party at the Jan Peerces' in New Rochelle in honor of Jan's father's 80th birthday. Yesterday morning, after I returned from conducting services at the (Brooklyn Jewish) Center, I walked into the "Gotenyu"* mother's bedroom only to find her in front of the mirror completely dressed in her evening apparel.
>
> "Where are you going?" I asked nonchalantly.
>
> "What do you mean!" she jumped on me quickly. "Aren't we supposed to go to a party tonight at the Peerces!?"

---

*An exclamation of affection or irony, informally invoking God's ear

"Sure," I said, a bit frightened, as I usually become when I see your mother looking directly at me. "But," I added, "I thought the party was tonight, not this morning."

"What's the matter with you, JERK!" she said, "do you think I will go to a party without rehearsing my clothers first?" Well. I went back to the kitchen. I made myself lunch. I ate, washed the dishes, I wrote a review of the Marian Anderson debut at the Met, I returned to the room where I had left her. When I walked into the room again, I found your mother still in front of the mirror, fully made-up, her face, her lips, her eyes, her hair-do in place.

I then took a two-hour nap and when I got up, she was getting ready to dismantle herself, after exposing herself to all conditions of various lightings. I asked her why she was taking her clothes off again, since by now so much time had passed that we would be leaving in an hour anyway.

"Go back to sleep, dope," she said. "You wouldn't understand. A woman must see what she will look like before she goes to a party. I have to hang up my dress so the wrinkles fall out first."

I nodded approvingly, having no alternative, and added under my breath, "I shall go without a dress rehearsal."

She began to change into a robe and then joined me in the kitchen. I looked at the clock and said, "Bet, I think you better get dressed. She looked at the clock, hit me, and, while running back to the bedroom, shouted, "Now, on account of you, I'll never make it!"

She got dressed again. Of course, I waited for her in the car downstairs in the bitter cold for half an hour, but she appeared, finally, with a few unfinished businesses in her hands. She entered the car with this warning: "Better drive slowly and put the light on—I have to finish getting dressed." Forty-five minutes later, when we arrived at the Peerce mansion, your mother crept into the back of the car, ordering me not to turn around. Believe it or not, within less than an hour, she announced, "I am ready. Let's go in."

Betty, an earthy and funny woman, was a willing audience for slightly off-color humor, but Sholom would blush. He was offended by blue language, and had a tendency toward priggishness. Betty was discouraged by Sholom from wearing makeup or revealing dresses.

The only time his sons ever saw Sholom visibly pained was when they fought with each other. Routine sibling rivalry was torment for Sholom to witness. If Gene or Shelly called each other "stupid" or tried to demean one another, Sholom would say, "Don't do that. Some day you'll only have each other." He would not tolerate any form of disloyalty between them. It grieved him when his sons would disagree with him as well, and so he would leave to Betty the chore of making them practice the piano or do their homework. Occasionally Sholom would be forced into disciplining them on some matter, and he would make his reprimand as brief as possible, in a manner that would leave his sons sputtering with rage.

"Sholom had a way of ending a conversation," Gene says. "He would say, 'You're wrong. Now forget it,' and walk away. It drove us crazy."

There were times when Sholom and Betty blended into one perfect, Jewish mother. Shelly recalls summers at Workman's Circle Camp when he would be required to wear a bathing cap and bathing shoes while swimming, as though a few laps in the lake were akin to being caught in the rain. When he was in college, Gene contracted mononucleosis, and had to convalesce at his parents' home on Fort Washington Avenue. Sholom wrote the following bulletin to Shelly about the younger son's condition:

His personal nurses—your mother and me—are at his bedside 24 hours a day. True, the female nurse complains about fatigue, nevertheless she is at her post constantly. The male nurse (me) has had to develop new talents, as a rule uncalled for by any nurse. Since the patient cannot indulge in any activities, he puts demands on his male nurse to furnish him with entertainment.

As a result, yesterday the male nurse performed, by special request, dances of all varieties: ballet, tap-dancing, soft shoe, interpretive and acrobatic. For an encore the patient requested imitations of all the symphonic instruments. The request was carried out to the best of the male nurse's ability. However, the great obstacle presented itself when the patient insisted that the poor, worn-out male nurse perform an imitation of a full symphony orchestra, playing *fortissimo*. This is when the nurse, to his advantage, collapsed, and was saved from an embarrassment.

In conclusion: Please God, make our patient well and in a hurry.

Although Sholom always had a car, his ego was in no way involved with its make or style or horsepower. His teenage sons, however, were very interested in the effect that their father's automobile would have on their buddies and girlfriends. And so it was almost jarring one year, to everyone but Gene and Shelly, to see Sholom purchase a Sunbeam Rapier—a red and white English sport coupe with stick shift—that at first he could only drive with their assistance.

When Sholom did turn down a request by his sons to buy something, it was agony for him. He tried to say "no" in a way that would sound like "yes." In 1954 Shelly wrote from Germany, where he was stationed, asking for money to buy a battery-operated tape recorder. Sholom responded:

I do not see the value in a battery recorder to the tune of $300. Be realistic, my son, $300 is a lot of money. Sure, if it can bring in return sufficient joy, pleasure and results to warrant such an extravagance, all right. That's what money is for. I am sorry, but in this case I fail to see eye to eye with you. Sometimes one of us has to be realistic and rational. This time, permit me to be the one. Quite often I weaken before your plea, and as a result we all feel sorry. There must be a limit to how extravagant any one may permit himself to be. You will agree with me, son, if you will make an attempt to seek the logic of my contention. You know very well that if I could but see a wee bit of sound reasoning in your arguments, I would not hesitate in filling your request.

"My father," Shelly says, "could write 5,000 words on how to butter a bagel."

Sholom's volcanic temper was displayed at home only when his sons failed to practice the piano. It was as much to avoid a confrontation, as it was a chore delegated to her, that Betty prodded them to keep up with their lessons.

Gene recalls:

Music was the only area in which Sholom would lose perspective.
He began hammering away at me when I was five about the piano.
I ran through a string of music teachers, beginning with him, and I
fought tooth and nail. I was a reasonably accomplished pianist, but
I wasn't extraordinary. He would blame Betty for my not practic-
ing because I'd want to go and play ball with the kids in the neighborhood when he wasn't home, and they'd have all kinds of alter-
cations.

One particular evening we had the worst emotional exchange. I
remember saying dreadful things to him, and he blew his top. I
don't remember any time that he ever blew up to that extent,
because he was a superindulgent parent. If I'd robbed a bank, he
would have said, "We'll work it out." But with music, he was absolutely rigid and uncompromising. It was a blind spot.

Next to his family, music meant more than anything to Sholom,
and he dragged his sons to concerts and opera performances. When
Sigmund Romberg died in 1951, Sholom made 16-year-old Gene go
to the funeral, saying, "Some day you'll remember attending this
great composer's funeral." In much the same manner he had said,
"Some day you'll remember seeing Toscanini conduct," or whatever
musical highlight it was that Sholom wanted to have remembered.
In the boys' bedroom Sholom hung up a picture of Beethoven
which Shelly tore down, replacing it with a picture of New York
Giants pitcher Carl Hubbell.
"We resented being taken to all the concerts, because we would
have preferred being with our friends," Gene says. "But today, I appreciate it. I know more about music and how an orchestra functions
than I would have had he not insisted on exposing us to fine music."

If Sholom had one failing as a father—and this failing is one that
many people would gladly have traded for their opposite experience—it is that he was too supportive of his sons. Because their
smallest achievements were heralded by Sholom as Nobel Prize
material, it was difficult for Shelly to take criticism well, and for Gene
not to be too critical of himself. All the same Sholom's encourage-

ment, however overstated, was appreciated by them.

When Shelly set up his own photography studio in Manhattan in 1965, he encountered the normal variety of setbacks that attend any one-man operation. Sholom wrote to Shelly, "So you are learning about hardships and business difficulties. It will do you good, I am sure. Just learn that nothing must go beyond the skin. Nothing must touch the heart. Nothing is worth it."

To Gene, whose first newspaper article fetched a paltry $25, Sholom wrote, "Don't worry about the price of your first publication. That means nothing. Think of the insignificant amounts other luminaries received for their first epics: Rachmaninoff sold his now-famous 'Prelude in C Sharp Minor' for 37 rubles, the equivalent at the time of $17. Think also of how little your old man sold his immortal 'Bei Mir Bist Du Schön' for. So what? There will come a time when people will read about you. It is only the beginning of a great career that will bring fame and glory to the name of Secunda."

⚎ THE CONCORD YEARS

In 1945 Sholom became musical director of the Concord Hotel, a Catskill Mountains resort in Kiamesha Lake, New York, a post he held for 28 years.

The Concord Hotel today is the largest resort hotel in the world. It is very different from the small hotel *cum* bungalows that it was in 1935, when Arthur Winarick bought it for $15,000.[1] The Catskills— its devotees called a vacation there "going to the mountains"—were accessible to New York City working Jews. Thanks to the influx of German Jews to the area in the 1880s, Jews in the 1920s and 1930s did not encounter anti-Semitic restrictions that were rampant elsewhere.

Set in the heart of farming country two hours from Manhattan, Catskills hotels, many of them former farms, could provide fresh food in enormous quantities. Dotting the back roads of the Catskills were bungalow colonies, tiny cottages where Lower East Side laborers could, for a modest fee, rent two to eight weeks of greenery and good air.

Arthur and his brother Nathan Winarick (and their progeny) made the Concord the envy of the resort trade because they knew their market. The Winarick brothers were born in Novograd-Volynskiy in the Russian Ukraine, and, to escape the Russian Army, emigrated to the United States in 1913. Arthur became a barber on the Lower East Side and in the early 1920s manufactured a hair tonic, called Jeris, with his brother, who was a chemist.

Arthur spent many summers at Gluck's Hotel across the road from the Concord, and in 1935 he bought the Concord, then called the Concord Plaza, which was bankrupt. (It was called the Concord for two reasons: first, the name of the man who developed the land was

Colcord; second, "Concord" sounded like Concourse, as in the Bronx's Grand Concourse, where many Jews lived, a step up from the Lower East Side.)

Arthur Winarick was an uneducated but brilliantly astute businessman. "His mind," says his sister-in-law, Frances Winarick (Nat's widow), "worked faster than his mouth. He came to a point more quickly than he could articulate it. If you didn't get the point, God help you."

He and his siblings grew up in Brownsville, Brooklyn, in a home that was Jewish but not religious. "Brownsville represented socialism," Frances recalls. "Jewish people as a minority of working class immigrants were, after unionism improved working conditions, like birds getting freedom. *Yiddishkeit* (Jewish culture and life) was not part of my life in Brownsville. We were running away from Jewishness. We did not keep kosher at home—my mother would have been an agnostic if she'd had the guts. Arthur was an agnostic."

Arthur set aside his religious views because he knew that Jewishness—hence keeping kosher—was good hotel business. And he was smart enough to hire experts in those areas about which he knew little. He kept on, as manager, Mrs. Sarah Jacobson, the Concord's previous owner. In 1940 he consulted with Al Beckman of Beckman & Pransky, the biggest Catskills booking agents. Beckman told Winarick, "You don't have first class property or nicer facilities than the other hotels. The way you'll attract attention is to feature fabulous stars and personalities."

During the season—which then lasted only for the summer months—one could see at the Concord Sophie Tucker, Milton Berle, the Ritz Brothers, Harry Richmond, Ethel Waters, Danny Kaye, Phil Silvers, Sid Caesar, Billy Eckstine and Billy Daniels. Beckman, who was also a Yiddish theater *patriot,* booked Aaron Lebedeff, Moishe Oysher, Jennie Goldstein and other Second Avenue stars to do variety shows.

Beckman & Pransky, who had been musicians in speakeasy bands during Prohibition, knew the entertainment business and the Catskills inside out. In the late 1930s and early 1940s troupes of performers would play all the hotels, one week at a time in each hotel. Beckman's widow, Ceil, recalls that "sometimes one act would be booked at three different hotels in a single day. Al terrified his acts with his driving. He drove from hotel to hotel at breakneck speed. He knew all the shortcuts through the forests so he could make it to the hotels on time.''

Alexander Olshanetsky was hired as the Concord's first musical director. He died in 1944, but he left his mark at the hotel by instituting pop and classical music concerts. ''Olshanetsky was a real swinger,'' Ceil Beckman says. ''He would drop an important deal if he saw a pretty girl.''

''It's true that Olshanetsky had a *schmecker*—a nose for girls'' says Jan Peerce (who had worked with the composer as a violinist in the Catskills in the 1930s), ''but he was also a first-rate musician.''

Arthur Winarick wanted a composer of equal stature, and he hired Sholom as Olshanetsky's replacement.

''Arthur knew what people wanted,'' says his nephew, Gordon Winarick, one of the Concord's managers. ''East Side immigrants wanted upper mobility. He built a resort for people who wanted better. The Concord gave them what they couldn't get at home or anywhere else. Arthur wanted culture, and his brother, Nat, found it in Sholom and others. And although he wasn't himself religious, he knew that people would follow well-known cantors, so he hired Sidney Shickoff and Oysher to sing during the holidays. Concert nights were Arthur's mandate. To be a patron of the arts was business logic. Sixty per cent of the hotel's guests showed up for those concerts, and many people from other hotels in the area.''

''It was very formal here in the early days,'' says Frances Winarick. ''The Concord represented status for a growing Jewish middle class. People wanted to show their affluence in the clothes they wore, so they dressed for dinner. Arthur knew how to attract those people. That's why each room has two bathrooms, to enhance that 'glamour.'''

The Concord became a year-round resort in 1944. The first winter, a meager 100 guests were registered, a figure that grew by a geometric progression in ensuing years.

As musical director, Sholom conducted an orchestra and choir for Passover and the High Holy Days and during the summer conducted concerts every Thursday night. His first Concord orchestra consisted of twelve musicians and no string section. The incumbent musicians were not eager to have a new, more demanding conductor than his predecessor had been. ''They resorted to any means to stop me from being employed at the Concord,'' Sholom wrote. ''Many of their tricks occurred during actual concerts. On one occasion, when I stepped onto the podium, my baton was missing, and I was forced to conduct without it. Another time, in the middle of Ravel's 'Bolero', I signaled the bassoonist to play at his cue. He pointed to his music stand, which was empty. He did not play.''

Ray Parker, Arthur Winarick's son-in-law and general manager of the Concord, offered to fire the entire orchestra, but Sholom, who was sympathetic to the sporadic livelihoods of musicians, declined. (Hiring needy enemies was a practice Sholom carried over from Second Avenue. Once, in the 1930s, a violinist he had engaged brought Sholom up on charges with the Musicians Union because Sholom had not conducted a given performance, which was customary once the show was set and the musicians knew their cues. The violinist filled in for him, which was also the custom, and he wanted to be paid an extra fee. Over the objections of his family, Sholom engaged the violinist for the following season, explaining that although the man was a rat, he was a good musician and had a family to support.)

Sholom asked Parker to give him the authority to at least threaten the musicians with dismissal, to which Parker agreed.

At first the programs for the weekly concerts consisted of semiclassical music, arranged by Sholom in concert form. The concerts did not, initially, attract a large audience. The Concord guests were more interested in the ''name'' stars who were booked on weekends. But Winarick, an amateur violinist, was committed artistically and commercially to serious music, and the concerts continued. Slowly they were better attended, and Sholom began adding the work of such composers as Mozart to the program. After one such concert, Winarick came backstage and said to Sholom, ''You see? They like Mozart! Next time, add a little Beethoven and Tchaikovsky—they'll love it.''

''Arthur,'' Sholom said, ''to play Tchaikovsky properly, you need a bigger orchestra.''

''Go ahead!'' Winarick shouted. ''Order a bigger orchestra! Get good soloists! We'll make Carnegie Hall out of this place yet!''

Sholom took Winarick at his word. Met stars such as Jan Peerce, Richard Tucker, Roberta Peters and Robert Merrill all made appearances at Sholom's concerts. Beverly Sills spent several summer evenings performing with him early in her career. Musicians from the Juilliard School of Music, the New York Philharmonic and the Metropolitan Opera Orchestra appeared. The orchestra grew from twelve musicians to 65.

For the High Holy Days and Passover, the Cordillion Room, which seated 4,000 people, was turned into a synagogue. Sholom hired a four-part choir of 16 voices for the holidays. Over the years cantors for services included Moishe Gentshoff, Jacob Koenigsberg, Sidney Shikoff, Jacob Barkin, Herman Malamood and Richard Tucker.

The ten days of holidays were billed as the "Annual Passover Festival." It included two services at the beginning and two services at the end of the period, with a Thursday night concert. A concert program could include "Procession of the Sardar (Caucasian Sketches)" by Ippolitov-Ivanov, "Ah Jeux Veux Vivivre," from "Romeo and Juliet" by Gounod, "Yesh Li Gan" by Secunda, "Israeli Symphony" by Olshanetsky, "Rhapsody in Blue" by George Gershwin, "Marche Slav" by Tchaikovsky, and excerpts, sung by soloists, from Puccini's "La Boheme."

The Concord grew to include 1,200 bedrooms, most of them with two bathrooms and two walk-in closets, on 3,000 acres, and a dining room capable of producing 3,500 kosher meals in one sitting with 120 items on the menu. The Imperial Room was added making it, at 24,000 square feet, the world's largest nightclub. Lectures, a card room and an enormous gameroom with pinball and other electronic machines contributed to the entertainment options of the guests. With its plethora of activities and Texas-style bigness, it wooed a clientele that today is mostly, but not necessarily, Jewish.

Sholom loved the Concord and especially its dining room. Year after year he and Betty sat at the same table with family and friends, and nearly always with the same waiter serving them. Dessert time was the pinnacle of the meal for him. If the waiter put anything without whipped cream or chocolate frosting in front of Sholom, he would say, "Cake? You call this cake? This is *bread!* Bring me a *real* dessert!" His favorite was anything chocolate and wet. When the dining room once failed for several days to produce chocolate pudding, Sholom stalked into the kitchen to demand an explanation.

As the Concord's profits grew, so did Sholom's budget for his artists (but never to the extent that the music personnel believed. Winarick saved the big fees for the nightclub stars, and Sholom had a comparatively small budget for his own soloists and choir members. He paid his performers the top dollar he could manage, and the most he himself ever received for an entire year of work at the Concord was $8,000). The choir was expanded to 24 voices, and in 1955, Winarick said he wanted a singer of international reputation to be the cantor during the holidays.

"How about Richard Tucker?" Sholom suggested (Tucker was not only an opera superstar, he was also a deeply religious man and in great demand as a cantor).

"That's the man!" Winarick thundered. "What a combination! Tucker, Secunda and the Concord!" (Subtlety was not a part of Arthur Winarick's personality.)

Tucker told Sholom he was interested in the offer, and that his fee was $20,000 for the 10 days.

"Ruby," Sholom said, "that's a fortune."

"If Winarick wants Tucker," Ruby replied, "he'll pay."

Winarick paid.

"That's when the Secundas and the Tuckers really became close," says Sarah Tucker, Richard Tucker's widow. "Richard said that his friendship with Sholom was like a good marriage. They shared the limelight. It was not just Richard who did a service, it was Sholom and Richard. If Richard received a compliment, he would say, 'Well, Sholom and I did it together.'"

The Tucker and Secunda families always ate their meals together at the Concord. On the mornings following a concert or service, Sholom and Tucker would march arm in arm into the dining room, and the guests would give them a standing ovation.

But even with his old friend, when it came to music, Sholom could be a tyrant.

"When they were on stage during a concert," Sarah Tucker recalls, "Sholom would get very angry if Richard gave more than he should. When you're an artist, and you're going strong during a performance, you go stronger because you're inspired. So Sholom used to look at him and point his little finger at him, which meant, 'Enough, already.'"

Over the years of their friendship Sholom composed the majority of the liturgical music Tucker sang at the Concord, as well as two oratorios in later years, recorded for television and Columbia Records. If Sholom learned that Tucker performed a program of Jewish music not his own, he would say to Tucker, "How can you sing that *junk*?"

It was nearly impossible for Sholom to ask Arthur Winarick for more money for himself. But Tucker insisted on getting a raise each year and pushed Sholom into fighting that particular battle. By the seventh year of their Concord association, Tucker was demanding $40,000 for the High Holy Days and Passover. Arthur Winarick refused to pay it, and Tucker resigned.

At Tucker's last service at the Concord, the members of the choir were on the verge of tears, as was Sholom. Sylvia Snyder, who was an alto in the choir from 1949 until 1974, recalls the speech that Tucker gave the Concord audience at the conclusion of his farewell concert.

"This is my last holiday here," Tucker said. "I love this place. The reason I'm leaving is because I asked for more money and the management wouldn't give it to me."

"It was their last time together there," Sarah Tucker says, "and to see the chorus people cry was really heart-breaking. Sholom was miserable knowing that Richard was not coming back. But Richard made up his mind that he had to go. He adored Sholom, but he couldn't stay on if he was unhappy."

Tucker was succeeded by Jacob Barkin in 1962. In 1967 Herman Malamood became the Concord's cantor for the holidays, a post he still holds.

Most singers and musicians stayed with Sholom at the Concord for many years. Once auditioned and accepted, it was virtually impossible for them to get fired. Part of the reason was Sholom's extraordinary (and occasionally misplaced) loyalty. He had a keen awareness of financial struggle, especially for musicians. Sholom also hated discussions of money, and for a member of the chorus to raise the subject struck him as ingratitude. Disloyalty struck him as betrayal. Once, one of his sopranos told him that it was causing difficulties within her family for her to travel so far to appear at the Concord, and that she wanted to accept a position with a choir in New York. Sholom told her that if she resigned, he would see to it that she never sang anywhere again.

The result of Sholom's attitude was a mixed bag of musical talent. "As forceful as he was," Sylvia Snyder says, "he was really a soft touch. There was one woman in the choir who was totally irresponsible—she once fell asleep by the indoor pool and got locked in, so she missed a performance. Sholom said, 'I'm finished with her, finished!' But next year, there she was again. We all had husbands and wives and children, and he'd let us bring up our families and he'd work out either free rooms or minimal room rates.''

Sholom might have been a soft touch when it came to personalities, but when it came to music, he had a short fuse.

Herman Malamood, who not only worked with Sholom as the Concord's cantor but was also a principal of the New York City Opera, says of Sholom,

He was the toughest son-of-a-gun I ever ran into. If I made one slight mistake, he would not let me go ahead. He would yell and bang the piano. He would make me grab a chair and sit next to him, and I never got so close to a teacher banging and screaming in my ear, but he was very insistent. Especially in his vocal runs. His runs were so difficult because they weren't made for the average singer, but were based on the coloratura.

After doing four or five years of his runs I started to master them, not perfectly, but well enough that he would talk to me reasonably. Tucker studied those runs too and to the end of his life he performed Sholom's runs.

Sholom was the one who really made a musician out of me. He'd say, "You must study. Don't come here unless you've studied." He was so tough. I'd say, "I've got to make a living, when I get home, I'm tired." He'd say, "No excuses. You've got to work hard if you want to make it."

I studied with him four or five times a week in New York. I had to work four times harder for him than in the opera. Once during a service, I veered off and made a mistake, and he picked up the score as though he were going to throw it at me.

But he was a tremendous interpreter not only of his own music but of anything. He knew his music and opera. He helped me tremendously in learning many of my first roles, and he was instrumental in getting my first operatic experience—with the Israeli National Opera. He was proud of my opera career, but he was demanding. One time he saw me in Pagliacci and he said he didn't like it, that my voice was constricted. I thought I had done a good performance and I wondered, why is he depressing me like this? But you know something? By telling me what he did, it made me work harder. He was the biggest musical influence of my life because of that early negativism.

"Talk about Toscanini and his batons!" Sylvia Snyder says. "Sholom broke plenty of them, too. He also brought decent singing into the liturgy. When we sang poorly, he'd curse us, saying we sounded like 'dog-catchers,' his favorite term for lousy musicians and conductors. He threw chairs to a point that made me very, very nervous."

Sholom was equally demanding of his orchestra. Because of rising costs in hiring extra musicians for the holidays or a concert, he had to use as the nucleus of his orchestra the regular band that played for pop singers and provided dance music in the nightclub. They were not always up to the precision of classical music, nor were the occasional supplementary musicians who were hired by a jobber.

Danny Marsik, a classically trained violinist, bassist and guitarist who plays year-round at the Concord, remembers, "Once there was a trumpet player from Buffalo who was hired for a concert. He murdered the '1812 Concerto' during the performance. Sholom whispered at him, 'You son of a bitch!' in front of everyone. The whole fiddle section broke up laughing.

"Another time during a rehearsal we were playing the Tchaikovsky Fourth Symphony badly. Sholom stopped the rehearsal and said, 'Excuse me, gentlemen, what key are we playing in?'"

Occasionally Sonny Rossi's Latin band, a regular Concord fixture, was featured during a concert with the orchestra. Once during a rehearsal, the Latin band missed its cue, and Rossi suggested to Sholom that the group give a grunt, Latin-style, as the downbeat.

"Are you crazy?" Sholom yelled. "I have a baton, and you want to *grunt*?"

Many of the members of the band and orchestra remember the years with Sholom as the most professionally satisfying, as well as the most fun, of their tenures at the Concord. Frank Pertocelli, clarinetist and saxophone player, recalls a rehersal during which the piano soloist complained to Arthur Winarick, "This piano is terrible."

"Don't worry!" Winarick said. "We'll paint it up! It'll be fine!"

"All the performance soloists were asked to take a bow by Sholom at the conclusion of a piece," Petrocelli says. "Jerry Nazar, a brilliant clarinetist, always had a solo. Once Sholom pointed to Jerry to stand up after his solo. Jerry whispers to me, 'He means you. Stand up!' Like a schmuck, I did. I felt like a jerk. The guys fell down."

Sholom praised the band musicians when they played well during a concert, but did not conceal his contempt for their other, "pop" work. "After a concert," Petrocelli says, "I was packing up my clarinet and unpacking my sax because I had a band date. Sholom strolled by and said, 'That's not an instrument.'"

Danny Marsik, on rehearsals with Sholom:

Sholom could be a pain in the ass. He'd holler a lot. Boris Malina was in charge of contracting the other musicians, and if the section screwed up, Sholom would yell up at Boris, who was 6 feet 6 inches and weighed 9,000 pounds. "You rotten dogs with a disease" is the most polite way I can translate his Russian description of bad musicianship—I speak Russian. The women in the choir he'd call "street walkers" and "whores." In Russian, of course.

Sholom had trouble firing loyal regulars, but not freelance "dog-catchers." Once he called a rehearsal for 3:00 p.m., and by 3:15 he had fired the trumpet section. On another occasion he fired the entire string section.

According to long-time members of the band, Sholom was an old-world professional. He expected his musicians to know the musical literature. He couldn't comprehend that, as a hotel band, they were a different breed. "We were," says one musician, "a multi-national, all-purpose, jazz-oriented orchestra. But we learned."

"I miss the concerts," says another band player. "I was trained to be able to play anything. I'd think I was doing okay with the classical stuff until I heard a real player on WQXR Radio, like Julius Baker, flute soloist of the New York Philharmonic. I wanted to crawl into the woodwork then. But at least with Sholom, during the concerts I had practical application for my training. My playing improved."

The greatest test Sholom ever gave his musicians was in their ability to decipher his orchestrations, which were written, as one of them put it, "like chicken scratchings." When an error was Sholom's, he would make light of it.

"Once I complained about the sloppy manuscript," Marsik says, "and Sholom said, 'Make it up.'" To another complaining musician, Sholom said, "Just listen. You'll figure it out."

Ginetta La Bianca, a soprano who in 1950, at the age of 15, was the youngest opera singer ever to make her professional debut (at the Teatro dell-Opera in Rome), was for years a soloist with Sholom at the Concord, performing there two or three times a year. Sholom asked her to perform Yiddish music as well as her opera repertoire, and taught her the difference between cantorial and aria singing.

"I learned all my Yiddish and Hebrew from him," La Bianca says. "And if I didn't do something right, he'd hit me on my knuckles, and it wasn't a light tap either. You made sure you didn't make the same mistakes. For the High Holy Days I sang the 'Yehi Rotzon,' a cantorial piece by Secunda. That is more difficult than an aria because it takes so much out of you. You can't just sing it lightly and beautifully. You've got to give emotionally, otherwise it doesn't come across. Sholom taught me how to do that. He never charged me for all those lessons. Whenever I called and needed help with the language or the music, he never said no."

The marriage of Sholom Secunda and a huge Catskills resort in the 1940s and 1950s was one made in heaven. Sholom was a symbol for immigrant and first-generation Jews who prospered sufficiently to afford a summer at the Concord. He shared their East European roots, their Lower East Side misery, their struggles with the English language and American ways. "He sprouted with them," Frances Winarick says. And, as a Yiddish theater celebrity and classical musician, he was to them a hero.

On Thursday nights Sholom would conduct a 90-minute concert in the Imperial Room. Before each piece of music Sholom would tell the audience about its history, and occasionally had the orchestra play themes to demonstrate their development through the work.

For one concert Sholom decided to make a minor alteration in Tchaikovsky's "1812 Concerto." The music called for cannons during a final section of the piece. "So I hired policemen from Kiamesha Lake and Monticello," Sholom told Douglas Watts of the *New York Daily News,* "about twelve men in all (who would fire their revolvers, loaded with blanks, instead of cannons), and put them under the hotel security officer who asked me if he could play 'first gun.'"

Those annotated concerts were probably Sholom's finest hours. "Guests here were in awe of him and his knowledge," says Ceil

Beckman. "In the lobby he would be mobbed, but he would bow and smile, bow and smile."

"If you or I saw Leonard Bernstein on the street," says Sylvia Snyder, "we would not have the courage to go over and say hello. But the Jews possessed Sholom Secunda. If he was conducting at the Concord, you had a right to go over and tell him how marvelous he was. And the charm about him was that he would never be rude to anyone. There was no privacy there for him. People would stop at his table, and that smile of his appeared on his face."

Sholom was especially favored by the women who visited the hotel. Once there was a convention of 2,000 members of the National Women's League. Sholom conducted his usual Thursday concert, and at its conclusion, the conventioneers asked that a piano be brought into the lobby so that Sholom could play for the women. He did so, and the women took their shoes off and danced around the piano, pausing to kiss Sholom between selections.

"His face was just one smear of lipstick," Betty Secunda recalls. "He was always called 'the mezuzah' because women were always kissing him. I sat on the side, laughing and smiling at all this. A woman came over to me and said, 'I don't understand you, Mrs. Secunda, all these women hugging and kissing your husband, and you're smiling.' I said, 'This has been going on since I married, and I love it. In numbers. I have no fear of numbers.'"

Sholom ate up the attention. In a 1954 letter to Shelly, he wrote, "Generally speaking, I believe this season has been the most successful of all. If the administration did not appreciate it fully, it is indeed a consolation to know that the guests who attend the concerts show a real appreciation and demonstrate their feelings vociferously. What more do we artists need?"

Although the ten High Holy Days would continue to be the most solidly booked week in the Concord calendar, the Thursday night concerts were not to last. "It was a matter of economics," says a former Concord employee. "A concert in the Imperial Room would cost the hotel from $1,800 to $2,000, depending on the soloists and the size of the audience. And, of course, the concert audience didn't drink, so that revenue was lost. When Arthur Winarick went to those concerts in the 1950s, most of the guests attended as well. But by the late 1960s the concert audience dwindled to around 500 people. Management continued the concerts out of respect for Sholom. After

Sholom became terminally ill, they stopped.''

The era of the intellectually hungry, easily dazzled immigrant was, by the 1960s, over. Jews no longer spent the summer in the Catskills in the numbers they once did, and a drive through the area today is like driving through a series of ghost towns. Most of the old hotels and bungalow colonies are boarded up and ramshackle. A few have become residential facilities for mentally retarded adults.[2] The Catskills resorts, which once employed thousands of local people, had passed their prime, and residents have sought employment elsewhere or moved away.

The big hotels—Grossinger's, Kutsher's, Brown's—linger on, but none of them with the flashiness and big budget public relations of the Concord. The kitchen still serves kosher food, but the emphasis now is on packages that draw a multi-ethnic crowd—conventions, singles weekends, ski weekends.

The deathknell for the Catskills was cheap airfare to Florida and points south. As second generation Jews became more successful, they changed their vacation habits. The Caribbean—not the Catskills—was the chic place to sojourn.

Arthur Winarick died in 1964, and with him the Concord's commitment to an immigrant class, which no longer existed. His son-in-law, Ray Parker, and then his grandson, Bobby Parker, took over the hotel, updating its image.

''Arthur's thinking was to make money,'' says Frances Winarick. ''To attract Jews to the Concord—another world, a make-believe world—it had to be Jewish. But times and the hotel's management have changed. Would the concerts have continued if Arthur were alive? Arthur was too practical a man not to have gone with the times.''

🎵 YIDDISH THEATER TWILIGHT

Sholom went back to Second Avenue, after his hiatus with Maurice Schwartz, in 1942. He was engaged at the Second Avenue Theater by William Rolland, who scored a coup by signing comedian Menashe Skulnik. Skulnik was to become a familiar name to radio (and later, Broadway) audiences: he was Uncle David to Gertrude Berg's Molly Goldberg on "The Rise of the Goldbergs," an enormously popular program. Rolland repeated the combination of Secunda-Skulnik the following season.

But in 1944 Joseph Rumshinsky was hired as Rolland's composer, replacing Sholom. "I was publicly good-natured about it," Sholom wrote, "but privately, I was mortified." Not so Betty, who felt that Yiddish theater was on its deathbed and that Sholom should take the rejection as a sign that it was time to move on professionally.

He began making the rounds of radio stations in New York, hoping to get on the music staff. One afternoon at NBC, he overheard Ben Yost, star on NBC Radio of "Ben Yost and His Chorale," telling some of the other musicians that his arranger had not yet begun doing the arrangements for that Sunday's broadcast, and that the Chorale had nothing to rehearse. One of the musicians introduced Yost to Sholom, who offered to do the arrangements on the spot.

Yost had nothing to lose by taking Sholom up on his offer, and within an hour and without the use of a piano, Sholom had completed the work. An assistant copied out the singing parts and the rehearsal began punctually at 3:00 p.m. Sholom was hired as Yost's new arranger. Every Sunday a "new Ben Yost arrangement," ghosted by Sholom, was presented on NBC. It wasn't Second Avenue *shund*, but it galled Sholom just the same. Still it was a living, a better living that he had made in the Yiddish theater.

Sholom's defection by degrees from the Yiddish theater was well-timed. By the late 1940s there were only six Yiddish theaters left in New York City, four for legitimate theater (the Second Avenue, the Yiddish Art Theater and, in Brooklyn, the Parkway and the Hopkinson), and two for Yiddish vaudeville (the Clinton and the National). Alexander Olshanetsky died in 1944, leaving Joseph Rumshinsky, Abraham Ellstein and Sholom as the remaining, prominent Jewish composers. Most Jewish societies were taking their benefits to Broadway, and the remaining theaters occasionally had to rely on financial loans from the Hebrew Actors Union to stay afloat.

Yiddish theater was running out of an audience that spoke Yiddish. The legendary Celia Adler said of that decline toward the end of her life,

Once two girls and a small boy came to see me after a performance. I asked if they understood what was going on, and the girls said the little boy had been translating from the Yiddish for them. But such a small boy. And I turned to the little boy and I said, "Where, my little boy, did you learn Yiddish?" And he was very shy, but he said, "At home. My *bubby* (grandmother) speaks to me in Yiddish."

And I thought to myself, it's all right. As long as the *bubbies* are here, Yiddish will last. But when the *bubbies* go, the Yiddish theater will go.[1]

Second Avenue producers tried valiantly to compete with Broadway. In 1942 the Rodgers & Hammerstein musical "Oklahoma" premiered. Downtown Sophie Gaby and Harry Schlecker mounted their Yiddish operetta, "A Wedding in Oklahoma" three years later.

Yiddish producers were also responding to the war abroad for timely—and, hopefully, commercial—subject material. In October 1944, Jacob Ben-Ami, an actor known to Broadway as well as to Second Avenue audiences, produced "Miracle of the Warsaw Ghetto" at the New Jewish Folk Theater on 12th Street, for which Sholom wrote incidental music.

Unlike most actor-managers, Ben-Ami cast himself in a role that did not eclipse the powerful theme of the recent (April) resistance in Warsaw. Although the dialogue was in Yiddish, actor Sam Jaffee provided entr'acte commentary in English. *New York Post* critic Wilella Waldorf said of the production, "Surrounding himself with a large and competent company, Mr. Ben-Ami has directed a well-thought-out production. . .We thought Sholom Secunda's music helped a good deal. . ."

The following year Sholom composed the score for "Hard to Be Honest," produced at the Hopkinson Theater, a combination of vaudeville and ethnic pride. The *New York Post* critic cited Max Wilner, Henrietta Jacobson and newcomer Fyvush Finkel for their adroit comic touches, but Sholom got the lion's share of praise:

> Mr. Secunda is known as a composer of classical music and much of his time, furthermore, has been spent in synagogues. When he turns to popular songwriting he can come up with a tune that the audience finds itself whistling after the show, and he knows how to manipulate rhythms that help put over dance numbers. Yet there is often an echo of Jewish church (sic) music about his work that gives it a quality quite apart from the usual Tin Pan Alley product. Mr. Secunda's synagogue background colors his popular songs as definitely as Sir Arthur Sullivan's choir boy training makes itself felt in the Gilbert and Sullivan operas.

It is interesting that Sholom's best Second Avenue work occurred at the ebb of Yiddish theater. He had reached a stature equal to the egomaniacal actor-managers of his youth. Sholom's heart was certainly elsewhere—his classical music and cantorial composition occupied most of his time—and he was finally in a position to write music for Second Avenue that pleased him artistically.

Still, Yiddish theater clung to *shund* in such productions as "The Hired Bridegroom" (score by Secunda), "A Wedding in Fallsburg," "My Golden Bride," and "Marriage by Request"—matrimony was still a popular theme. Yiddish theater retained some of its original *patriots*—the ones who were still alive—and Sholom felt obliged to do at least one score yearly for them.

Sholom's Concord years gave him exposure to devotees of Jewish music who no longer attended Yiddish theater, and he began to receive invitations to give lectures at Jewish organizations and at New York universities and colleges.

Gene Secunda on his father's speaking ability:

He could speak on any subject extemporaneously—it was a gift. Once I had to do a speech on Wendell Willkie in high school and I asked Sholom to help me with it. He knew a little bit about Willkie—he read the papers every day and when the news was on the radio we had to shut up. But he certainly wasn't an authority on Willkie.

Anyhow, he delivered 15 minutes on Willkie, beginning with the line, "I'm glad you asked me that question," to show me how easy it was.

In time the lecture circuit took Sholom to other cities and states. In 1946 Sholom was asked by Chaim Ehrenreich of the *Daily Forward* to become a music critic for the Yiddish newspaper. Sholom's reviews of Metropolitan Opera performances and classical concerts appeared each Friday. He believed that, although these reviews were not of Yiddish theater or Jewish music, they would nevertheless have an audience with the *Forward's* readers. He wrote in his memoirs:

All of Jewish history is filled with melody and song. When we read chapters of the Psalms, it's hard to find one that doesn't talk about "a pleasing voice," or "a new song" or "praise Him with the blast of the horn," "with psaltery and harp," "with timbrel and dance," "with stringed instruments and the pipes," "with loud-sounding cymbals." A people raised on song, whether a folk song, a popular theater song, an art song or a symphonic work, must find these subjects interesting. Judging from the letters I receive from my readers, my assumption is correct.

"It wasn't money that drove him to write," says Simon Weber, the *Forward's* editor today. "It's because he had an interest in writing, and he liked to see his name in print. Just like every other writer."

According to Weber, Sholom began his association with the *Forward* by ghost writing. Weber, who was then a staff writer, says, "Occasionally I would go to see an opera, and I would have to show the Met that some review had appeared. But I told Sholom that it would be ridiculous for me to write a piece because I didn't know anything about opera. Sholom said, 'Don't worry. Go. I know the opera and I know the people in it.' He would give me three or four paragraphs about the opera. If I saw something, he wrote it.''

Sholom continued his pattern of workaholism. His work week included a trip to the Concord for special performances during the winter, two concerts or an opera performance to be reviewed for the *Forward*, a lecture in the city or suburbs, and weekend services at the Brooklyn Jewish Center or the East Midwood Jewish Center.

In 1945 Sholom began his association with the Entertainment Bureau of America, owned by Beckman & Pransky, sharing their offices in the Hotel Woodstock. Through EBA, Sholom wrote music and conducted the orchestra for All Star benefits at Madison Square Garden which helped to raise money for such organizations as the United Jewish Appeal, the Jewish War Veterans, and others. His income helped to defray new expenses at home: Shelly had graduated from the Bronx High School of Science and had been accepted at UCLA; in five years Gene would be college-bound.

In his lectures and articles Sholom deplored the fading interest in Jewish musical heritage and traditions. And so, too, he reproved himself, and decided to compose a string quartet, a form of music he had not employed since his graduation from the Institute of Musical Art in 1919. Sandwiching composing between his other commitments, he completed his four-movement "String Quartet in C Minor" within six months. The music was based on Jewish themes and cantillations in the tradition of Sholom's mentor, Ernest Bloch. BMI agreed to publish the work.

Arturo Toscanini was then conductor of the NBC Symphony Orchestra, which had been formed for him a decade earlier and had become, under his baton, a world-renowned orchestra. Its string quartet frequently performed on Toscanini's weekly Sunday radio program. On a hunch Sholom called Max Hollander, first violinist of the NBC String Quartet. Hollander was familiar with Sholom's work and agreed to look at the "C Minor Quartet" with an eye to performing it on NBC Radio. A month after receiving the manuscript, Hollander called to say that NBC would play its premiere on Sunday, March 2, 1947. It was repeated on subsequent broadcasts.

Sholom wrote increasingly for the East Midwood and Brooklyn Jewish Centers, and his catalog of liturgical music expanded and was published by Mills Music under the aegis of Norman Warembud. Richard Tucker recorded Sholom's "Kol Nidre" and his arrangement of "Cantorial Jewels" for Columbia Records. His music was also performed in concerts at Town Hall and Carnegie Hall. But he was not finished with Second Avenue altogether. He supplied songs for Maurice Schwartz's Yiddish Art Theater production of "Yosele, the Nightingale," an adaptation of Sholom Aleichem's folk novel, *Yosele Solovey.* In 1949 he wrote the score for "Every Girl's Desire" for actors Irving Grossman and Irving Jacobson, producers in partnership at the Parkway Theater in Brooklyn.

In 1951 Sholom's music was performed for the first (and last) time on Broadway in "Bagels and Yox," an American-Yiddish review produced by Al Beckman and Johnny Pransky. Presented at the Holiday Theater on Broadway and 47th Street, the lyrics for the songs were written by Hymie Jacobson. The principal players were veterans of Second Avenue and the Borscht Belt: the Barton Brothers, Lou Saxon, Marty Drake, Larry Alpert, Rickie Layne and Velvel, Mary Forest, Patrice Helene and Jan Howard. According to Brooks Atkinson in *The New York Times,* the only redeeming virtue of the show was Sholom's music. Atkinson wrote:

> . . ."Bagels and Yox" maintains an even level of noisy mediocrity. With one or two exceptions, the material is commonplace. The exceptions are two or three bits of Jewish religious and folk music. What they are doing in this resort floor-show is hard to say. For this ancient music is beautiful. It is overflowing with humanity. Someone could make a memorable musical show out of these songs by taking them seriously and not throwing them away in a tasteless revue desperately coagulated around a microphone.[2]

Sholom was delighted with Atkinson's praise, but wrote him a letter to correct the critic's assumption that the melodies were "ancient," instead of, as they were, original. Atkinson wrote back, "You fooled me. I thought that music was right out of the synagogues. I salute you for having given me such an exalted impression."[*]

---

[*]The problem of writing music that sounded traditional haunted Sholom all his working life. In 1973, for instance, when a song of Sholom's called "Wus Die Wilst" (What You Want) was used in a scene of the film, "The Heartbreak Kid." Sholom received a fee only after the oversight was brought to the attention of the film's producers.

In its continuing effort to lure Broadway theater-goers downtown, Yiddish theater used increasing amounts of English dialogue in its scripts. In 1952 Herman Yablokoff produced an English translation of Benjamin Ressler's book, "Uncle Sam in Israel," with Yiddish punch lines. Sholom's songs, with Chaim Tauber's lyrics, were praised in the *New York Times* review, as was comedian Michael Rosenberg, who starred. The critic added, "The description of the production as an English-language offering is not entirely accurate. The basic dialogue and lyrics are in English, but there is a bit of Hebrew and quite a little Yiddish in 'Uncle Sam.' Perhaps it's a good thing, too. The Yiddish punch lines were the ones that seemed, as they say uptown, to be fracturing the patrons last night."[3]

Yablokoff's "experiment," as he himself put it, to attract a young Jewish audience unfamiliar with Yiddish offended Yiddish theater purists. The Yiddish press, he said, accused him of "putting the last nail in the coffin of Yiddish theater," because of his use of English. In his effort to please everyone, it seems, he pleased no one.

Although Sholom and Yablokoff generally worked well together, Yablokoff, a man of no small ego, occasionally got on Sholom's nerves. One of the plays for which Yablokoff engaged Sholom to do the score was presented at the National Theater on Houston Street. On top of the theater was an enormous clock. One afternoon, following a matinee, Sholom and a friend were standing in front of the theater. Sholom's friend recalls,

The clock was maybe six stories high. You could tell what time it was on 14th Street, 14 blocks away. It was a landmark. Yablokoff leased the theater and he covered the clock with his picture. He lit it and everything—he was a big publicity type man. So we're standing outside and a man who doesn't know that that's Sholom Secunda goes over to him and says, "Can you tell me what time it is?"

Sholom looks up and says, "It's half-past Yablokoff,"

Still, Sholom had fun working on "Uncle Sam." Yablokoff gave him total freedom with the score, unlike the old, star-dominated days, and later he transformed the music into a symphonic poem called "Yom B'Kibbutz," parts of which were performed in concert by such artists as Richard Tucker and Roberta Peters. Like a journalist-turned-author, Sholom's theater music was grist for his serious compositions, and he frequently borrowed themes from his Second Avenue work for other forms of music.

Herman Yablokoff was not the only target for salvos from the Yiddish press for the use of English in scripts. In the 1950s Julius Adler was a Yiddish theater producer in partnership with Irving Grossman and Irving Jacobson. Due to skyrocketing labor and production costs, the weekly budget for mounting a show grew from $14,000 to $22,000 (when it reached $55,000, they stopped producing). Because of theater economics and chancy receipts, compounded by its minority language, theirs was a business of enormous risk. "When the weather was bad," Adler says, "our eyes popped out hoping the audiences would come." He continues:

> When I produced, our scripts were 40 per cent English. One day Chaim Ehrenreich of the *Forward* came backstage to see me, and he criticized me for using so much English. I pulled him by the lapels into the alley outside and I said, "Why do you knock me for making a living? If you want pure Yiddish theater, why don't you invest your *own* money in it? Young members of benefit organizations are threatening to take their benefits to English theater because they don't understand Yiddish. If I don't use some English, there will be no Yiddish theater!"

In 1953 there occurred an event that even the most die-hard *patriot* could not ignore: the Cafe Royal closed. In its place, redecorated with chrome and plate glass, K&S Cleaners opened. The loss of the Cafe punctuated the end of the immigrant era, of East Side intellectual life, and not simply the poor health of its theater. Harrison Salisbury, in a touching ode to the place in the *New York Times,* wrote:

> For many years the course of the Cafe Royal had led but one way—downward. No longer did the stars of the Jewish theater congregate on the sidewalk terrace on a summer evening. In fact, the Jewish theater itself was virtually extinct.

> No more did rising young doctors and professional men make known their names and budding talent by the innocent device of being paged at the Royal.

And long since had vanished the youthful artistic rebels, the brilliant socialists, the eccentrics and anarchists who poured their talents so lavishly into Great Causes like the Russian Revolution. . .

Actors and actresses, Mrs. Sirotkin (the owner of K&S Cleaners) said, still stop by to ask about the Cafe Royal.

"I tell them," she said: "Well, the Cafe Royal isn't all gone. See the mirror there? That's your mirror from the cafe. You can still look in it and see yourself—just like the old days." The mirror from the cafe is almost the only memento of the great days along Second Avenue. You will look in vain for a restaurant that serves tea in a glass. . .[4]

By 1953 Sholom had achieved a degree of professional and personal harmony for which he had longed for years. At the age of 59, he was respected as a composer. His son Shelly had graduated from college, and Eugene was a student at New York University. Sholom and Betty were contentedly alone and free to travel extensively.

In the 1950s it was still common practice among Jewish fraternal and professional organizations to give banquets at the slightest provocation. Every time Sholom and Betty went on a trip, some Jewish society would throw a dinner for them. "It got to be," says Shelly, "that they seemed to be given a farewell dinner when they took a ferry to Hoboken."

In 1953 on the eve of their first trip to Europe, which included a visit to Israel, Sholom was the guest of honor at a banquet sponsored by the American-Israeli Club. A series of toasts was proffered, and a variety of Jewish and non-Jewish entertainers performed material from Sholom's repertoire.

Speeches were given by members of various Jewish organizations and Yiddish theater unions. Abraham Ellstein, a board member of the Society of Jewish Composers (of which Sholom was president), who was known as a witty speaker, was asked to say a few words. This night, however, he was in a serious mood.

After outlining Sholom's contribution to music and culture, Ellstein paused, and said to the attentive audience, "I'm going to tell you something about Sholom that you may not know. Only a handful

of people are aware of an incident in his life that could have made
him a lot richer than he is.''

Ellstein told of Sholom's decision twelve years earlier to remain in
the Society of Jewish Composers, rather than join ASCAP, at great
financial sacrifice. Sholom was deeply touched by Ellstein's remarks.

Betty, from whom Sholom had kept his decision a secret, was stunned. For the rest of the evening she made no comment about
Ellstein's revelation. But on the way home she exploded.

"It's unbelievable to me that you could be so stupid!" she
shouted. "None of them would have done that for you!"

On May 21 Betty and Sholom boarded a BOAC flight to London,
the first stop of a seven-week, grand tour of Europe. It was Betty's
first trip abroad, and the first for Sholom since his trip to Europe with
Hymie Jacobson in 1923. Travel with Betty was vastly different. She
was full of fun and *kvetches,* she was a tireless tourist (as was he), and
she was Sholom's alone for companionship.

Well, almost. Accompanying the Secundas were two more Secundas—Isadore and Sadie, known to the family as the Pittsfield Secundas (they lived in Pittsfield, Massachusetts). Although they could
never document it, Sholom and Izzy believed they were distant cous-
ins—Sholom's grandfather had come from Lithuania, as had Izzy's
father. On this and subsequent trips abroad Izzy and Sadie traveled
with Betty and Sholom. For this trip the itinerary included London,
Brussels, Paris, Rome, Tel Aviv, Naples, Florence, Venice, Lugano,
Milan, Nice, Geneva, Paris and home on *HMS Queen Elizabeth.*

Sholom wrote to his sons every day—the letters served as his diary
for articles on his trip for the *Forward*—pages and pages of observations and expressions of love.

Sholom chronicled the highlights of each stop in letters home.
From Paris he wrote:

Everyone is raving about Betty's beauty, and I am running short of
mirrors for her to look at and convince herself—but I must admit,
the kid looks great.

From Rome:

We had a "private" audience with the Pope. The star appeared
with plenty of light effects, and throne and a chorus of extras—

Swiss guards exquisitely costumed. It was a production worthy of Ziegfeld or Yablokoff.

But the letters from Israel were rhapsodic. In Israel Sholom felt as though he had come home:

No art, no sculpture or music is comparable to God's wonders here. We visited Beer Sheba, the Negev and S'dom where we were given a lesson in natural sculpture. See Israel and become a Jew. No pages in history can match the heroism and accomplishments in so short a time as that of Israel.

It was the first of five trips Betty and Sholom would take to the Holy Land.

By the time they returned to the United States, Shelly had been drafted into the Army. Sholom continued to chronicle his activities in letters to his son. His duties for the *Forward* now included theater and concert reviews. Occasionally Sholom refused to cover a cultural event. "Gieseking gave two Carnegie Hall recitals to oversold houses," Sholom wrote, "and, of course, I did not go to hear him. I doubt whether that calls for an explanation." (The explanation is that German pianist Walter Gieseking, who made his American debut in 1926, had returned to Germany in 1939 and was prevented, after World War II, from performing in America because of alleged Nazi collaboration. He was cleared of charges and permitted to renew his performances in the United States, but Sholom was unforgiving.)

Sholom had a banner year in 1954. He joined ASCAP. Most of the members of the Society of Jewish Composers were either dead or no longer active, and Sholom no longer felt a division of loyalty. His income was greatly abetted by his share of the ASCAP royalties for "Bei Mir Bist Du Schön" (receiving equal shares were Sammy Cahn, Saul Chaplin and Jacob Jacobs), which was still popular, if not on its 1938 scale. He wrote to Shelly:

I recently appeared on the Latin Quarter program on ABC, of all things, and was interviewed in connection with a new mambo recording of "Bei Mir." I collected a goodly number of ASCAP credits. They played five different recordings of various versions of the song. Each playing, if only a few measures, collects credits and adds to the Secunda treasury. The interview was the general routine. Nothing exciting, besides the plug of the number and the name of S.S. on a national hookup, which at no time can hurt, unless it's tied up with a criminal offense. . .

The same year Richard Tucker recorded Sholom's arrangement of an Israeli song, "Shir Hapalmach," for Columbia Records and performed it on the Ed Sullivan television program, mentioning Sholom's involvement with it on the air. ("On Monday," Sholom wrote to Shelly, "so many people were anxious to congratulate your mother—it seems everyone heard it.")

Sholom's "Psalm 118" was also performed by Alfredo Antonini and his orchestra on CBS in December. That month he picked up more ASCAP credits on the Dean Martin-Jerry Lewis show with a dance version of "Joe and Paul," a tune he had written in the 1930s as a commercial for a clothing store. Now that he was a member of ASCAP, every piece of Sholom's music was a potential moneymaker.

"Some day," he wrote to Shelly, "you will be buying *Chanukah* presents for your kiddies with the royalties that these psalms and others of my songs bring in. Upon your return, for your own good, you should familiarize yourself with this material. From now on, every broadcast means credits at ASCAP and checks at the end of every three months."

Sholom was still trying to write a non-Yiddish, non-Hebrew hit. Jan Peerce, a close friend of Sholom's (and Richard Tucker's estranged brother-in-law—they were not on speaking terms), had recorded a sentimental, inspirational tune called "Bluebird of Happiness" in 1937. It became Peerce's signature (and was the title of his memoirs, published in 1976). The song was a hit for Peerce, and Sholom thought he could repeat the formula of that song, however derivatively, with a song of his own called "Faith Alone."

Tucker recorded "Faith" for Columbia Records (the producer of the record was Mitch Miller). It was a frank imitation of "Bluebird," including phrases that Tucker recited dramatically, rather than sang. The timing for such sentiment was poor—such songs by the 1950s were old-fashioned—and the song was a financial disappointment.

Although Sholom was close to both singers, a discussion about one with the other was not encouraged. The Peerce-Tucker fallout was a source of pain for Sholom, who loved them both.

"Sholom and I took the position," said the late Norman Warembud, "that there were too few Jewish creators around, and that unless we all stuck together and made peace with one another, we could not nurture Jewish culture. Each of us tried desperately to bring those two together. I remember once Sholom and I walked Peerce down Broadway and up 7th Avenue, trying to convince Peerce to make the first move, or at least to be receptive to a move if we could get Tucker to do it. It would make us wince when Peerce would refer to Tucker as 'my brother-in-law'—Tucker adopted the same terminology for Jan. They wouldn't dignify each other by calling each other by their proper names."

Sholom was reunited professionally with Maurice Schwartz in 1955 when Schwartz mounted "The Shepherd King" at the National Theater. Schwartz's Yiddish Art Theater was slipping in its artistic supremacy of Yiddish drama. Of the production, the *New York Times* critic wrote, "...South of Fourteenth Street...audiences bring a quota of enthusiasm that is rare on Broadway. For them it did not seem to matter that Leizer Treister's play wallowed in dialogue that was somewhere between Italian and soap opera. . .To help Mr. Schwartz, Sholom Secunda has shaped an intelligent, sympathetic score and a number of actors did the best they could. . .''⁵

The blame for the play's failure rests with Maurice Schwartz. This production was the first Yiddish Art Theater presentation in six years after 31 years of superb theater. In an effort to revive it, an alliance of Yiddish newspapers and Jewish political and social organizations attempted to subsidize Maurice Schwartz's theater. "They were creating," write Nahma Sandrow in *Vagabond Stars*, ". . .a subsidized community art theater. They even guaranteed Schwartz himself a minimum wage. Almost four hundred people subscribed for season tickets.''⁶

Herman Yablokoff, who was executive secretary of the group, recalls that although Leizer Treister wrote the book for the play, it was Maurice Schwartz who adapted it for a musical production. When Schwartz had completed his adaptation, he invited Yablokoff and

Sholom to his apartment on Eighth Street so that he could read it to them. Of the meeting Yablokoff said:

> After Schwartz finished, we didn't have the heart to tell him what we really thought. Instead, we told him, "Well, it's only a first draft, you'll work on it." I had my car downstairs and I offered to drive Sholom home. "I can't go home," I said. "I won't be able to sleep." I took him home and we never exchanged a word between us. Sholom was so downhearted. We knew it was no good. And I'm sorry to say that we were right. The theater was closed shortly after that.

In 1956 Joseph Rumshinsky died. During his lifetime he had been an artistic tyrant, a theatrical demigod, a Yiddish theater manager who left his company and staff either in tears or in a rage. But always he was a consummate musician. He had an eerie sense of what his audiences wanted, and his melodies were ranked by many people as unparalleled in lyricism.

His death shook Sholom to his shoes. "My God, I'm the last of them," Sholom said when he heard the news. With Olshanetsky and Rumshinsky dead, and Ellstein no longer working in the Yiddish theater, he felt his roots were withering. Now when Jewish producers wanted to mount a musical production, they had only Sholom to turn to. He couldn't say no.

"Why do you do it?" Yablokoff once asked him. "You don't need it."

"What can I do?" Sholom replied. "I've worked with these people all my life. There's nobody left to write for them, so they come to me. What do you expect me to do?"

Sholom's explanation to Richard Shepard of the *New York Times* was this:

> . . .It's my duty. I owe it to the Yiddish theater. . .It gave me my start. I had Broadway offers but I never considered them. In its heyday, the Yiddish theater paid me $250 a week and my contract guaranteed me a six-week vacation. That's when Broadway paid a conductor $100 a week.

And so he cranked out a show a year—"It's a Funny World" (1956), "It Could Happen to You" (1957), "Nice People" (1958).

Sholom's contribution to the Yiddish theater in 1959 was a treat for him rather than an obligation. He got to work with Molly Picon— the greatest musical comedy star on Second Avenue in a career that began in 1905. Sholom had known Molly and her husband, Jacob Kalich, since the early 1920s—at Loch Sheldrake in the Catskills and in Paris, where she and Jacob toured and lived, and at assorted professional functions over the years. But it wasn't until 1959 that she appeared in a Sholom Secunda operetta.

The play was "The Kosher Widow," produced by Irving Jacobson and Julius Adler at the Jewish Anderson Theater. Jacob Kalich and Louis Freiman wrote the book, and the play was directed by Kalich. Molly Picon, as was her habit, wrote the Yiddish lyrics, and was the star. She was assisted by a cast of Yiddish theater veterans—Irving Jacobson, Mae Schonfeld, Julius Adler, Henrietta Jacobson, and Kalich.

Of the production, which opened in October, Lewis Funke of the *New York Times* wrote, ". . . it is good to have Miss Picon back. A performer of charm, warmth and the desire to please, she makes 'The Kosher Widow' a real delight. The fact is that this is one of the best musicals to adorn the dwindling Yiddish theater in years. The book is full of humor, wit and farce, and Sholom Secunda has provided a tuneful score in which, indeed, there may be a hit or two."[7]

"The season with Molly and Yankele was the most enjoyable one of my long career," Sholom wrote. "Although Molly was certainly more musical than all the other stars, she didn't try to rework my music, and at the rehearsals she was a disciplined actress, without pretensions."

"Sholom had a little trouble writing for me," Picon says, "because by the time I worked with him, I had very little voice left." Her range may have been limited, but she had no trouble drawing an audience of 1500 nightly.

Molly knew her audience and played to it with an intimacy that was a hallmark of the Yiddish theater and is rare on Broadway—it was as though she and her audience were having a party. Gene Secunda attended one of the performances of "The Kosher Widow," and of Molly's performance, he says:

She was singing a number and suddenly there was this unbelievable crash outside the theater. Somebody had smashed a car into a
store window or something, and there was this tremendous com-
motion and sound of things breaking.

Molly turned to the audience and said, "Ah, the *kinder*
(children)." It broke up the house.

During the run of the show, Sholom conducted the orchestra every
night, for which he was paid $750 weekly. When "Kosher Widow"
closed on January 10, 1960 (because Picon had a commitment to do
"Majority of One" in London), Irving Jacobson and Julius Adler split
$75,000 in profits. "It was the most money we ever made," Adler
says. No one has matched this Yiddish theater success.

♫ TRAVEL

"The Kosher Widow" was the last money-making gasp of the Yiddish theater, and when it closed, Sholom announced he was finished with Second Avenue (nevertheless, in the 1960s he would write the scores for at least eight operettas).

His challenges were now with serious music alone, and he had sufficient income from royalties and elsewhere to pursue them. In 1960 he took a trip around the world with Betty, a journey that would inspire two lengthy, ambitious oratorios, the works that he considered the most important of his life.

The itinerary was, again, frenetic: London, Lisbon, Madrid, Barcelona, Tel Aviv, Athens, Istanbul, Vienna, Odessa, Moscow, Leningrad, Helsinki, Stockholm, Oslo, Copenhagen, Amsterdam, and Paris—17 cities in 71 days. And, as before, Betty and Sholom were accompanied by Izzy and Sadie Secunda.

"Everything so far is great," Sholom wrote from Madrid. "Still, every once in a while I get annoyed because of some incompatibility. I get over it quickly, but the accommodations are too ritzy for my taste."

The combined Secundas stayed at deluxe hotels, because Izzy insisted on American efficiency. Sholom would have preferred spending less money on quarters that were almost solely for sleeping. In addition, Sholom, who was very European in character, was appalled by the behavior of some of the Americans he encountered in those hotels. From Stockholm, he wrote, "The natives of the countries we have visited pay dearly for every American dollar. The average Jewish tourist, to my regret, assumes a sense of superiority with the handing over of every green bill."

He was distressed especially by the poverty he saw in Madrid (as everywhere), which may have reminded him of his early years in Russia. "Beyond the city limits," he wrote, "the shacks remind you of Indian reservations. People draw water from community wells. Kids stand outside waiting for tourists, pointing to their mouths and begging for centimas. But inside the cathedrals and churches there are riches—gold, silver and priceless jewels—enough money for valuables, but not for homes or bread for the poor suckers."

But Israel—another land of immigrants—had an urgent appeal for Sholom. The enormous body of work he had produced in his 66 years gave him great satisfaction, but still he was profoundly aware that whatever goals remained for him had to be tended to soon, work that would make a statement not only of his musical creativity but of his being part of an historical—and Jewish—continuum. Israel spurred that awareness.

Sholom was esteemed in Israel, and he was met at the airport by Issacher Miron, composer of the popular song, "Tzena, Tzena," and by a representative of the Israeli Ministry of Culture. In Jerusalem Sholom was invited to speak before an audience of Israeli composers and music critics, and he had a recording session of two of his symphonic pieces—"Yom B'Kibbutz" and "Concert Freilachs."

While Sholom was in Israel, Maurice Schwartz, who was then living in Tel Aviv, had a heart attack and died on May 10. Sholom had become the unofficial eulogizer of Yiddish actors and producers, and he gave Schwartz's final tribute at a memorial service in Bet Sokoloff.

"The press here resents very keenly the fact that Schwartz's body will be flown to the U.S. for burial," Sholom wrote to his sons. "They argue that real Jews leave wills stating that they be buried in Israel, and here is a Jewish artist who wishes to have his body returned to be buried among *goyim,* even though he was privileged to die in Israel. Oh well. . ."

"There is no youth in the (Yiddish) theater," Schwartz had written in a letter shortly before his death, and the reality of that fact was hardly lost on Sholom.[1] Certainly Schwartz's passing represented for Sholom his mortality, and his need to make his musical mark about larger issues of Jewishness—Jews of the Talmud, and Jews of the future.

Sholom's trip to Russia underscored that urgency. Russia, the place of his birth, was inhospitable to his nostalgia. Betty and Sholom were permitted to visit Odessa, Moscow and Leningrad, but were not allowed to visit Nicholayev, where Sholom had lived as a boy.

In one of a series of *Forward* articles on his travels, Sholom wrote of visiting the Tsar's palace in Leningrad:

. . .In 1905, I lived through a pogrom as a small child in my city of Nicholayev, which may have been approved by someone in this same palace I was about to visit. . .In order to save their children from persecutions and pogroms, my parents had left behind their brothers and sisters in Tsarist Russia and fled to America, where we could breathe freely as Jews. Now, after more than half a century, I was again in Russia and taking a walk through the rooms of Nicholas' house. . .I thought of one thing. . .How I wish that Nicholas could see me now, one of his former victims, strolling around his palace. . .

When we left the palace, I said to my wife, "Let's ride back to the hotel on a trolley." We boarded a trolley on Nevsky Prospekt, and I stood next to the motorman. I asked him in Russian how to get back to the European Hotel.

"Ah, you're an American?" he asked.

I said I was. He told me he had relatives who lived on the East Side in New York. . .He looked around and then said to me furtively, "I would like to give you the address of my relatives. If you don't mind, would you relay greetings to them for me?" I said I would.

Again he looked around and asked me to write my name and room number at the hotel on a piece of paper and he would bring me the address. I quickly did so and put the piece of paper in his hand. He took the note and said, "You should have been more care-ful—everyone saw you. It's dangerous."

"Why?" I asked, but he didn't answer. A few minutes later he said, "You get off the trolley when it stops."

On the way to the hotel, I asked my wife, "Do you think he'll come?"

"He won't come," she replied.

I was embraced by the same gloom I had noticed on the motor-man's face, and I began to long for the freedom to say what I wanted, to go where I wanted, to write what I wanted.

Of their Odessa visit, Sholom wrote the following letter, which he mailed only after leaving the Soviet Union because he feared that its contents would be censored:

We went to a synagogue. The Jews there are frightened to death, and for good reason. There is one Jew there who is a spy. His job is to make sure that if a foreigner comes in, he gets no chance to talk to any of the worshipers. This spy sat next to me all the time and made sure no one spoke to me. If I asked someone a question, he looked directly at the man who immediately turned away from me.

During the recess (Reading of the Torah) I walked into the cantor's room, where I found a Jew having a conversation with the cantor. When I introduced myself, they began to question me about the U.S. Before long, the spy was in the cantor's room. When I asked a man a question, he started to answer, but the spy told him, "Hey, why don't you take a drink?"

When the man obediently took a drink, the spy remarked, "Keep the water in your mouth." When the poor guy swallowed the water and returned to me, the spy, believing I hadn't noticed, signaled to the man to get out.

In Kiev Betty and Sholom visited another synagogue, and the experience was nearly identical. During the service, they managed to sit some distance from an official assigned to keep them from speaking with the congregants. Sholom wrote,

I quietly questioned some Jews sitting next to me. Some had locks on their lips, some murmured a few dispassionate answers, such as "nit gut" (not good), "schver" (hard), "fregt nit" (don't ask), and "me tor nit redn" (one mustn't talk). . .During the course of the services, I learned that the lot of the Jew is far from good, that anti-Semitism still plays an important role in the official government, that life for Russian Jews is one of woe, depression and persecution.

In Moscow there were isolated happy moments. "In all the restaurants," Sholom wrote, "there is an orchestra. Last night we went out for a midnight snack to a restaurant, and we heard the orchestra strike up 'Bei Mir Bist Du Schön.' Naturally, I went over to the conductor and introduced myself, which caused some excitement among the musicians."

But Sholom's gloom was perpetuated by more frustrations. He wrote,

Our Intourist guide, Miss Kislova, told me if there was anything the Ministry of Culture could do for me, her assistant, Mr. Alexeyev, would be of service. To test her good will, I expressed a desire to meet Mr. Weinberg, composer of the score for the Russian film, "The Cranes are Flying." After much persistence, Mr. Alexeyev agreed to set up a meeting. Your mother and I appeared promptly for the meeting at the Home of Friendship. A young man introduced himself as the interpreter for Mr. Weinberg and presented the composer to me. I assured the young man that I could spare him the job of translating since I speak Russian. He said he would not in the least mind translating anyhow.

We all sat down for our conversation—in Russian, in the presence of the interpreter—and when I told Mr. Weinberg I had an excellent article about him which the *Forward* asked me to give to him, he said quickly, "I'm sorry, I neither read nor write Yiddish."

I knew he was lying, since he had been a pianist years before in the Warsaw Jewish Theater. It was not possible that he didn't know Yiddish. His face was as white as a sheet, and sweat ran down his cheeks. I felt as though we were destroying him.

Outside on the street the interpreter agreed to take a picture of Weinberg and me. While we were posing, Weinberg said softly to me, "My whole family was wiped out in Warsaw." I winked at him to show that I understood.

Fortunately, the trip did not end on this melancholy note. Betty and Sholom unwound in the Scandinavian countries, and on July 2, they had a lavish dinner in Paris on the eve of their return to the United States. Still, Sholom came home with a sense of unfinished business—he would return to Europe to visit Germany three years hence to complete his inner picture of what it means to be a Jew.

One morning in the fall of 1960 Sholom received a call from William Starr, director of copyright and licensing of Harms Music Company, which owned the rights to "Bei Mir Bist Du Schön."

"How come we haven't seen you?" Starr said amiably.

Recalling the months in 1938 when he had haunted the Harms office, trying to get an appointment, Sholom replied curtly, "I've been busy."

"You're welcome here any time," Starr said. "Do you have any new songs? We'd like to hear them."

"If I have time," Sholom said, "I'll stop by."

Sholom put on his coat and hurried to the office of his friend, Norman Warembud, whose company, Mills Music, now published all of Sholom's work. He related his conversation with Starr. Warembud, who had had many years of experience in contract negotiation, looked at his friend's beaming face.

"Don't be in such a hurry," he said temperately. "Don't visit Starr and don't call him. Wait for him to call you. Don't worry, he'll call. The copyright to 'Bei Mir' expires next year. He needs you more than you need him."

Sholom was keenly aware of his bargaining position and had kept track of his hit song of 1938 over the years. Between 1937, when the Andrews Sisters recorded it, and 1961, "Bei Mir" had earned royalties of $3 million. By selling the rights to the song, Sholom personally lost over $350,000, which as composer he would have collected had he not done so. His joining of ASCAP in 1954 had improved his position only slightly—he had earned from it a total of $4,352.17 for performances of the song as of 1961.

Sholom knew that Harms was not eager to lose the publisher's share of a song that thirty years later still earned for the composer alone $5,000 (a quarter of the total shared by Secunda, Jacobs, Cahn and Chaplin) annually, and that he and Jacobs had the option at last of signing with any publisher.

Warembud's prediction came true. Starr did call, several times. Each time Sholom was polite but distant, pleading a busy schedule. Finally he agreed to an appointment.

At the meeting Sholom demanded a substantial bonus to sign with Harms, claiming that he wanted to recoup some of the revenue he had lost. Starr refused, saying that the song no longer had the earning capacity it had when Harms acquired it. The two men were not able to come to terms, and Sholom left.

The second conference was inconclusive, as was the third. After weeks of negotiation, Starr offered Sholom a bonus of $2,000 to be split with the original lyricist, Jacob Jacobs, which he accepted.

In the early 1960s such a gesture was rare in the music publishing business. In any case, it was enough to redeem Sholom's pride. Starr set February 3, 1961, as the date that the contract would be signed. Sholom relished the irony that a division of Warner Brothers, which had rejected the song when he visited Hollywood in the summer of 1937, was now giving him a bonus for agreeing to do business with them.

February 3, 1961, was a particularly grim day in New York. The sky was bleak, and frozen New Yorkers hurried past mounds of sooty snow to the warmth of their offices. It might as well have been spring for Sholom. Regaining the rights to his most famous song made him feel like a boy.

Betty shared his high spirits, muted somewhat by a powerful sense of retribution when it came to injuries to her family, which this day particularly symbolized. In the morning she went to the hairdresser's. Looking well, she reasoned, was the best revenge.

She returned to their Washington Heights apartment and changed into a new navy blue suit and fashionable hat. Betty always dressed with understated chic, as though her appearance were to be judged by an audience, as it had been three decades earlier when she had been a dancer in the Yiddish theater.

Betty slipped into her mink coat and, against her better judgment vis a vis boots and double pneumonia, she put on her new suede pumps. Sholom stood impatiently at the door wearing his coat and hat. It was still the family joke, Betty keeping everyone waiting as she rehearsed her clothes and carefully applied her makeup, which Sholom referred to as "paint" if it was too noticeable.

"Hurry up!" Sholom called from the front door. "What's taking so long?"

Betty gave her hair a final pat and, pulling on her gloves, joined her husband at last. They walked to the 181st Street stop of the IND Subway and emerged, 25 minutes later, at 59th Street and Columbus Circle. "Let's take a taxi the rest of the way," Sholom said expansively. Betty looked at him quickly and stifled an impulse to question this uncharacteristic splurge on private transportation. The cab pulled up to 488 Madison Avenue, and Betty and Sholom went up to William Starr's office.

"Well, Sholom" Starr said, "it's an historic day, isn't it?" On Starr's desk lay a contract between Sholom and Harms outlining new royalty terms of "Bei Mir Bist Du Schön." Betty removed her coat and sat down on the couch in Starr's office. Having shared her husband's anguish over "Bei Mir" for so long, it seemed appropriate for her to witness the contract signing. Sholom was asked to sit behind Starr's desk, flanked by Starr and Betty. A photographer documented the moment Sholom affixed his signature to the contract.

In the afternoon Sholom was interviewed by Arthur Gelb of the *New York Times* and was photographed for the story. Gelb's feature piece, recounting the history of the song, ran in the *Times* the following morning. The headline read, "Composer Regains 'Bei Mir Bist Du Schön.'"

At breakfast Sholom studied the story as though it were the commutation of a prison sentence. He did not want to be known as a one-song composer, and Gelb was faithful to his subject:

Mr. Secunda. . .has. . .earned a living writing Yiddish musicals for Second Avenue and liturgical music for Columbia Records; serving as music critic for *The Jewish Daily Forward* and acting as music director for the Concord Hotel in the Catskills, where he conducts a sixty-five-piece orchestra in the summer. About his loss, he is philosophical.

"Actually, it bothered everyone else more than it bothered me," he said. "I've been more interested in the symphonic music I'm writing. 'Bei Mir Bist Du Schön' has commercial value, but I wouldn't compare it too favorably with some of my symphonic compositions."

Sholom and Jacob Jacobs used the copyright reversion to get more mileage out of the song. In October they mounted a musical at the Anderson Theater called "Bei Mir Bistu Schoen (sic)," starring Leon Liebgold, Jacob Jacobs, Miriam Kressyn and Seymour Rexsite. For the production, Sholom wrote a counter-melody to "Bei Mir" called "Hob mich lieb (love me)." Of the operetta, Milton Esterow of *The New York Times* wrote, "Now, perhaps, Mr. Secunda will make some money out of 'Bei Mir Bistu Schoen.'"

The most fun Sholom derived from his controversial song was during a visit to the Far East with Betty in 1963. On May 12 they were in Tokyo, Japan. Still addicted to travel, he was consumed with curiosity about the customs and history of the country, and he wanted to know all about the Jews who lived there. A Tokyo "Turkish bath," as he called it, seemed to be the perfect amalgam of Jewish and Japanese life, a bit of logic that was peculiarly Sholom's.

A friend in New York had advised him, "A Turkish bath in Japan is not at all like a Turkish bath in Warsaw or Odessa. There are baths and there are baths."

Sholom was a man to find out such things for himself. He questioned bellboys, waiters and Japanese guests at the Imperial Hotel—where he and Betty were staying—about which Turkish bath was the best. Sholom's research turned up one intriguing fact: the massages were rendered by women, even to male patrons. Some baths were more elegant than others, he learned.

"I'd come such a long way," he later said wryly, "so it would have been foolish not to try one, right?"

Armed with a name and address given to him by a Japanese friend, he took a cab to Tokyo's most luxurious Turkish bath—with Betty's permission, of course. Sholom would dine out on the experience for years:

As I entered the bath, I was welcomed by a young Japanese man dressed in a well-tailored suit who spoke English like a Harvard professor. He led me to a room and read a list of the services and fees. I requested a massage, and was invited to pay in advance, for which I was given a receipt.

Then he rang a little bell and a beautiful, young Japanese woman of about twenty years of age entered. She bowed deeply and beckoned me to follow her. We went into another room, and she locked the door. I felt like a twelve-year-old. Her sympathetic smile took the edge off my nervousness, and she helped me remove my jacket, which she hung up.

I was frozen to the spot. With hand signals she told me to take off my shirt. It would have been rude to give her an argument. I took off my shirt. Then she showed me to a chair. In a businesslike manner, she undressed me, and I was left as naked as the day of my birth.

Then she took me by the hand and led me into another room. She sat me down in a cabinet and closed the doors so that only my face was showing. She turned on the steam and I sat there, perspiring, unsure of the source of heat—the steam or the young lady. After the steambath, she stroked me with a cold towel.

Next, she sat me in a bathtub and began washing me the way a mother washes a baby—I was in her hands, so to speak. I was then led to a long bench and I lay down on it. I had had massages before, but I can still remember how powerfully this young, slender Japanese girl kneaded me. It felt as though she were counting every bone in my body. The small of my back still aches.

As the young lady massaged, she hummed a variety of Japanese songs. Since she couldn't speak English, it occurred to me that we might communicate through music. "American song?" I said. "Sing American song?" I sang a scale and she seemed to understand.

She thought for a moment, and then she began to sing "Bei Mir Bist Du Schön," in Japanese.

I nearly dropped off the bench. I was halfway around the world, in a totally foreign culture without a stitch on, and this lovely young woman was singing a song I had written 32 years before.

I gleefully began pointing to myself, trying to say, "I'm the one who composed that song." Suddenly she stopped massaging, she quickly took me back to where my clothes were hung, and helped me to get dressed. Then she went over to a telephone, spoke in rapid Japanese, and abruptly hung up, then unlocked the door.

In a moment, the Harvard-type Japanese man rushed in and said, "Is it true? Did you write that song?"

"Yes," I replied. "Why?"

"Are you kidding?" he shouted. "How long will you be in Tokyo? Where are you staying?"

I answered all his questions and finally left, ushered to the door by the young man and the charming masseuse. Two days later, I bought a copy of the Asahi Evening News, a daily English-language newspaper. The headline read: COMPOSER FINDS OWN SONG AT A TOKYO TURKISH BATH.

It is worth noting that "Bei Mir Bist Du Schön" earns more foreign ASCAP royalties in Japan than in any other country.

The rest of the 1963 trip, which took Betty and Sholom around the world again, was less ebullient. Sholom looked for and found Jews and Jewish culture in Bangkok, New Delhi, Hong Kong and Istanbul.

But looking for Jews in Germany was anguishing, although it was the purpose of his trip. In a letter to his sons, Sholom wrote: "We were both in a bad mood as we disembarked from the plane and walked on the bloody soil once occupied and governed by the damned Nazis, where Hitler developed his brutal policies. Your mother wanted to take the next plane home. It is hard to tell here who is Jewish and who is not. After many phone calls I located a cantor, Mr. Reiss. I told him who I was, and he insisted on coming to collect us in his car so that we could visit his home. . .The sun is trying to greet us, but the German clouds are anti-Semitic and are in the way. Those Germans never change. How they bow constantly. Do they know I am a Jew, and hate them every time they bow and say 'bitte schon'?''

The following day Sholom wrote, "We are leaving Munich with mixed emotions. The natural feeling is one of hatred. The cantor picked us up to take us to Dachau. We approached it with palpitating hearts. After all, it is not an easy place to face, but it is a harder place to omit. We saw enough to make your blood curdle—the bridge of death, the chambers before the death, the eternal smoke coming out of a tall chimney in memory of those who burned there. It was unbearably depressing. . .''

Sholom and Betty found respite in Israel and returned to the United States with almost palpable relief. Sholom began an extended tour of lecture appearances, in which he stressed the connection between Jewish modes and other forms of music.

"I don't have much fondness for popular music," he told AP writer William Glover for an article about Sholom's trip to the Far East. Nevertheless, in 1964 he had another internationally popular song.

In 1964 Theodore Bikel recorded an album for Elektra Records called "More Jewish Folksongs." Included in the album was the song, "Dona, Dona, Dona," which Bikel had heard sung in Yiddish by inmates when he visited Displaced Persons camps in Europe at the close of World War II. Bikel recorded the song, assuming it was a traditional (public domain) folksong.

A short time later, Joan Baez, then at the peak of her folksinging career, included "Dona" in an album she recorded for Vanguard. She had had an English lyric written and, within a few months of the release of the album, "Dona" was firmly entrenched in the repertoire of every guitar-playing flower child in America.

When the Bikel recording came to Sholom's attention, he wrote to the singer, who was an old friend, informing him of the song's true authorship. Having his songs thought of as ancient or traditional melodies was nothing new to Sholom. Brooks Atkinson had made the same mistake when reviewing "Bagels and Yox.''

Fortunately for Sholom, no one had offered to buy the rights to "Dona" from him. He had written it in 1940 for the score of "Esterke," with Yiddish lyrics by Aaron Zeitlin. Sholom owned the copyright and asked his son, Shelly, to do the English lyric. In 1956 Shelly had joined his father as a member of ASCAP, with two recorded songs of his own. Mills Music published the English version of "Dona" in 1964.

It was subsequently recorded by the Chad Mitchell Trio, the Everly Brothers, Chad and Jeremy, Patty Duke, Martha Schlamme, Yaffa Yarkoni and twice by rock singer Donovan, in 1969 and again in 1978. It was published and recorded in many languages and, like "Bei Mir," it earned its greatest foreign royalties in Japan. Over the years, "Dona, Dona, Dona" was to become second only to "Bei Mir" as a revenue producer for Sholom, and to enjoy enormous popularity with a generation that had never heard of "Bei Mir Bist Du Schön."

♫ ORATORIOS

By 1964 Sholom had been elected a fellow of the International Institute of Arts and Letters and was listed in Who's Who in America, in the World, in the East, in Music and in Jewry. He had released another album called "Sing A Little Something," a compendium of popular Yiddish and Israeli songs such as "Hava Nagilah," "Tzena, Tzena, Tzena," and his own "Shabbat Shalom" and "Dona, Dona, Dona." He was, you might say, a Jewish star.

Thus he was in great demand on the lecture circuit. Early in the year he was engaged to give a talk at the Beth El congregation in Rochester, New York, about Yiddish folk music and its influence on art songs.

Sholom's host in Rochester was Samuel Rosenbaum, cantor at Beth El. Sholom had known Sam since 1933 when, as a young man of 13, he had sung on Yiddish radio station WLTH, for which Sholom was musical director. The two men had seen each other sporadically over the years. Sholom went to Rochester at Sam's invitation, and that trip was the genesis of Sholom's first oratorio.

While in Rochester Sholom told Sam that he was looking for a good English translation of Isaac Lieb Peretz's "If Not Higher." Sam had done a translation of the work, which he gave to Sholom to take home. When he returned to New York, Sholom called Sam to say that he would like to set music to Sam's translation and, further, that he would guarantee that Richard Tucker would perform it.

It was a rash promise, typical of Sholom's enthusiasm. "Arranging an appointment with Tucker," Sholom wrote, "was not the easiest thing to do—one day he'd be singing at the Met and the next day he'd be off to Italy for an appearance." Nevertheless, Tucker was available the day after Sholom's call.

With pianist William Gunther, Sholom went to Tucker's apartment in New York (Tucker had a house in Great Neck, Long Island, as well) to audition the oratorio. Sholom had completed the 45-minute work in five months, including orchestration. Tucker agreed to perform the piece as soon as his schedule permitted.

Sam Rosenbaum began preparations for the premiere of the work in Rochester, and Norman Warembud began working on Jack Mills of Mills Publishing to publish it. The premiere was set for November 18, 1964.

The personnel for "If Not Higher" were Richard Tucker in the tenor role, Norman Atkins, baritone with the New York City Opera, Millard Fargo and Margaret Sage, both of the choir of Rochester's Third Presbyterian Church. Theodore Hollenbach conducted the Rochester Civic Orchestra and the Rochester Oratorio Society. Cantor Rosenbaum was the narrator.

Three days before the premiere, Sholom and Betty flew to Rochester to supervise the final rehearsals with the soloists and choir and generally to assist Hollenbach. The day before the premiere, Sholom got a phone call from Sarah Tucker.

"I don't know how to tell you this," Sarah said, "but Richard has come down with a cold and his voice is hoarse. His doctor has advised him not to leave the house. Would it be possible for you to get another tenor for the premiere?"

"Sarah," Sholom said, trying to sound composed, "the music is extremely difficult. We can't possibly get someone else to do it on such short notice. We'll just have to postpone the premiere."

Tucker got on the phone. "Don't do that," he whispered. "The doctor is coming over and I'll get him to do whatever is necessary. I'll sing the piece without a rehearsal—I know it very well. You do the rehearsal without me. I'll call you tomorrow."

The rehearsal went on as scheduled, with Sholom singing Tucker's part. The next morning at 10:00, Tucker called Sholom. "I'm at the airport," he said softly. "The flight leaves in an hour."

Sholom and Rosenbaum met Tucker at the airport and took him directly to his hotel. Hollenbach came over in the evening to go over the score with Tucker, and Tucker then went to bed.

As they were leaving Tucker's hotel, Hollenbach dropped a bombshell on Sholom and Rosenbaum. He had to fly the following morning to Washington for a rehearsal for an upcoming concert, which he had promised Rosenbaum weeks before that he would get out of. He vowed he would be back in time for a 3:00 p.m. camera rehearsal.

"The oratorio was to be videotaped for CBS television," Rosenbaum says, "and we had thirty thousand bucks' worth of camera equipment and personnel and two big trucks from CBS and everyone in the world at the temple, and I thought, 'My God, if Tucker hears this, he'll blow his top and turn around and go home.' Hollenbach said he couldn't break his rehearsal date. So at his own expense, he hired a plane to take him and bring him back in time for the rehearsal. It was a foggy day. Three o'clock came, and he didn't show. At 3:30 I called my friend Sam Adler at the Eastman School of Music and asked him to come over. He had never seen the score, but he conducted the camera rehearsal. And Tucker was as sweet as he could possibly be. At 5:00, as they finished the last chord of the rehearsal, Hollenbach finally came in.

"I said to him, 'You better watch out, because if Tucker gets hold of you he'll kill you, and if he doesn't, I will.'"

That night Temple Beth El, which has a capacity of 1500 seats, was filled to overflowing. The program was to have begun with a song recital with Atkins and Tucker, but was replaced, to avoid strain on Tucker's voice, with a performance by the orchestra of Ernest Bloch's "Shelomo," featuring cellist Ronald Leonard. After the intermission Rabbi Abraham Karp gave the audience a synopsis of "If Not Higher," the story of a devout rabbi in Russia who is always absent when the Jews of Nemirov gather to pray each night. The rabbi is believed to go to heaven during those prayers. A Litvak visits the town and questions that belief. He follows the rabbi and discovers that during prayer time he is in fact chopping wood for an impoverished Gentile widow. Contrite, the Litvak, when asked if the rabbi goes to heaven each evening, replies, "Yes, to Heaven—if not higher."

"As soon as Tucker began to sing," Sholom wrote, "our nervousness disappeared. His voice was clear and shone like a gem. When he finished his first aria, a storm of applause broke out from the audience."

Tucker's singing of anything written for him by Sholom brought out the best in each. "The greatest ability Sholom had," Rosenbaum says, "was that he knew how to write for the voice. He was a rather primitive arranger, but he knew where the voices should go and how to display the best colors of that particular voice. For Ruby Tucker's voice, he was made to order.''

Richard Tucker sang inspirationally that night, executing the built-in passion of cantorial music with technical precision and restraint. Cantor Saul Meisels had flown from Cleveland for the premiere and after the performance invited Sholom and the principals to perform the work at his temple, the Temple on the Heights. It was performed there on January 19, 1966, with the Cleveland Orchestra and the Robert Shaw Chorale, under the direction of Shaw. The work, with an entirely new cast (save Rosenbaum), received good notices from the *Plain Dealer* and elsewhere.

The third performance of ''If Not Higher'' was on March 1, 1967, at Atlanta's Ahavath Achim Synagogue with the Atlanta Symphony and the Atlanta Singers. Sholom conducted the performance himself. The oratorio was also performed in Springfield, Massachusetts; Portland, Oregon; Detroit, Michigan; and Paterson, New Jersey. It appeared on ''Lamp Unto My Feet'' on CBS Television and, in 1966, Mills Music published the work.

The warm reception of ''If Not Higher'' by critics and performers gave Sholom a sense of vindication from the years when he had been written off as a Second Avenue composer. ''It bothered him that he was not a top contemporary composer,'' Warembud said, ''and that composers with far less talent were making big money. He wanted to try to bring his melodic talents instead to writing works of more lasting importance. Especially since we had a guy like Richard Tucker in our corner, for whom these works would become works of standard performance.''

Indeed they were. Tucker recorded an album for Columbia called ''Welcoming of the Sabbath,'' which included Sholom's ''Friday Evening Service.'' Sholom conducted the chorus and orchestra for Tucker's other Columbia liturgical albums—''Cantorial Chants,'' ''Israel Sings,'' and ''A Goldfaden Album.'' Tucker performed Secunda songs on the Bell Telephone Hour on NBC Television in the spring of 1966.

Of ''If Not Higher,'' Sholom said to a reporter from *The New York Times*, ''I hope it will stop people from introducing me as the composer of 'Bei Mir Bist Du Schön.'''

Sholom's final trip to Europe in 1966 was a melancholy one. "I had a need to visit countries behind the Iron Curtain—Romania, Hungary, Poland, Czechoslovakia—to find out what life was like for these persecuted Jews."

In Budapest, Hungary, Sholom was astonished by the size and relative freedom of the Jewish community, as well as the sophistication and latitude of the general cultural life. He attended two opera performances, and was interviewed by the editor of a Jewish bimonthly newspaper which, in Hungarian, reported on Jewish life in Hungary and elsewhere.

"The editor escorted me to the Jewish museum," Sholom wrote, "and there I saw heartbreaking scenes. The museum was built on the spot where Dr. Theodor Herzl (founder of modern Zionism) was born. There are original documents that were issued by Nazis ordering Jews to wear the yellow star, forbidding them to leave the ghetto, pictures of the inquisitors instrumental in the operation, including Eichmann. There are pictures of crematoriums and the burning inside of naked boys, starved to the degree that you can count each rib, before they marched into the ovens. 560,000 Jews were killed during the period, and 3,000 were buried in the courtyard of the big synagogue as a symbol of Nazi persecution."

Betty and Sholom's visit to Poland was a sentimental journey. Sholom had not been there since 1923, when he had appeared with Hymie Jacobson as guest stars of the Kaminska Theater, there befriending Esther Rokhl Kaminska, her daughter Ida, and granddaughter Ruth.

The reunion with the Kaminskas was moving for Sholom. Ida Kaminska was a "public idol," as he put it, in Warsaw. Born in 1899 (she died in 1980), she began her theatrical career at the age of 4, and she began directing when she was 17. "My father," she later told a *New York Times* reporter, "Avrahm, who started his theater before the 1900s with my mother. . .a great actress, told me you have to do it, and I did."[1] Ida achieved international fame when, in 1964, she starred in "The Shop on Main Street," a Czech film directed by Jan Kadar. During World War II she and her family had fled to Russia, returning to Warsaw at the end of the war.

While Betty and Sholom were in Poland, they were taken to see the Warsaw ghetto. "We visited the cemetery where the great notables in Jewish literature and the arts are buried. The graves face the site where hundreds of thousands of Jews were destroyed, where the homes were bombarded, where the heroes of the ghetto were stubbornly determined against a more powerful, barbaric enemy. We visited the courtyard where 300,000 were driven, only to be piled into specially built trains and transported to the crematoriums. It was a sorrowful, painful experience.''

Ida's husband, Meir Melman, took them to visit Warsaw's only synagogue. ''Imagine,'' Sholom wrote, ''a city this size and only one synagogue. We went at 9:30 in the morning, and the congregants were still waiting for a tenth man to complete the minyan so the service could begin. We filled the quota. We sat and watched the pathetic old men praying. It was so sad.''

The wretchedness Sholom and Betty felt at witnessing the evidence of Nazi destruction of Polish Jews and of their diminished numbers was alleviated somewhat by the gaiety of Ida Kaminska's home. The elegant apartment was filled with her intellectual, charming friends. Vodka and traditional Jewish meals were plentiful.

''Did we drink!'' Sholom wrote of his living up to his reputation for being able to consume quantities of alcohol with no visible effect. On the other hand, ''The mother (Betty) got pickled.'' (The Kaminskas' privileged status was not to last. A wave of official anti-Semitism on the part of the Polish government in 1968 forced them to leave their country. They settled in New York.)[2]

On the day of their departure from Poland, Melman appeared at Betty's and Sholom's hotel to help them with last-minute packing. He escorted them to a private car for their ride to the airport. There they were touched by the surprise appearance of Ida and her daughter, who were there to give them a farewell gift and proper sendoff.

In Czechoslovakia Sholom met Jan Kadar. Sholom wrote, ''Jan and his wife took us to a synagogue and showed us the cemetery in the courtyard where the names of thousands of martyrs who were murdered by the Nazis were written on the wall. There I recalled the deep pain we had felt at Dachau, in Hungary at the Jewish Museum, and at every step in Warsaw. Looking at the spot where the Tlomatske Synagogue had once been, walking down Leshno Street where Jewish culture had once flourished, sad thoughts brought me much heartache. I couldn't free myself of them. I began to think to myself, how often do we recall the extermination of the Jews? Once a year? Maybe less? I felt a need to make good a debt that I and millions of other Jews in the United States incurred by sitting with folded arms while European Jews were being slaughtered.''

The day after he and Betty returned from Europe, Sholom called Sam Rosenbaum and asked him to do a libretto on the Holocaust. He wanted material with which Rosenbaum was familiar—Rosenbaum's father had spoonfed him on Yiddish literature while other children, he says, "were reading Little Red Riding Hood." Rosenbaum had an impressive collection of memorial books, called Yiskor books, written by survivors of the Holocaust, showing how their communities were before and after they were destroyed.

"After reading all that material," Rosenbaum says, "I felt as though I had been there. I wrote 'Yiskor' over the summer in Cape Cod, and I remember crying constantly as I wrote it."

He sent the finished manuscript to Sholom. It was perfect. It captured in eloquent, moving poetry the sense of horror that Sholom wanted to express in music—poetry nearly too painful to hear but too powerful, too beautiful to ignore, as these passages from the libretto illustrate:

> In all the realms
> of silence
> more silent than all
> are the stones of the ghetto.
> Silent and cold to the touch.
> In their silence
> one remembers
> how Warsaw
> burned like a sea of flame.
> How the streets,
> the courts,
> the alleys,
> quiet now in their orphan loneliness
> gasped and quivered and died.

In the silence
you see again
the ghetto
screaming, exploding—
ebony smoke
rising as from an altar
darkening the sun.
Below,
in the seething, fuming,
coughing, choking
cellars and sewers
the remnant,
the stubble,
the pitiful shadow
of proud Polish Jewry
crawled from fire to fire,
clawed the walls
for one more breath—
one more heart-beat,
one more surge of blood
to throw a grenade,
to press a trigger,
to bar the way
for the foe. . .

The night—
the long, bitter night,
is now yesterday.
The fingers of dawn
so long in coming,
dapple the earth
with new light.
Slowly—
oh, so slowly
the earth warms,
drying the tears of the night.
They, the slaughtered six million,
bought for us this day.

> Without their awesome agony
> we should have all died
> shamed,
> unconsoled,
> unavenged. . .
>
> It is time for Yiskor,
> A time to remember!
> For it was they,
> the slaughtered six million,
> who charged us
> with remembering.*

Sholom, too, was possessed by the work. "In the orchestral introduction," he wrote, "I felt the agony of death, right up until the last note." Betty had always been Sholom's standby critic, and he played the opening choral passages for her.

"Sholom, it's too strong," she said. "People won't be able to bear it."

"Good!" Sholom said. "That's why I'm writing it."

"For Sholom, 'Yiskor' was a turning point," says Rosenbaum. "His music was inspired—there's no other word for it. It was the most sophisticated writing he ever did. It was Puccini, but damn good Puccini—Jewish Puccini."

Sholom was worried about the commercial appeal of "Yiskor," but Norman Warembud was not. "It should be performed soon," he told Sholom, "and every year thereafter."

Sholom played the work for Cantor Saul Meisels of the Temple on the Heights in Cleveland, who asked that the work be premiered there. Three days later, Meisels telephoned Sholom to say that one of his congregants, Harry Givelber, would commission the work. The premiere was set for Sunday evening, February 25, 1967, with Arthur Koret in the tenor role and Meisels as the baritone soloist. Sam Rosenbaum would narrate and Sholom would conduct the premiere himself.

Because of the oratorio's subject matter, the committee set up to arrange the premiere felt that an important figure in Jewish life should speak. Isaac Bashevis Singer agreed to appear.

On the night of the premiere the performers sang "Yiskor" flawlessly. The oratorio lasted 37 minutes, and the audience was silent throughout. "It seemed to me that they had stopped breathing," Sholom recalled later. "When it was over, I put down my baton. Everyone seemed frozen. It was certainly a full minute before the audience got up from their seats to applaud. Only then did I turn to face the audience and take a bow. They were still applauding after we had all left the stage."

"Yiskor" was performed for the second time at Sam Rosenbaum's Beth El Synagogue in Rochester on March 25, 1969, where reviews were glowing. Sholom was especially pleased by an editorial in the *Times-Union* that appeared in the same edition as the very favorable review. The editorial said, in part, "Remembering alone is not enough. We must recognize the fact that mass murder can yet remain humanity's mass failure and undoing."

"Yiskor" was next performed in Atlanta with the Atlanta Symphony Orchestra and chorus under the baton of Robert Shaw, with soloists Barbara Cien, David Ag, and Cantor Isaac Goodfriend (who, with his wife Betty, had survived concentration camps during the war, and who would later sing "The Star Spangled Banner" at President Jimmy Carter's inauguration in 1977).

But the best performance was still to come, Tucker's performance of "Yiskor" which was televised on ABC. That performance, and preaprations for it were a race against the clock. In 1967 Sholom's health had begun a steady deterioration due to a series of illnesses that would slowly kill him.

▥ FINAL DAYS

At the age of 73 Sholom had been blessed with nearly a lifetime of splendid health. He had not been in a hospital since his bout with typhus in Russia in 1907 and, save for colds, had not been bedridden since 1908 when he contracted diphtheria shortly after he arrived in the United States as an immigrant.

In the winter of 1967, however, his prostate gland had to be removed. The operation went smoothly, as did Sholom's twelve days in the hospital. (What he did not know was that he had cancer.) His recuperative powers were good—he began taking walks every day upon his return to Washington Heights, and in six weeks he was fully recovered from the surgery.

Over the summer of 1967 Sholom continued his commitment at the Concord for weekly classical concerts. He felt no strain in his work and began making preparations for the High Holy Days. In September Betty and Sholom drove to the Concord for the ten days of *Rosh Hashanah* and *Yom Kippur*. The first two days of services were uneventful. On Friday, the morning of *Yom Kippur* eve, Sholom went to the dining room with Betty for breakfast. Afterwards Sholom wanted to take a walk, and told Betty it would be his last opportunity to get some fresh air before the evening services. Betty occasionally accompanied him on these walks—but this time, he went outdoors alone.

Without warning, Sholom felt a horrible, stabbing pain in his chest. His first thought was that he had eaten breakfast too quickly and was paying for it with heartburn. Still, as he walked, the pain increased. He returned to his room to rest, but whichever position he assumed on the bed, the pain persisted. Again he opted for silence about his symptoms.

Sholom conducted the afternoon rehearsal, trying to conceal his torment from the choir. Although they said nothing to him, several of his veteran singers knew something was amiss. He did not yell at them for their mistakes, but, rather, simply ran through the music without stopping.

"Don't forget," says Sylvia Snyder, "if you wanted a picture of a temperamental artist, Sholom was usually it. But that day there was no carrying on and throwing of chairs. During the services, he conducted, this dynamic man, using his arms, for an entire day. It must have been eight solid hours he conducted."

(Sholom admitted later that his stoicism had less to do with the show going on than with fear. His father had died of heart trouble, and his younger brother, Jack, had recently died of a heart attack. Sholom was disinclined to make the connection between those events and his chest pains.)

The next day he told Betty about his pains, which had not diminished, and asked her to phone their son, Shelly, in New York, and his heart doctor, Dr. Elmer Pader. While she did so, he returned to the synagogue to finish the next portion of *Yom Kippur.*

The following morning, Shelly drove his father and mother to Mt. Sinai Hospital in New York City where Sholom was admitted and placed under an oxygen tent in his room. He lost consciousness. When he awoke, three days later, his wife and two sons were in the room.

Sholom stayed in the hospital for four weeks and was permitted no visitors save the immediate family. There were two exceptions to the "no visitors" rule: Richard Tucker, who was en route to a concert tour, was allowed a few minutes with him. Jan Peerce went to the hospital too, and was told that Sholom was on the critical list. Peerce managed to obtain permission to see for himself that his old friend was not dying.

Sholom's doctors advised him to take a trip south for the winter months where he could regain his strength in the sunshine. He was eager to conduct the premiere of "Yiskor" in Atlanta on February 25, and was willing to do whatever his doctors said in order not to miss the event.

Betty and Sholom had spent many winter vacations in Puerto Rico, beginning in 1955. Generally their stay was three weeks, but in 1967 they stayed for six. Pablo Casals and his wife, Marta, had for years been residents of the Island. Casals had sworn he would never return to Spain, his homeland, while Franco ruled. Sholom had been introduced to Casals by Walter Damrosch years before when he was a student at Juilliard. Over the subsequent 50 years, Sholom had followed Casals' career and attended his New York concerts.

Through a mutual friend, Sholom arranged for a visit with Casals at Casals' home. Because of the great cellist's age—he was 91 when he and Sholom saw each other in Puerto Rico for the first time—Mrs. Casals arranged for visits of short duration.

Betty's and Sholom's first visit with Casals was on February 22, 1967. "It was my day!" Sholom wrote exuberantly to Shelly. "Good old Pablo and I had a grand time. He agreed with my view of avant-garde music—I hate it. We exchanged general opinions and reminiscences of the days when I was a student. Our appointment was for 15 minutes, but it was extended to more than an hour. At the conclusion he and his charming young wife escorted us to the gate and asked us to come again. What a thrilling experience!"

In all their annual visits, Casals exhibited interest in Sholom's work, inquiring about Sholom's varied career, about where his music had been performed, about who conducted and who sang. For his 93rd birthday, he asked Sholom to bring an audio tape of "If Not Higher." Casals' tape machine was out of order, and he had rented a Sony recorder for the occasion.

"You should have been there!" Sholom wrote to his sons. "As Casals listened, he read the score, conducting, even singing portions of it. He kept on murmuring 'impressive,' and 'how dramatic.' When he got through with the work, he asked to hear 'Yiskor,' but I declined. Too much for one session. I promised to bring that tape the next time we visited."

Sholom's Puerto Rico vacations were restorative. As his strength returned, so did his sense of humor. He loved the mock bickering between himself and Betty, and wrote to his sons about an incident that exemplified their banter over nearly 50 years of marriage:

On the street the other day, your gorgeous blond mother and I were taking our usual walk. I grabbed her arm and playfully began to pinch it and to sing one of my by now famous arias—"Yookesil, Mookesil, Kookesil, Tookesil." Since I heard no reaction from your mother, such as "shut up, jerk!" I became suspicious. I looked up and what did I see, but a white head of hair and a face I did not recognize belonging to the body I was pinching. What's more, your old lady was observing the scene from a distance and laughing up to high C or maybe D—she had slipped away from me and I hadn't noticed. That's your mother for you.

Sholom was a lifelong sun worshiper, and in Puerto Rico he could sit for hours in blistering heat, tanning his skin to a mahogany brown, while Betty kept her sensitive skin under wraps or indoors. The leisure time was used productively all the same. "I am very glad I took along plenty of homework," he wrote. "I do more composing here than at home. I'm amazed at how much music I am turning out, and certainly not at the expense of sunshine."

By 1970 Betty and Sholom had made the Diener Tower Hotel in San Juan their winter residence. Nearly every winter, his sons would visit, and Sholom would arrange rooms for them at the Diener. Shelly was prospering as an advertising photographer, and Gene was en route to becoming a vice president at the J. Walter Thompson advertising agency. Gene and his wife, Shirley, had two children, Ruthanne and Andrew, Sholom's only grandchildren.

These family reunions were joyous for Sholom. He was as doting and proud as any other picture-toting grandpa around the hotel's pool. He reported on his grandchildren in a letter to Shelly:

About Avramele Andy, I can only tell you that he is a holy terror. The Grubby Mother (Betty) named him Mr. Destruction and justly so. He comes to our room, moves all the furniture around and demolishes everything he can put his hands on. When he is denied something, he either tries to win you over with his irresistible smile, or he punches you on whatever part of the body he can reach. As for Ruthanne, you should see her swim. She already jumps from the diving board and swims across the pool. Now, what do you think of that?

Sholom loved holding court in Puerto Rico. Simon Weber, editor
of the *Jewish Daily Forward* in New York, and his wife, Sylvia,
visited the Secundas several winters in a row. Sholom obtained rooms
for them at a discount at the Diener.

"We spent most of our time with Betty and Sholom," Weber says.
"He took two-mile walks every morning and I accompanied him. In
the evenings we'd go across the street to the Sheraton to gamble—but
Sholom would seldom actually play."

Weber, who had shepherded Sholom's early writings for the *Forward*, had become editor of the paper in 1968, and began running
pieces about Casals and others that Sholom would send from Puerto
Rico.

In 1971 he began serializing Sholom's memoirs. "I ran them not
only because Secunda was an interesting man," Weber says, "but
also because he had things to say that should not get lost, and I realized he was getting on in years. I never rewrote him, and I edited very
little. He brought back the flavor of the surroundings he was describing, whether Russian Jewish flavor or American flavor. It ran for more
than a year."

Sholom had a reputation for penuriousness which was taken for
granted by his friends when the bill arrived at a restaurant. Once, he
had had dinner out with Betty, Irving Grossman and his wife.
Sholom complained about the prices on the menu. When they left
the restaurant, Irving brought up the rear, carrying the restaurant's
cash register, saying, "You see, Sholom? It wasn't a total loss."

Sholom's thriftiness was an attitude that Weber understood, because he had grown up in desperate poverty in Poland, as Sholom had
in Russia.

"Childhood poverty affects people in two ways," Weber says. "I
was a child in Europe during the first World War, and the only thing
I remember is the hunger. During the Depression, when I lived in
Detroit, as soon as I earned a dollar, I went to a restaurant and ate a
meal for 85¢, which at that time was a tremendous meal.

"The effect of poverty on Sholom was quite different. He was
tight. He earned good money, but he didn't want to spend too
much. He could not stand spending for food—he knew that you
could eat at home for less money than a restaurant meal would cost.

"Another thing. It's a Jewish trait for people to be really stingy with themselves. Your children get everything—it's an attitude of 'what I didn't have, let them have.''"

(Weber's assessment of Sholom's fiscal policies is accurate. Betty's reaction to childhood poverty was identical to Sholom's, and when she needed a new dress, she would shop for hours for bargains and come home empty-handed. Sholom was generous with her where he could not be with himself. He coerced her to buy over the years two mink coats and an assortment of jewelry. If his sons asked for a new car, or a camera, or help with the purchase of a speedboat, Sholom could be persuaded to foot some or all of the bill. But fine clothes for himself held no appeal, and to take a taxi when there were subways was offensive to him.)

Sholom wrote his *Forward* pieces in longhand and in Yiddish, a language he would lapse into when conversing with Weber. They both had a deep respect for Yiddish, but pure Yiddish.

"In Yiddish, when you read Abraham Cahan's early memoirs," Weber says, "it's written almost in lyrical poetry. It's beautiful literature. Then he comes to America and the language becomes jargon. It's not Yiddish any more and it's not literature. Cahan's early Yiddish dealt with his background in Vilna, the people he knew best. You can never get to know an acquired people like those you were born with.

"It was the same with Secunda. Secunda could be in all the Broadways and Hollywoods, in all the satin places of the world. His writing wouldn't be the same as about Alexandria, where he was born."

Sholom's purism about language was matched with his purism about music, and he licked his chops when writing criticism of less than traditional music. His most glowing reviews were for music composed by the masters—Beethoven, Mozart, Brahms—but anything that smacked of modernism he impaled in print. The only modernistic music he could stomach was that of Stravinsky.

Some of Sholom's *Forward* chores, when he was not in Puerto Rico, included reviewing liturgical music. Cantor David Putterman of New York's Park Avenue Synagogue annually commissioned music for a Friday night service from esteemed composers such as Leonard Bernstein, David Amram, Morton Gould, and Sholom Secunda. One of the services was by a young composer named Gershon Kingsley, which Sholom was scheduled to review.

Kingsley wrote his service for the Moog synthesizer, an electronic keyboard attached to a machine that imitates tones of musical instruments and the human voice but that sounds frankly mechanical.

On the night of Kingsley's service at the Park Avenue Synagogue, the sanctuary was full of complicated gadgetry. Norman Warembud and his wife, Ruth (who was also a musician and composer), accompanied Betty and Sholom to the service. Warembud recalled the evening:

> After the service, Sholom was boiling mad. He got in the back seat of my car—we were driving them home—and as little as he was, I thought he would explode any second and make a hole in the roof.
>
> Betty says, "Sholom, take it easy." Sholom says, "I never heard such an outrage in my life! That goddamn amateur! Who does he think he is?" He keeps on like this for ten minutes.
>
> My wife, who was sitting next to me, whispers to me, "Ah, he only likes Ernest Bloch."
>
> We get to the West Side Highway and I turned around to Sholom and said, "Sholom, don't you want Jewish music to grow?"
>
> "Grow!" Sholom says, "you call that 'grow'? That's not growing, that's putting it back!" And I said, "Electronic music is putting it back? What's the matter with you?"
>
> "Well," Sholom says, "all I can say is wait until you read my review on Monday. You'll see what I do to this guy."
>
> By the time we reached 590 Fort Washington Avenue, Sholom had cooled off. He gave his word to me that he would not say anything bad about the music.
>
> Sholom kept his promise. In the entire review, he not only did not say anything bad about the music, he didn't say *anything* about it. Oh, he described who was at the service, he described the synagogue. He wrote that Putterman was commissioning works. But he didn't mention Kingsley's music at all.

On August 21, 1969, two days before his 75th birthday, Sholom experienced one of the happiest nights of his life. That night, on the Mall at Central Park, a Yiddish Theater Festival was held under the auspices of the Workman's Circle Education Department in cooperation with the New York City Department of Parks. Sholom conducted the event. Stars of the Yiddish radio and stage—150 of them—appeared, an orchestra from the Musicians Union, Local 802, and the Workman's Circle Chorus.

The concert, which was free, was mobbed—an estimated 30,000 New Yorkers and suburbanites showed up. A highlight of the evening was a segment called "Nostalgia From the Yiddish Theater" consisting of popular songs from Second Avenue productions, many of them by Sholom.

The evening was covered by camera crews from local television stations. Sholom was presented to the crowds by the then Mayor John V. Lindsay. As Sholom conducted, he turned to face the cameras with his radiant smile. That evening he was an indisputable star, mobbed by elderly Yiddish theater *patriots* who just wanted to shake his hand.

The next day he was described in a *New York Times* article about the event as "The Yiddish Leonard Bernstein," a redundancy that made him helpless with laughter.

The years 1970 and 1971 were contented for Sholom. His son Shelly had finally married (although the marriage was short-lived) and his winters in Puerto Rico were filled with social events. He spent his summers conducting concerts at the Concord, reviewing concerts at Tanglewood for the *Forward,* and making trips to Fire Island, off the coast of Long Island, where both of his sons had summer houses.

One hot summer night in July of 1971, Betty called Shelly at Fire Island, her voice trembling, saying that Sholom was experiencing agonizing pains in the groin. Dr.Irving Shulman, his urologist, was on vacation and couldn't be reached, she said. Sholom had seen instead Dr. Selwyn Fried of Montefiore Hospital in the Bronx (he was, coincidentally, Celia Adler's son).

"Fried says Daddy has to have radical surgery," Betty said.

"What does that mean?"

"It means he wants to remove Sholom's testicles."

That night, Shelly says, was a nightmare. "I went over to Gene's house. We finally located Shulman on the phone, and he said the radical wasn't necessary. We called Fried, who insisted that it was mandatory. We called Betty, and she told us that Sholom and she wanted Gene and me to make the decision. Can you imagine being asked to decide a thing like that?''

Gene and Shelly discussed the question for an hour, and were inclined to agree to the radical. Dr. Shulman fortuitously called during their discussion—he had conferred with Fried by telephone, and Shulman now concurred with his colleague. Gene and Shelly called Fried and told him to go ahead.

The operation was performed the next day at Montefiore. Sholom never discussed his mutilation with his sons, or with anyone. None of his friends or colleagues can recall a single complaint about it, either then or during the next three hideous years.

During the summer of 1972, Sholom seemed to have made a complete recovery. He and Betty visited Izzy and Sadie Secunda in Pittsfield, as they did during many summer weekends so that Sholom could attend and review concerts at Tanglewood. One of the performances took place on a dark, rainy evening. Izzy's Cadillac was in the shop for repairs, so he drove his wife's considerably smaller Rambler, with Sholom in front on the passenger's side. Sadie sat behind Izzy with Betty next to her on the back seat.

Izzy came to a stop sign at an intersection of two main streets. The rain blanketed his windshield, reducing his visibility. After looking in both directions, Izzy slowly proceeded. Suddenly a car, racing toward them from the left, plowed into the driver's side of the car. Izzy and Sadie were thrown violently against Sholom and Betty. Betty was knocked unconscious, and Sholom suffered severe bruises and contusions on his left side. Izzy and Sadie were unharmed.

Within minutes, two ambulances arrived, and everyone was taken to a nearby hospital. Betty and Sholom were both hospitalized. While in the hospital, Sholom suffered another heart attack.

Betty and Sholom were released three weeks later, and Shelly took a bus to Pittsfield to drive them home. After two weeks of convalescence, Sholom felt able to drive again. Out of prudence, Shelly suggested they take a test run in the car together. At the first intersection, Sholom made a right-hand turn into heavy Manhattan traffic without looking to the left, and the car narrowly escaped being totaled by oncoming traffic. Shelly told his father, as gently as he could, that he should not drive again. He didn't.

By January of 1973 Sholom was well enough to return to Puerto Rico, but he was no longer up to taking his daily walks. Nor was he able to attend the most important night of his professional life—the January 29 taping by ABC Television of "Yiskor," with Richard Tucker, New York City Opera stars Bianca Sauler and Seymour Schwartzman, narrator Howard Da Silva, and the 46-voice Ithaca College Concert Choir and Orchestra, at Temple Beth El in Rochester. The oratorio was conducted by Thomas Michalak.

"Sholom had originally written the principal role for baritone," says Sam Rosenbaum. "When Tucker agreed to do it, Sholom had to rewrite it for tenor. So he took one of the long speeches that was in the narration and wrote two new arias for tenor. When he wrote it, his hand shook so much you could hardly read it, but he did it beautifully. It's not just pasted together. It's really a solid piece."

The *Rochester Democrat and Chronicle* critic wrote of the production, "Performances like last night's lift a work with such epic pretensions to first-rate dimensions." George Kimball of the *Times-Union,* wrote, ". . .Sholom Secunda's score, in a conservatively modern style that reminds of certain richly harmonized works of Ernest Bloch, deftly alternates music and narrator, solos and choir, small and large ensemble sequences. . .Tucker was magnificent. . .Miss Sauler and Schwartzman scarcely less effective. Da Silva's narration was crisp and eloquent. It was a quality performance that made the work's 30-minute duration seem shorter."

Late that night, Norman Warembud, who had come for the performance to supervise its recording for an LP album, placed a call to Puerto Rico, to read the reviews to Sholom.

"Everybody got on the phone that night," Warembud said. "Da Silva says, 'Sholom, you should have been here, you would have gotten a kick out of it.' Tucker gets on and says, 'I never sang better in my life.' I get on and read the reviews. I could hear Sholom on the other end, crying. He said to me, 'This is one of the great moments of my life.'"

Sholom and Betty returned from Puerto Rico in time to see it broadcast on ABC's "Directions '73" on April 29. It was nominated for an Emmy.

In spite of his progressive weakness, when he returned to New York, Sholom tried to maintain his work schedule. He continued giving singing lessons, although the number of his students was drastically reduced. Herman Malamood, who had become cantor for the Concord High Holy Days and, subsequently, a New York City Opera Company principal, periodically appeared at the Secundas' apartment for a lesson.

"I stayed on with Sholom until the end," Malamood says. "I'd push with Betty for a lesson because it made him work instead of hanging around. The depression he felt in the last couple of years was tremendous, so I'd come and all of a sudden he'd be a different man behind the piano. He was worried whether or not he could still play, that insecure feeling you get when you're sick, and I'd give him an argument. 'What do you mean?' I'd say if he hit a wrong note. 'What is this?' And he'd hit the right note. He and I switched roles at the end—he had had such high standards for me at the beginning of my career, and now I was doing that for him."

Sholom conducted High Holy Days services at the Concord in the fall. It was an Herculean effort for him to do so. His hands trembled, and the choir members and musicians were afraid that he would topple. It was his last appearance at the Concord.

"My position at the Concord was not an easy matter due to my present physical condition," Sholom wrote to a friend, "but I had lots of help. However, everything went well, although we cut out the Thursday concert which I used to do every holiday. Now we are back home resting most of the time."

His final speaking engagement was at the 92nd Street YM-YWHA in Manhattan on October 28, 1973. The afternoon lecture was about Yiddish theater music, specifically that by Alexander Olshanetsky, Joseph Rumshinsky and himself.

The following night his final Yiddish operetta was mounted at the Eden Theater on Second Avenue—"It's Hard to Be a Jew." It was a musical version of a play by Sholom Aleichem that had first opened on Second Avenue in 1921.

"He was desperately ill when he wrote that score," recalled Sholom's old friend, Chaim Miller. "We tried to stop him. First Betty tried, and then she came to me and asked me to talk to him. He told me, 'I'm the last of the Mohicans and it has to be done. Somebody has to do it. There's nobody else, so I'm it.'"

Sholom and Betty attended opening night, but Sholom was unable to conduct. In his *New York Times* review, Richard Shepard wrote, "If you're one of those who think of Yiddish theater in terms of bygone art, by all means get down to the Eden Theater, on Second Avenue, the original Broadway of the art, and see one of the more lively shows in town, 'Hard to Be a Jew'. . .This new version has been adapted from the author's original play into a sparkling new Yiddish musical with melodies by Sholom Secunda." Joyce Wadler, in her review for the *New York Post*, wrote, ". . .the show. . .was totally professional—from the performance of veteran Yiddish stars Joseph Buloff and Miriam Kressyn to the warm, lovely music of Sholom Secunda. . ."

Buloff won an Obie, the highest award for off-Broadway theater, in 1973 for his performance.

Sholom's condition deteriorated in 1974. "I am in poor health," he wrote to a friend, "ever since that miserable accident in Tanglewood. You will remember it started last winter in San Juan. Unfortunately, they could not find the trouble. Here they did. I have spent many weeks in hospitals and even now I am still under doctors' care."

The trouble, according to his doctors' diagnosis, was that Sholom now had bone cancer. It was diagnosed in the winter of 1974. Betty and Sholom had flown to Florida rather than Puerto Rico to spend the winter months because, Sholom felt, it was preferable to be near an American hospital. In addition, Izzy Secunda had an apartment in Hollywood, Florida, and would be on hand in case of an emergency.

One night Sholom had had an attack of unspecific, blinding pain, and he was rushed from his motel to a hospital. Because of his aversion to solitude, round-the-clock nurses were hired to provide company for him during those hours that Betty slept at night.

During the weeks of January and February, while he convalesced in Florida, he realized that he could not honor his Concord commitment for Passover. Alan Chester, his old friend and colleague, was in Miami on vacation, and Sholom asked him to come to his motel. Chester was, at the time, Richard Tucker's conductor for his Passover engagement in Chicago. Nevertheless, Sholom asked Chester to take on the conducting responsibilities at the Concord for him.

"I'm not going to be able to do anything anymore," he confided to Chester. Chester could not relinquish his responsibility to Tucker, but when he returned to New York, he made arrangements for Jonathan White, who had appeared as a singer for Sholom over the years, to conduct the services.

If Sholom knew that his condition was terminal, he did not tell anyone, at least not for the moment. Simon Weber, who had flown to Florida to see Sholom, came to visit.

"It was the last time I saw him alive," Weber says. "He was sitting in front of the motel in a courtyard. One leg was swollen, and it was resting on a chair. It was tragic to see him so sick."

Betty and Sholom flew back to New York in early March, and Sholom underwent a series of radiation treatments.

"I took him for his first treatment," Shelly says, "and I had to help him undress. It killed me to see him like that, dying and looking emaciated, but he was so good about it."

One of Sholom's few remaining pleasures was Fort Tryon Park, near his Washington Heights apartment, and Shelly would push Sholom's wheelchair along the lovely walks, looking for signs of spring.

Sholom summoned the strength to make a final public appearance at Richard Tucker's Carnegie Hall concert in March. By coincidence, Sylvia Snyder, who was still a member of the Concord choir, attended the same concert.

"I walked in and there in the rear row were Betty, Gene, Shelly and Sholom, who was in a wheelchair. It was quite an evening. All the people who sang with Sholom were there because they were part of Ruby's entourage. At intermission they all came to the back of the Hall to speak to Sholom. At the end of the concert, Sholom asked me to tell Ruby that he didn't feel up to going to his dressing room. Mind you, the man's at death's door, and he's apologizing to Ruby because he could not come up to say what a beautiful concert it was."

In the final weeks of his life, Sholom was being treated by a heart specialist, an oncologist and a radiologist, but he missed the presence of his personal physician and friend, Dr. Jack Lefkowitz, who himself was quite sick. Into this void stepped James H. Barnum, Jr. Barnum, an advertising executive with the J. Walter Thompson Company, was also a medical doctor on the staff of Columbia Presbyterian Hospital. He was an admirer of Sholom's, whom he had met through Gene. Dr. Barnum visited Sholom frequently (without charging a fee) and he was available to the family day and night. It was a great comfort to Sholom to have a physician who personally cared about him.

By May Sholom was taking massive doses of painkillers. He still received visits from old friends, and at those times he was able to rally himself in order to chat and charm. But when he and his family were alone, Sholom listened to the tape of "Yiskor" or slept.

Sholom entered Columbia Presbyterian Hospital at the end of May, from which he did not emerge. Under heavy sedation he began losing track of time. He asked Betty to put the earpiece of his portable tape recorder into his ear so that he could listen to "Yiskor."

"He didn't care anymore," Shelly says. "All he wanted to do was listen to 'Yiskor.' He was so drugged that he rarely opened his eyes. I had just finished my first book—a children's book of photographs of Zero Mostel—Dad had always wanted me to be a writer—and I took the first copy I got from the publisher straight to the hospital to show him. He roused himself and asked Betty to put his glasses on for him. I turned the pages of the book and he chuckled at the photographs. 'Let me see the back of the book,' he said, wanting to make sure that I had been given proper credit. Then he closed his eyes and never opened them again."

"I knew the end was near on June 13," Betty says. "That day he said only one word: 'Betty.' He died at 1:00 in the afternoon with the earpiece of his recorder in his ear, listening to 'Yiskor.'"

With Betty at the time of Sholom's death were her sister, Lottie, and Lottie's husband, Lou Weintrop. Lottie called Gene and Shelly. Ruby Tucker was on his way to the hospital to make his daily visit to Sholom. When Tucker arrived, Betty met him in the hall and told him that Sholom had died.

Tucker broke down. "He was heartbroken," Sarah Tucker says. "Sholom and Ruby went way back together. When Ruby first started, I can truly say that not everybody thought he was the greatest. But Sholom felt there was something great in Richard. And when you have somebody to back you like that, when you begin your career, that's what brought them close. It was something—a love and respect—I can't describe."

Sholom had been a father-figure to Tucker. He had shared with Ruby roots as children in synagogue choirs. Sholom was a link to Tucker's youth, and Tucker was a link to greatness for Sholom because of his willingness to perform whatever Sholom wrote.

And so it did not surprise Gene and Shelly, when they arrived at the hospital less than an hour after their father's death, to hear Ruby

Tucker say, "I would like to be the last person to be with Sholom."

"At first we were offended," Gene says, "but then we realized that although Sholom's family was his first priority, Ruby was probably the most important person in his life. Ruby, the greatest tenor in the world, had added a luster and importance to Sholom's image of himself. They had shared Sholom's most rewarding professional moments—his oratorios. How else can you explain Sholom's need to have the sound of Tucker singing 'Yiskor' in his ear up until he died?"

Betty, Gene and Shelly went into Sholom's room and kissed his face. Then Tucker was left alone with Sholom's body for ten minutes to make his own, private farewell.

Betty and her sons went to Lottie's house to begin funeral arrangements and to contact the newspapers. The Weintrops' eldest daughter, Sondra, left her office and came to her parents' home. When she arrived, she told Betty that Sholom a year before had taken her aside and sworn her to secrecy about what he was going to say to her.

"There are some very serious things I have to tell you," he said. "They don't know that I know I'm dying. I don't think I'm going to live through the year. I can't discuss my funeral arrangements with Betty or my sons. They aren't up to that."

"Why me?" Sondra asked.

"Because you're like a daughter to me," he said. He gave her a piece of paper and pencil so that she could take notes. He told her he wanted Ruby Tucker to sing at the funeral and for Sam Rosenbaum to give the eulogy. He also wanted Rabbi William Berkowitz to officiate.

"They keep telling me I have arthritis, but I'm not stupid," he said to Sondra, and added, "If only I had more time."

Sholom had cleverly orchestrated his last public moment by making his own arrangements. He wanted to be the star at his own funeral, and to be honored by first-rate speakers and singers. His last wishes were nearly sabotaged.

The night before the funeral, during visitation hours at the Park West Chapel on West 79th Street, Gene and Shelly were cornered by Yiddish actors, managers, and union leaders, all of whom wanted to speak at the services the next day. "We didn't care what they wanted," Shelly says. "We were going to carry out Sholom's wishes even if we had to punch somebody. But it wasn't necessary. It was a hell of a funeral.''

Indeed it was. William Gunther played a medley of Sholom's songs on the organ as over 1,000 mourners filed into the chapel. Alan Chester spotted members of the Concord choir and pulled them aside. On the spot he organized a choir of 20 voices to sing during the service, handing out copies of liturgical pieces by Sholom that they knew.

''I was told to stand at the foot of the coffin,'' Chester says, ''and the choir stood at the head. Herman Malamood and Tucker sang, and the choir sang background harmony. All the singers were crying, but they were glorious.''

Shelly says, ''As I listened to the choir, I said to myself, 'So how come you never sounded that good for Sholom?'''

Then Rosenbaum stood to give his eulogy—he was by virtue of his closeness to Sholom and his gifts as a writer the best qualified person to do so—a chronicle of Sholom's personality and achievements. Rosenbaum appeased the representatives of various groups who wanted to speak with this line: ''The organizations to which he gave time and thought and attention were legion: Yiddish Theatrical Alliance, Hebrew Actors Union, Musicians Union, Local 802, *Jewish Daily Forward*, Workman's Circle, Farband, ASCAP, Ethnic Music, Society of Jewish Composers, Artists and Friends, Actors Club, Cantors Assembly, and the Concord Hotel.''

Rosenbaum concluded,

In my heart of hearts I am convinced that if Man is ever to fulfill the vision of the Prophet he will first need to learn to hammer his strident voices into the mold of Sholom's gentle melodies; to laugh, to dance and to sing together, brother trusting brother.

The long, exciting journey from Alexandria in the Ukraine is almost over; the traveler rests. Sholom is, as his name, complete and at peace. And our remembrance of him will never be merely a passing flutter of regret, but a flame with which we will illumine the dark passages of our own lives.

Hundreds of friends and colleagues formed a cortege that took the coffin to the Old Montefiore Cemetery in St. Albans, Queens. There, beside his parents and brothers, Sholom was buried among other Alexandrians in a plot purchased when Sholom's father first came to the United States.

No rabbi officiated at the graveside. Instead, Ruby Tucker, who himself would be dead within six months, and Herman Malamood sang a *kaddish* (mourner's prayer) in tandem, each singer singing alternate lines. Tucker threw the first shovelful of earth into the grave, followed by Malamood and the other male mourners, in the Jewish tradition of burials.

It was a majestic, intimate, musical sendoff.

🎵 EPILOGUE

There are few tangible reminders today of Sholom Secunda's life and work, no monuments and no legends. His legacy is subtler. That legacy is best summed up by Broadway producer Emanuel Azenberg, a first generation American Jew. Of Sholom, he says,

> We grew up in a very volatile and anti-Semitic time, the 1930s and 1940s, when if you announced you were a Jew, somebody would punch you in the mouth.

> But Sholom was the guy who stood at the piano when we were kids and made us all sing Jewish songs and *like* it. Thirty-two years later, it is what we are. We are Jewish. In that sense I can say, Sholom, you did it. You made me Jewish.

> As for the lasting impact of Sholom's music, I don't know that anyone could ask in this world to be so significant that four thousand generations are going to recall your contribution. I think if you have accomplished it with the next generation, that's all your obligation is.

> With me, Sholom succeeded in that. He affected many of our lives. We know who we are because of him. He was the Pied Piper of Jews.

NOTES

Chapter 1

1. Joel Cang, *The Silent Millions: A History of the Jews in the Soviet Union*, Taplinger Publishing Co. Inc., New York 1970, p. 23.
2. Robert K. Massie, *Nicholas and Alexandra*, Atheneum, New York 1967, p. 94n.
3. Dan Rottenberg, *Finding Our Fathers: A Guidebook to Jewish Genealogy*, Random House, Inc., New York, 1977, p. 199 ill.
4. *Evreiskaia Entsiklopediya* (Jewish Encyclopedia), St. Petersburg, 1910, Vol. I, p. 765.
5. *Kratkaya Geographicheskaya Entsiklopediya* (Short Geographic Encyclopedia).
6. Massie, *Nicholas and Alexandra*, p. 94n.
7. Nathan Ausubel, *The Book of Jewish Knowledge*, Crown Publishers, Inc., 1964, p. 344.
8. Cang, *The Silent Millions*, p. 24.
9. Bernard Pares, *A History of Russia*, Definitive Edition, Alfred A. Knopf, Inc., 1968 (new edition of 1926 original), p. 430.
10. Ausubel, *The Book of Jewish Knowledge*, p. 343.
11. *Ibid.*
12. Massie, *Nicholas and Alexandra*, p. 41.
13. Pares, *A History of Russia*, p. 430.
14. Ausubel, *The Book of Jewish Knowledge*, p. 345.
15. *Evreiskaia Entsiklopediya*, p. 765.
16. Leo Trepp, *A History of the Jewish Experience*, Behrman House, Inc. Publishers, New York 1962, revised 1973, pp. 260-261.

Chapter 2

1. Massie, *Nicholas and Alexandra*, p. 97.
2. Jesse D. Clarkson, *A History of Russia*, Random House, Inc., New York 1961, p. 383.
3. *Ibid.* p. 386.
4. *Ibid.*
5. *Voshkod*, St. Peterburg weekly, 1904, no. 19.
6. *Evreiskaia Entsiklopediya*, p. 765.
7. *Voshkod*, No. 18.

Chapter 3

1. Irving Howe, *World of Our Fathers,* Harcourt Brace Jovanovich, Inc., New York, 1976, p. 38.
2. John Maxtone-Graham, *The Only Way to Cross,* Macmillan Publishing Co., Inc., New York, 1972, p. 155.
3. *Ibid.,* p. 156.
4. *Ibid.,* p. 120.
5. *Ibid,* p. 1.
6. *Ibid,* p. 156, 157 ill.
7. Howe, *World of Our Fathers,* p. 39.
8. Maxtone-Graham, *The Only Way to Cross,* p. 153.
9. *Ibid.,* p. 154 ill.
10. Ronald Sanders, *The Downtown Jews,* Signet 1977 (Harper & Row, Publishers, Inc., New York 1969), pp. 29-30.
11. Howe, *World of Our Fathers,* p. 45.
12. *Ibid.,* p. 44.
13. *Ibid.,* p. 69.
14. *Ibid.,* p. 133.
15. *Ibid.,* p. 276.
16. Lulla Rosenfeld, *Bright Star of Exile: Jacob Adler and Yiddish Theatre,* Thomas Y. Crowell Company, New York 1977, p. 276.
17. *The New York Times,* July 8, 1973.
18. Hutchins Hapgood, *The Spirit of the Ghetto,* Schocken Books, New York 1976 (Funk & Wagnalls, New York 1902), pp. 27-28.
19. Howe, *World of Our Fathers,* pp. 274-275.
20. *Ibid.,* p. 277.
21. *Ibid.,* p. 167.

Chapter 4

1. Sanders, *The Downtown Jews,* p. 228.
2. Howe, *World of Our Fathers,* p. 461.
3. Sanders, *Downtown Jews,* p. 229.
4. Howe, *World of Our Fathers,* p. 461.
5. *Ibid.,* pp. 461-462.
6. *Ibid.,* p. 462n.
7. *Ibid.,* p. 184.
8. David S. Lifson, *The Yiddish Theatre in America,* Thomas Yoseloff, New York (A.S. Barnes & Company Inc.) 1965, p. 173.
9. Howe, *World of Our Fathers,* p. 479.
10. *Ibid.,* p. 58.
11. Lifson, *The Yiddish Theatre in America,* p. 177.
12. *Ibid.,* p. 548.

13. Howe, *World of Our Fathers*, pp. 544-545.

14. Irving Howe and Kenneth Libo, *How We Lived: A Documentary History of Immigrant Jews in America 1880-1930*, Richard Marek Publishers, Inc., New York 1979, p. 264.

15. Hapgood, *The Spirit of the Ghetto*, pp. 116-118.

16. Mark Slobin, *A Survey of Early Jewish-American Sheet Music (1898-1921)*, Working Papers in Yiddish and East European Jewish Studies Number 17, YIVO Institute for Jewish Research, New York 1976, p. 15.

17. *Ibid.*, p. 13.

18. Rosenfeld, *Bright Star of Exile*, p. 335.

19. Howe, *World of Our Fathers*, p. 466.

20. Harold Clurman, *The Fervent Years: The Story of the Group Theatre and the Thirties*, Alfred A. Knopf, Inc., New York, 1945, p. 4.

21. Macy Nulman, *Concise Encyclopedia of Jewish Music*, McGraw-Hill Book Company, 1975, p. 210.

22. Howe, *World of Our Fathers*, pp. 130-131.

23. *Ibid.*, p. 132.

24. Sanders, *Downtown Jews*, p. 365.

25. Howe, *World of Our Fathers*, p. 489.

26. Rosenfeld, *Bright Star of Exile*, p. 209, 211.

27. Hapgood, *Spirit of the Ghetto*, pp. 139-140.

28. Rosenfeld, *Bright Star of Exile*, p. 253.

29. David Ewen, *A Journey to Greatness: The Life and Music of George Gershwin*, Henry Holt & Co., New York 1956, p. 44.

30. *Ibid.*, p. 311.

31. Nulman, *Concise Encyclopedia of Jewish Music*, p. 38.

32. *The New York Times*, April 20, 1980.

33. Nulman, *Concise Encyclopedia of Jewish Music*, pp. 37-38.

Chapter 5.

1. Rosenfeld, *Bright Star of Exile*, pp. 183-184.

2. Sanders, *Downtown Jews*, pp. 227-228.

3. *The New York Times*, June 17, 1953.

4. Rosenfeld, *Bright Star of Exile*, p. 286.

5. Nahma Sandrow, *Vagabond Stars: A World History of Yiddish Theater*, Harper & Row, Publishers, Inc., New York 1977, p. 297.

6. Rosenfeld, *Bright Star of Exile*, p. 325.

7. Maxtone-Graham, *The Only Way to Cross*, p. 169.

8. *Ibid.*, p. 170.

Chapter 6

1. Howe, *World of Our Fathers*, p. 481n.

Chapter 7

1. Rosenfeld, *Bright Star of Exile*, p. 332.
2. *The New York Times*, Nov. 3, 1936.

Chapter 8

1. Robert H. Stanley, *The Celluloid Empire: A History of the American Movie Industry*, Communication Art Books, Hastings House, Publishers Inc., New York 1978, p. 109.
2. Harry M. Geduld, *The Birth of the Talkies: From Edison to Jolson*, Indiana University Press, Bloomington, Indiana 1975, p. 255.
3. *Ibid.*, pp. 253-256.

Chapter 9

1. Sandrow, *Vagabond Stars*, p. 154.
2. Howe, *World of Our Fathers*, p. 237.
3. Leo Guild, *Zanuck: Hollywood's Last Tycoon*, Holloway House, Los Angeles 1970, pp. 114-115.
4. Sammy Cahn, *I Should Care: The Sammy Cahn Story*, Arbor House Publishing Company, New York 1974, p. 44.
5. *Miami Herald*, March 3, 1974.
6. *Life Magazine*, January 31, 1938, p. 24.
7. *Ibid.*, p. 49.
8. *Ibid.*, p. 34.
9. *Miami Herald*, March 3, 1974.
10. Cahn, *I Should Care*, p. 33.
11. *Life Magazine*, January 31, 1938, p. 39.
12. *New York Journal American*, Feb. 26, 1938.

Chapter 10

1. Alan Levy, *The Bluebird of Happiness: The Memoirs of Jan Peerce*, Harper & Row Publishers, Inc., New York 1976, p. 88.
2. Rosenfeld, *Bright Star of Exile*, pp. 308-309.
3. Howe, *World of Our Fathers*, pp. 487-488.
4. *The New York Times*, Jan. 20, 1980.
5. Howe, *World of Our Fathers*, p. 357.

Chapter 12

1. Joey Adams with Henry Tobias, *The Borscht Belt*, The Bobbs-Merrill Company, Inc., New York 1966, p. 98.
2. *The New York Times*, May 27, 1979.

Chapter 13

1. *The Village Voice*, March 10, 1975.
2. *The New York Times*, Sept. 13, 1951.
3. *The New York Times*, Dec. 8, 1952.
4. *The New York Times*, Sept. 30, 1955.
5. *The New York Times*, Oct. 13, 1955.
6. *Vagabond Stars*, Sandrow, p. 300
7. *The New York Times*, Nov. 1, 1959.

Chapter 14

1. Lifson, *The Yiddish Theater in America*, p. 373.

Chapter 15

1. *The New York Times*, Dec. 29, 1979.
2. *Ibid.*

INDEX

263

271